Bronze Pillars

An Oral History of African-Americans in Flint

Bronze Pillars

An Oral History of African-Americans in Flint

by Rhonda Sanders

The Flint JOURNAL

Copyright © 1995 by The Flint Journal and
Alfred P. Sloan Museum

All rights reserved.

ISBN 0-9649832-0-6 12.95

Printed in the United States of America.

First Edition
Book design by Richard L. Watkins Sr.

*All photographs are from collections of The Flint Journal and
Alfred P. Sloan Museum, and may not be copied or reproduced.*

Foreword

In Bronze Pillars, as with any book, the author's name and that of the publisher will be prominently displayed. What follows is an acknowledgement of the other people and organizations - whose names you may see only once - who made this book possible.

We wish to thank, first of all, the African American Collection Committee of the Sloan Museum. Their insight, work and good wishes kept us all inspired. The committee included:

Catherine Alexander
Charles Hamilton
Ezra Artis
Lolita Hendrix
Mancine Broome
Sondra Rawls
Norman Bryant
Edith Prunty Spencer
Ruth Owens Buckner
Joan Stapleton
Craig Carter
Debra Taylor
Dolores Ennis

We are also grateful to the financial supporters of this project, who contributed funds to support the printing and distribution of the book. They include:

St. John Street Reunion Committee, Inc., Phyllis P. Dobson, Omogene Spencell Truss, Mrs. Anne N. Gregory, Jay & Martyann S. Edwards, Milton C. Port, Robert A. Rails, Mancine Broome, First Trinity Missionary Baptist Church, Edith Prunty Spencer, Delta Sigma Theta

Sorority, Inc., Flint Alumnae Chapter, Lenore Croudy, President; Alpha Kappa Alpha Sorority, Inc., Zeta Beta Omega Chapter, Jean Conyers, Basileus; Dr. Orlando J. Roberts & Hon. Ramona M. Roberts, Omega Psi Phi Fraternity, Inc., Omicron Rho Chapter.

Those who were interviewed and those who donated photographs were, of course, critical to this project. A heartfelt thanks to you all.

The Trustees of the Friends of Sloan Museum deserve special appreciation for their moral and financial support.

Finally, although their work on this book was part of their regular jobs, we wish to offer thanks to our staff members who gave the extra effort needed to bring Bronze Pillars to the public. From Sloan Museum, we want to especially thank Wanda Howard, African American Collections Project coordinator, meeting organizer, photograph collector and researcher, who kept the details of this project in order. Thanks are also due to Sloan staff members David White, Jeff Taylor, Stephen Laux and Sandra Houston. At The Flint Journal, the work of John Dickson, Richard Watkins, David Larzelere, M. Teresa Calkins and Sherry Compton was indispensible to the project.

Finally, for special services, we would also like to thank Lewis Driskell, owner of Union Printing Co., who helped with advice on printing; Lawrence R. Gustin, who provided editing advice; Maxie and Dezeray Brandon, who drove Rhonda Sanders and Wanda Howard on a historical tour of Flint; and Lenore Croudy and Loretta Milo, who advised us on marketing.

Tom Lindley, Editor	Steve Germann, Director
The Flint Journal	Alfred P. Sloan Museum

Preface

In keeping with somewhat of a tradition for books about African-Americans, this book's title comes from the Bible. The Book of Kings I (Revised Standard Version) describes in detail the twin bronze pillars at the entrance to the temple for God built by wise King Solomon.

The expression "pillars of society" refers to people whose contributions provide a solid foundation and strong support system similar to architectural pillars.

They are among the ones referred to by prominent African-American educator and civil rights advocate Benjamin E. Mays, who said: "We, today, stand on the shoulders of our predecessors who have gone before us."

Flint's bronze pillars have been people from all walks of life. Many have held leadership positions. Some have pioneered "firsts" in every aspect of community life – business, education, entertainment, sports and more. Others were ordinary men and women who serve as living testimony to the virtues of hard work, persistence and patience.

During the 15 months I spent working on this book, I often compared it to making a quilt. It was a slow process requiring a great deal of patience and attention to detail.

This finished work has been woven from many colorful pieces of African-American life in Flint.

The book's design began to take shape in 1992 when the Sloan Museum conceived an exhibit called "Flint and the American Dream," to recap life in the 20th century.

To help gather artifacts, photographs and information about blacks for the exhibit, Sloan formed the 15-member African-American Collection Committee. As part of that initiative, more than 200 hours of personal interviews were recorded by Wanda Howard, a Sloan staff member.

A desire to preserve those conversations in a book led to a partnership between Sloan Museum and The Flint Journal in the summer of 1993.

Then I was asked and accepted the honor of assembling this record of Flint's black community life. So little has been written that the work of finding and compiling missing pieces proved quite a challenge for Howard and me.

Oral history, as this format is called, reflects an old African tradition. A village historian called a "griot" was responsible for memorizing tribal records and lore to pass on by word of mouth to successive generations.

I kept that imagery in mind as I sifted through stacks of recorded and written transcripts, selecting some stories based on historical significance and others because they gave insight into the thoughts and day-to-day experiences of ordinary men, women and children.

One of the big surprises for me was finding out how much I have yet to learn about this community I've called home for nearly 16 years. There are so many inspirational stories of personal and collective achievement that need to be told.

The people interviewed, many of whom I've never met, now seem like "kinfolks" to me. Many of their stories rekindled sentimental memories of stories handed down in my family. That personal touch makes the oral sharing of history seem like watching a good movie starring people you know personally.

Because oral history is less formal than a scholarly approach, what is presented here are "real people" stories, told as often as possible in their own words.

Great effort was made to correct inaccuracies, but an oral history, by definition, relies heavily on accurate memories.

Still, even the sharpest memories are not perfect, and thus, much that should be remembered was never recorded and has been lost.

That further underscores the importance of having this written record now. It ensures that at least a portion of a remarkable heritage will be preserved and passed on to future generations.

My hope is that these stories will say to our children and their children, "you can do it." Despite whatever hardships they may face, they are standing on the proud, strong shoulders of bronze pillars.

The pillars seen throughout this book are from Flint's Northbank Center, 432 N. Saginaw Street. These grand pillars originally framed the entrance to Union Industrial Bank, built in 1923. Renamed the Metropolitan Building in 1948, the structure provided a community gathering spot for basketball games and dances, in addition to office and retail space. Restored and expanded in 1986, the building was renamed Northbank Center.

Overview

Fewer than 300 "colored" people were known to be living in Flint 100 years ago, census records show. That meant that in a city of about 10,000 people, only one resident in every 300 or so was black.

But from 1890 to 1990, Flint's black population swelled to 67,485, nearly equal to the 69,788 whites.

Back in 1894, a black population of 289 in all of Genesee County did not rank among the top 10 in the state, according to the census of the state of Michigan.

Of 16,240 blacks living in Michigan in 1894, census records indicate that most were clustered in 10 counties including Wayne, Cass, Washtenaw, Kent, Jackson and Kalamazoo.

Blacks represented less than 1 percent of the state's 2.1 million population in 1890. Most of them lived in one of 70 incorporated cities, including Flint. But of the 41,000 residents in Genesee County only 239 were black, including two black males living in Gaines Township and one in Forest Township.

Though the 1890 census did not provide separate information about black employment or housing, it sketched an overview of what the city was like a century ago.

Flint was far from being a one-industry town. Factory jobs included sawmills and flour mills; marble, stone, wagon and carriage works; cigar, brick and tile, and box makers; printing and publishing and dairies. Most factories employed fewer than 40 people, and a day's pay ranged from about 70 cents for unskilled workers in printing and publishing to $2.33 for skilled laborers at sawmills.

Ninety-three percent of county land in 1894 was used for farming, the census reported. That included 26 acres of apple orchards in Flint, 28 acres of vineyards and 27 acres of nurseries. Some city-dwellers also kept livestock.

The census reported 295 dwellings in Flint in 1894, averaging about four people per household. In comparison, the 1990 count found nearly 59,000 housing units in the city.

Also, the census showed one African Methodist Episcopal church in Genesee County, among 18 known to exist in the state. In all, there were 79 congregations of various denominations in Genesee County. Two "Baptist Regular (colored)" churches were reported for the state but none in Genesee County.

Comparatively, Flint's black churches numbered well over 100 by the early 1990s.

A century's passage has made a big difference in many other ways.

"Flint is 100 percent different now than it was (even) 60 years ago," said James Wesley, who first visited Flint as a child in 1929 and moved here permanently in 1956.

"You can go anywhere you want to go now and buy anything you want to if you have the money. ... Living back then was safer than now. When you go to bed at night now, you don't know if you're going to wake up alive."

From the early 1900s until the early 1940s, the main jobs open to blacks were domestic ones such as cooking, cleaning or chauffeuring for wealthy white families. A few worked in trades as barbers, furniture finishers, barn builders, doctors or lawyers. Most black men who worked in automobile factories were janitors, although some worked at Buick's hellish foundry.

Like many cities nationwide, Flint has had its share of racial problems, which affected the quality of life for blacks. Conditions were nowhere near as oppressive as in the Deep South where lynchings and voting restrictions were common practices until the early 1960s. But many public facilities in Flint were segregated until the late 1940s. Blacks could not stay at hotels or eat at certain restaurants. They were allowed to use recreational facilities only on designated days and couldn't partake of entertainment at the downtown IMA Auditorium until midnight, after whites had left.

Black schoolchildren in the early 1900s received a good basic education, although a common complaint was that few of them were being prepared for college or professional jobs.

Blacks could not live anywhere they wanted until a legal mandate in 1968. However, many blacks and whites lived in the same neighborhoods before World War II and formed close friendships.

Up until the mid-1960s, crime was so low that people walked all over the city day and night and slept or left home without locking doors.

Changes in lifestyle were reflected in fashions. Across the century, hemlines roamed from ankle to thigh level and back and black hair styles went from braided or natural to chemically straightened and back. Moral standards roamed right along with them from prim to promiscuous and back again.

But when automobile plant production lines were running on overtime, the bountiful wages compensated for many of Flint's flaws and drew new residents as surely as an accumulated lottery jackpot. For the better part of the century, black folks flocked here steadily from all over North America.

Frankie Wynn, now a retired educator, was a teen when her family came from Oklahoma as part of a war-generated jobs boom in the early 1940s.

"My father wanted a better life for his kids," she said. "He already had a brother here who told him they wanted workers."

Ruth VanZandt had arrived in 1927 from Arkansas with an aunt and uncle who raised her after her mother died.

"They came here because of the chance of better work," she said. Her father followed later drawn by higher pay at Chevrolet than what he was earning as a maintenance man at a small black college in Little Rock, she said.

In 1921, Katie Ellis Harper's grandfather became the first of several in his family to move from South Carolina to Flint. Ellis Harper was born and raised in Flint but lived in Pennsylvania for a few years during the Great Depression of the 1930s when her parents moved there after losing their jobs and home.

Ruth Owens Buckner, born in 1911, is also a Flint native. Her grandfather escaped slavery in Kentucky by hiding in a crate and allowing himself to be shipped north. His "Man in the Box" story became something of a legend.

Buckner traces her family tree on both sides to some of Flint's earliest black residents. Many of them came here because of the Underground Railroad route to Canada, she said.

"There's an awful lot of history in the southern part of Michigan," she noted, adding that she once toured one of the Underground Railroad's former hiding places in Marshall.

Watching the made-for-TV movie "Queen," about an ancestor of "Roots" author Alex Haley, brought back many memories of stories Buckner said she heard as a child.

Her husband's family came to Flint in the late 1800s from Nicodemus, Kan., a black settlement steeped in its own rich history about the black Buffalo Soldiers regiment of the U.S. Cavalry and other pioneers of the Old West.

Many blacks who migrated to Flint found the better life they sought but, for some, the city's golden reputation eventually lost its allure.

Marion Wright Quinn, a resident since 1929, complained that dwindling General Motors jobs prompted a massive exodus of young people in the 1980s. Her eldest son works for GM in Denver, Colo., another lives in Ohio and two in California.

Some who chose to remain in Flint have also been critical of it.

"I always thought Flint was such a country town, not progressive enough," said Lois Shaw, a retired registered nurse. She attributed it to "a General Motors mindset."

Not until many years after Shaw moved to Flint in 1946 did city fathers develop the Flint Cultural Center and other enrichment programs for children, she said.

Despite such growing pains, as time passed, Flint saw improvements in employment, housing, education, politics, business, religion, race relations and many aspects of community life.

Blacks progressed from having a narrow selection of neighborhoods during the first two-thirds of this century, to living wherever they pleased. They now occupy about 23,000 of the city's 59,000 total housing units, according to the 1990 census. About half are homeowners and half are renters.

From political impotence in the 1930s, such as having to elect a symbolic mayor, blacks have seen three black Flint mayors seated from the 1960s to 1990s among a host of elected city, county and state representatives. Also, an evolving political outlook has influenced identity changes from colored people to Negroes to blacks to African-Americans.

From segregated dining, dancing and death rites, the city has integrated at virtually every social level.

Menial job opportunities have broadened to a full scope of white-collar professions. The 1990 census reported that nearly 3,000 of about 19,000 black Flint workers, ages 16 and up, hold professional specialty or administrative jobs. About 8,000 work in service or manufacturing jobs.

As for the prosperity index, about 7,000 of 23,000 black household incomes exceeded $50,000 a year in 1989 though about 6,000 black families lived below poverty level.

From schools having few black students and no black teachers or black history lessons, the predominantly black Flint School District now embraces multiculturalism. More than 10,000 of black Flintites in 1990 were high school graduates. Only about 3,000 reported having less than a ninth-grade education while roughly the same number were college graduates.

Flint is or was home to many African-Americans of national or international renown. They have made their mark in moviemaking, modeling, music, professional sports, entrepreneurship and more.

As the 20th century draws to a close, Flint boasts far more black churches, social outlets and general opportunities than when the century started, despite interruptions by five wars, the Great Depression and a sometimes volatile civil rights movement.

Interviews with about 90 black Flint residents of all ages and walks of life reveal that the Vehicle City owns a remarkable history of black progress. Let's walk with them down memory lane to see how much Flint has come of age as a desirable place for blacks to live, work, worship and pursue happiness.

Contents

Chapter 1
Neighborhoods
1

EARLY FLINT:
"We didn't know anything about being black until the war came."
4

ST. JOHN:
"The good, the bad and the ugly"
10

SOUTH SIDE:
"Most of the houses ... in that area were built by blacks."
16

INTEGRATION:
"Would you live some place you weren't wanted?"
22

PUBLIC HOUSING:
"It's not what you have, it's how you keep what you've got."
27

LIFESTYLES:
"We were poor but we didn't know we were poor."
32

CRIME:
"That would have been big news, somebody getting killed."
40

REINVESTMENT:
"You have to use all the money you can borrow."
44

Chapter 2
Jobs
49

SHOP TALK:
"It took WWII to put black men in the shop on production."
56

SELF-EMPLOYED:
"... always looking for a slot he could fill to make money."
65

PROFESSIONAL GROWTH:
"I had to be twice as good as anyone else."
74

THIS AND THAT:
"You can't keep a good, determined person down."
89

DISCRIMINATION:
"They said the job was filled."
92

Chapter 3
Education
95

EARLY DAYS:
"They'd tell the black girls they'd make good hairdressers."
99

FIRSTS:
"They were advertising for teachers and I couldn't get (hired), so I went to work at Chevrolet."
102

QUALITY RATING:
"At least when we came out of school, we could read and write, which a lot of them can't do now."
108

SUCCESS STORIES:
"No such thing as I can't."
118

HIGHER GROUND:
"You didn't pass any black person on campus without speaking."
124

Chapter 4
Churches
129

ORIGINS:
"All the blacks attended one church."
135

LEADERS:
"He took time with all people."
138

CHURCH WORK:
"The church could get more involved in problems facing our black youth."
141

OTHER FAITHS:
She became a Christian Science practitioner – healing through prayer.
146

Chapter 5
Social Life
149

IMA:
"We had to wait until the whites left."
153

NIGHTCLUBS:
"It was wall-to-wall people."
156

AMUSEMENT PARKS:
"We went separate from the white kids."
163

MOVIES:
"There was a theater on every corner."
165

APPEARING LIVE:
"It's not all glamour and glitz."
168

CLUB AND SERVICE ORGANIZATIONS:
"We started meeting from house to house."
176

DOWNTOWN AND OTHER SOCIAL VENUES:
"Downtown was beautiful to me."
184

Chapter 6
Athletics
191

PLAYGROUNDS:
"I lived at Berston."
197

IN THE BALLPARK:
"It was rough but it was fun."
203

SHOOTING HOOPS:
"Everybody in the stands went crazy over it."
213

FOOTBALL GREATS:
"If we won, we had bragging rights."
219

ON TRACK:
"We might see another state record fall."
230

HER STORY:
"The McGee twins revolutionized women's sports here in Flint."
235

IN THE RING:
"He taught us that you couldn't just go out into the streets and fight."
241

Chapter 7
Race Relations
249

PREJUDICE:
"I didn't know my dad was that way."
254

DISCRIMINATION:
"You knew where you could go and couldn't go."
265

ON THE JOB:
"The last hired and the first fired"
269

LEADERSHIP:
"A common man trying to do common good."
276

PROTEST:
"No one had ever dared to challenge the establishment."
298

Neighborhoods

Having a bike in the mid-1940s when many blacks still did not own cars was a status symbol for Addie Roselyn Leonard, daughter of funeral-home owner Ailene Butler.

"When I first came to Flint, there was no such thing as a black neighborhood," recalled William Hoskins, who arrived in 1936 from his native Mississippi. "The Italians, Polish and everyone else (including blacks) lived together."

In some cases, black and white families shared one house. One family lived upstairs and the other down. But there were no walls between friendships. The families stuck together, often ate together and freely visited back and forth.

Children played together, uncaring about the difference in their skin colors. Some blacks said they were so close they learned to speak foreign languages from their ethnic playmates.

In some memories, interracial living in the early part of this century was harmonious. But memories can deceive. Flint as a whole was not happily integrated.

As near as many old-timers can remember, no blacks lived west of North Saginaw until after World War II. Flint's small black population lived in two neighborhoods. The older was on the south side, just north of Thread Lake. The other was on the north side, east of the Buick factory complex in the legendary St. John Street community.

St. John was the ethnic melting pot Hoskins described. It was a bustling self-contained neighborhood, convenient to jobs at Buick. It was home to thousands of southern blacks like Hoskins who had migrated to Flint seeking better-paying jobs and freedom from racial oppression.

Flint had two major black migration booms, according to census data. The first was from about 1910 to 1929, before the Great Depression. The second was during and after World War II, from about 1940 through the mid-1950s.

At the turn of the century, only about 300 blacks lived in Flint compared to an overall population of about 13,000. But by 1960, Flint's black population had grown to about 35,000 of 197,000.

With the steady flood of new arrivals, the original two neighborhoods where blacks lived were quickly outgrown. Blacks gradually moved outward, starting on the fringes of adjacent all-white neighborhoods.

But blacks were not free to live anywhere they chose until 1968. That's when Flint voters narrowly approved an open-housing ordinance. The hard-won Fair Housing Law was believed to be the first in the country approved by a referendum, and it opened the door for blacks to move to any neighborhood they could afford. (More details in race relations chapter.)

A downside of that victory is that it accelerated a common housing pattern. When blacks moved in, whites moved out.

Neighborhoods that were mostly white in 1968 were mostly black by 1988 – often much sooner. Few neighborhoods with a balanced racial mix exist in Flint today.

There is a social gap among blacks, too. As prosperity enabled some to move to better neighborhoods, a gulf developed between the haves and have-nots.

Many old-timers speak nostalgically of the era before open housing when the black community was like a close-knit family.

Black doctors, lawyers and other prosperous residents could afford to move but lived in the same neighborhoods as less-affluent blacks. They had no choice.

Some tried to move but were firmly blocked by owners who refused to sell or real estate agents who refused to show them houses in desired neighborhoods.

Tensions eased after World War II. Middle- and upper-income blacks moved to newer neighborhoods. Now some people don't look back on that as progress. Instead of a turning point, they say it harmed the black community.

Black professionals and prominent business owners had been leaders of the black community. What they did had a positive trickle-down effect on the black community as a whole. When they moved, they took with them a big chunk of community standards and culture.

In another sense, the black community had been psychologically separated long before that.

Many of Flint's oldest black residents regarded newcomers as intruders whose undesirable values and morals lowered the standard of living.

They spoke of a long-standing rivalry between north-side and south-side blacks. Some described it as petty and others as acute. The perception is that many south-side blacks consider themselves socially and economically superior to north-side blacks.

Yet, wherever blacks live in Flint, most tend to find that most of their neighbors also are black.

According to the 1990 U.S. Census, Flint's 67,485 blacks are 47.9 percent of the total population and growing.

If William Hoskins was moving to Flint today, unlike in 1936, he would not have much trouble identifying black neighborhoods. But one sign of progress is that black families now live in every quadrant of the city and neighboring suburbs.

"The only way they separate us now is by the price of the house and that's the way it should be," said Sam Williams, a Flint resident since 1927. "If I can afford to move in and take care of my property, I should be able to."

The old rule of "just as soon as we start to move in, they (whites) move away if they can" does not apply as much, he said.

"It's getting harder for (whites) to move away. I mean they gotta keep going further. Now they're going to Fenton. They can't go to Holly that much because we're in Holly. We're in Davison."

He knows one black family living in Grand Blanc's exclusive Warwick Hills subdivision, "right on the golf course. He can afford to live there and take care of his property. No problem. That would be unheard of years ago," Williams said.

EARLY FLINT:
"We didn't know anything about being black until the war came."

Bessie Owens Brooks was born in 1906 at 610 Kennelworth (then 11th Street) on Flint's south side.

"My mother was born here and her mother too. I have a certificate (to prove) that my great-grandfather was here in 1855," Brooks said. That was the year Flint was incorporated as a city.

Also among Brooks' keepsakes is a photo of her grandmother, Helen Hill Graves, who is believed to be the first black child born in Flint.

Brooks traces her father's history to Sarnia, Ontario, where he was born the son of a fugitive slave. After slavery ended in the United States, he migrated to Flint where he met and married Brooks' mother.

Some of the first blacks to visit Flint may have been fugitive slaves en route to Canada. Detroit was the most direct stopover on the Underground Railroad network that secretly led runaway slaves to freedom in Canada.

Flint is believed to have been an alternate route that directed fleeing slaves through Port Huron into Canada.

Many Michigan and Flint residents were actively opposed to slavery. Some white sympathizers went out of their way to thwart slave catchers.

Some escaped slaves may have settled in Flint, but there is no record of it because they kept a low profile to avoid slave hunters, according to historian Melvin E. Banner. His book "The Black Pioneer in Michigan," published in 1973, is one of few resources on Flint's early black history.

A barber named John Carter was one of the first blacks known to settle in

Blacks are among the construction workers shown here building houses in an area identified as Murray Hill, circa 1912.

Flint, according to Banner. Originally from North Carolina, Carter advertised his trade in a Flint newspaper in 1839 and was listed in the 1840 census. That was only about 20 years after the arrival of Flint's first white settler, Jacob Smith.

The 1840 census also listed John Patterson as another black settler, according to Banner. His occupation and origins were not given but the record indicates he had a wife and four children.

Banner's book is a good reference for history about blacks in Flint before 1900.

Some of Flint's little-known early black history has been pieced together from census records and newspaper archives. But the best remaining resource is older residents whose family histories have passed down to them by word of mouth.

Like Brooks' family, at the turn of the century, most blacks lived between Court Street and Lippincott Boulevard, southwest of Lapeer Road and west of S. Saginaw Street.

The streets were unpaved and toilets were outdoors. Nobody had a lot of money, but they knew how to make the most of what they had.

"My father had vacant lots around the house where we had gardens," Brooks said. "It was wide open. As long as it wasn't for sale, we were free to use it. Mother was a day worker and dad worked in the shop and drove a truck."

These crude barracks in what was called a Negro Camp were home to many black men who worked nearby at Buick in 1920.

Automobile manufacturing began in Flint in 1902, but few blacks could afford cars until the 1940s. They walked where they had to go, sometimes from the south side to the north side. Those who could pay the nickel fare rode the streetcar.

Few blacks owned homes. One who did was Alonzo Owens, the father of Ruth Owens Buckner. Like Brooks, who is her cousin, Buckner's parents both descended from Flint's early black families. Buckner was born in 1911 and grew up in a seven-room house Alonzo Owens had bought on Park Street.

"When I was little, in the neighborhood where we lived, there were only three black families," Buckner said. "(Flint) wasn't as segregated. It wasn't like everybody lived in a black neighborhood.

"There might have been one black person in a block, but there wasn't all that much prejudice. I don't think blacks were all that bold about going into unfamiliar neighborhoods, to avoid trouble.

"Nobody lived east of Lapeer from Court Street (south). Some of the more fair-skinned ones lived elsewhere, but the brown-skinned ones like us lived where we did.

"In my early teens, there was a black family on the corner. I thought that only black people owned houses because the white people came and went but the blacks were stable," Buckner said.

With the beginning of Flint's automobile industry, the city's black population began to spread. Construction of Buick Motor Co.'s factory on the old Hamilton farm in 1906 spurred the growth of the St. John Street neighborhood on the north side.

Minnie Simpson grew up there. Her father came to Flint in 1918 from Georgia and sent for his family a year later, after finding work at Buick and a place to live.

In 1920, Flint was a growing city of about 91,000 people, including about 1,700 blacks. Gaslights lined the streets. From her front porch on Carton Street, young Minnie could see outside the city limits across Stewart Avenue.

"There was nothing out there but open land," she said.

Theresa Crichton, now retired from General Motors, lived on Easy Street in the St. John area in the 1920s. Her grandfather had come to Michigan in 1902 and first settled in Pontiac.

Crichton's family lived in several houses in St. John over a 50-year span. During the early years, it was a colorblind neighborhood.

"Neighbors felt free to drop in to borrow an iron or a cup of flour or sugar," Crichton said. "They left a note if no one was home. Nobody locked doors then. Neighbors trusted and looked out for each other.

"There were two buggies on the street. Everybody shared them.

"When my mother had twins, everybody came and made diapers and booties. They'd sit on the porch and help make baby quilts.

"We didn't know anything about being black until the (second world) war came."

Before 1910, there were fewer than 400 black families in Flint. They

A bird's-eye view from a Buick factory window takes in the surrounding residential area along Industrial Avenue.

knew each other by name and exactly where they lived. A boom time between 1910 and the start of the Great Depression in 1929 boosted the black population to nearly 6,000, still less than 4 percent of the whole.

Few new black families moved to Flint between 1929 and the late 1930s. During those Depression years, black families already living here struggled to survive.

"I can remember the Depression very well," Anna L.V. Howard said. She grew up on Flint's south side. "In fact, my mama and daddy lost their house but then the war came and that's when people started to get back on their feet.

"It took World War II, to put black men in the shop on production. Before then, they were janitors and did menial work. My husband got a better job. He came out of the foundry and got to be a finisher.

"During the war, you could go anyplace and get a job. They almost dragged you in there."

The auto factories hired black women for the first time because so many men were gone to war. Howard went to work on production at AC Spark Plug. AC hired few blacks before then, she said.

Seemingly overnight, Flint's black population doubled as newcomers poured in to grab prized jobs paying unprecedented wages. Rent ran as high as $25 a week because housing was in such high demand.

"That's how blacks got ahead, got money to buy their homes," Howard said. "Working and saving. It was good money."

With prosperity came a new attitude. After the war, blacks began to look for homes in previously forbidden territory. Returning war veterans felt that risking their lives for their country had earned them the right to live where they pleased.

The Sugar Hill neighborhood was built. The nickname was probably patterned after a legendary, upscale black neighborhood in Harlem, N.Y. Flint's Sugar Hill developed on vacant land south of Lapeer Road between Burr Boulevard and Dort Highway.

South-side blacks proudly use the name as a status symbol. But some north-side blacks use it disdainfully to ridicule the perceived snobbery of south-side blacks.

"There was always this north- and south-side rivalry thing," Katie Ellis Harper said. She was born in Flint in 1928.

"Basically, all the girls on the north side liked the boys on the south side and vice versa. Nothing serious," she said.

Apparently, some boys took it more seriously.

"They didn't allow me over there messing with their women (but) the north-side boys were always over here (south side) fiddling around,"

Once a beehive of recreational activity, the forlorn St. John Community Center building and a few street signs are all that's left of the neighborhood.

Layton Galloway said.

"They said the south side had the prettiest girls, so we ganged up on them if they came over here."

Some south-side parents would forbid their children to visit the "rowdy" north side, but that didn't stop them. Galloway would sneak over to visit his cousin, he said.

"They knew me as a south-sider so I couldn't go over there without him. I only went up there for sporting events. I wouldn't go to Berston (Field House) by myself," he said. Berston Field House is a community center on North Saginaw Street.

South-side girls sometimes sneaked over to the north side, too, to attend teen dances, Anna L.V. Howard said. And north-side youth attended south-side dances at the Clifford Street center, she said.

The rivalry thing continued into the 1950s when Sondra Rawls was a teen-ager.

"The south side was viewed as elitist," Rawls said. She lives on the south side now but grew up on the north side.

"I'm sure you can get a perspective from them as to how they viewed us," she said. "The guys from the south side would come to the north side and try to get a girlfriend and vice versa."

Sometimes fights broke out when the two sides met at community events such as dances at the IMA, she said.

ST. JOHN:
"The good, the bad and the ugly"

When this photo was taken in 1974, life was far from easy in this deteriorating neighborhood. But in earlier days, when businesses were thriving, the St. John Street neighborhood had been a desirable place to live and work.

There is a place that's dear to me. Not far, but near to me.
... No strangers walk these streets. ... No hunger here, for if I have food, so shall you. ...
Someone has stolen our happiness, our community and family lifestyle. ...
Is this better life what our forefathers wanted?

Bobbie Wells misses her old neighborhood so much, she wrote a poem about it. She's a member of the St. John Street Reunion Committee, formed in 1991 to preserve the closeness of the former neighborhood that was wiped out by urban renewal clearance in the mid-1970s.

The St. John neighborhood was between Stewart Avenue to the north, N. Saginaw, west; and the Flint River south and east. It was named for its main street, the spine of the neighborhood intersecting residential streets. Some fondly referred to the area as "across the tracks" because of the Grand Trunk Railroad line that separated the Buick factory complex from the neighborhood. To enter the neighborhood from the west, it was necessary to "cross the tracks."

"It was like being in a city of its own," said James Blakely. He lived there in the 1950s.

"Everything that blacks needed was right in that area. You didn't have to go out of that quarter, not even on weekends."

"St. John was a beautiful mixed neighborhood, a true melting pot," said Woody Etherly. "You had your Polish community, you had the black community, you had the Germans. You had everybody there and everybody talked to each other and everybody communicated with each other and everybody knew each other on a first-name basis.

"Now you don't have that here. That's lost and that's something I really hate. I mean black people had their businesses, they had their restaurants, they had their nightclubs. It was all right there in that community."

Despite blighted conditions, many blacks did not want to leave St. John because of its rich history, he said.

But not everyone remembers St. John nostalgically.

"Throw it out of your mind that the area was a nice place to be," James Wesley said. "It had some nice nightclubs but they didn't last long. There was too much fighting over there and off-the-wall businesses. No such thing as shopping over there. Nothing but joints. The only place to buy something decent was Papp's drugstore on the corner of St. John and Leith and he moved out as quick as he could."

With the exception of a few staple businesses such as dry cleaners, funeral parlors and restaurants, the primary enterprise in the St. John area was "more or less, pimps and prostitutes and things like that," Wesley said.

Sooty pollution from the Buick foundry and dust from unpaved roads blighted what age and neglect didn't get to first.

"People were suffering from all sorts of respiratory diseases," said Olive Beasley, director of the Flint district of the state Department of Civil Rights during the 1960s and '70s.

"Cars would get speckled, and the paint peeled off from the fallout. Houses peeled too."

Former residents described clouds of soot so thick, you couldn't see down

St. John Street. It blew across the entire neighborhood like a black plague. They couldn't hang laundry outside because it got dirty long before it got dry, they said.

Chemicals sprayed on the dirt streets to keep dust down would stick to shoes like chewing gum and get tracked into houses onto floors and carpets.

Those very different views of St. John reflect its evolution from a thriving community to a slum. By most accounts, the decline began about 1950 when white families moved out.

By the late 1960s, unfulfilled urban renewal plans had contributed to widespread blight. And by the mid-1970s, all the houses and businesses had been torn down and the vacant land turned into an undeveloped industrial park.

It is a stark contrast to the vital neighborhood that once thrived there.

St. John Street, the heart of the neighborhood, "was very much alive," Bill Hoskins said. "All along it were barber shops, shoeshine stands, entertainment. The whites ran the pharmacy, car repair shops and five-and-ten."

White-owned businesses had served the St. John community since the 1930s or earlier. But by the 1950s, the clientele began to change to mostly blacks or white Buick workers.

Papp's drugstore at Leith and St. John was one white-owned business held in high esteem. The Papps were a prominent Hungarian family. Elza Papp was a Genesee County Circuit judge. Her brother Zolton, a pharmacist, was president of the Hurley Hospital Board.

Their father, Kolomon Papp, gave many black youngsters their first jobs. He also made loans to customers short of cash between GM's biweekly paydays.

Two drugstores, McKain's on Stewart and McKeighan's on Leith at Industrial, were other white-owned businesses often mentioned by people reminiscing. (William H. McKeighan was Flint's mayor for five nonconsecutive terms between 1915 and 1932.)

From the 1940s to the mid-70s, the Beer Vault at Industrial and Leith was the convenience store of that era.

St. John residents lived convenient to the Catsman Coal Co., an ice house, a jail and a slaughterhouse.

At Bokor's grocery store on St. John Street, they bought on credit. All they had to do was sign their names in a large black ledger kept on the counter. In the 1930s, small neighborhood grocers like Bokor's flourished all over the St. John area. Competition from supermarket chains began to squeeze them out of business in the 1950s.

From The Balkan Bakery on St. John, the mouth-watering smell of baking bread wafted across the neighborhood. Three loaves cost a dime during the Depression. Doughnuts were 5 cents each in the 1950s.

A nickel also bought two scoops of ice cream at Shahidas Ice Cream Parlor, aka "the Double Dip."

You could get a hamburger smothered in grilled onions at Mrs. Kelly's or finger-licking barbecue dinners at Mr. Lucas' short-order restaurants.

If you wanted to see a good fight, or even if you didn't, the place to be was The Hut, a tavern on St. John. It was a dim, hole-in-the-wall establishment that attracted the sort of clientele quick to anger and settle it with a switchblade.

St. John was the hub of black entertainment. The Columbia and Richard movie theaters and nightclubs galore kept the streets awake day and night.

The Flint Community Center on St. John and later the St. John Community Center provided recreation and enrichment classes for youth and a meeting hall for adults.

Maxie Brandon lived two doors away from the Flint Community Building on Dewey Street, between North Street and Industrial Avenue. It was built in the 1920s by prominent blacks. The two-story building held medical, law and insurance offices, a drugstore, a funeral parlor and a gym. Basketball games, dances and civic meetings took place in the multipurpose gym.

When the yellow brick St. John Community Center was built in 1950, it had an auditorium, gymnasium and kitchen. The center is the only building from the old days still standing. The city of Flint police department uses it as a training facility.

Woody Etherly regrets not understanding the consequences of urban renewal. He was Third Ward city councilman from 1970 to 1983.

The relocation took advantage of many blacks by not paying enough for their homes to keep pace with rising inflation, Etherly said. The $15,000 maximum buyout was not a lot of money when you considered moving expenses and the price of homes in nicer neighborhoods, he said.

(Families bought out decades earlier during a Buick property acquisition fared much better, Sam Willlams said. His father paid $1,900 for a house on Everett Street in 1930. Buick paid owners like him $15,000 or more for their homes. "When Buick was buying, a lot of people made out real good and were able to purchase nice homes," Williams said.)

Critics of the government buyout, such as Etherly, argue that ghettos are not created by blacks, who seldom move into new neighborhoods, but by age and neglect. By the time blacks pay for older homes in established neighborhoods, the decline cycle usually is already under way, some said.

Catherine Alexander shudders to remember her family's first home in the St. John area. Her parents moved from Arkansas to Flint in 1950 when she was 3.

"We stayed in a house that had three or four families in one room," Alexander said. "There was no yard and the back yard was full of bottles and stuff. For a little child, accustomed to having a yard to play in, it was a big shock."

"It was a time when too many people lived in one area. There was lots of fighting."

Archie Parks, Flint's first black police officer, patrolled St. John and the north side for 11 years, beginning in 1931. He was Flint's only black officer for nearly eight years.

Parks was a big man – 6-foot-2, 220 pounds. He patrolled the area on foot. Some said he was allowed to arrest only blacks but often helped the detective division solve crimes.

St. John in the early years was "an immigrant area of muddy streets and little shacks," Ruth Owens Buckner said.

"When GM sent south for people to come (during World War II), the majority of the men who came weren't family men. They were roustabouts. That was the origin of the belief that the south side was better than the north. Lots of the men weren't married so lots of whores moved in.

"The whole street – Michigan Avenue – was nothing but prostitution. (But) there were whores on the south side too."

Buckner, a lifelong south-sider, recalled her first visit to the St. John area in about 1916.

"We never saw that many black people growing up so we wanted to go meet them," she said.

"The doors were standing wide open, flies were going in and out and the men sitting around drinking. Lots of those who came didn't have good morals so that carried on through the years. (Despite) people there who were good, more were bad. At one time, every Saturday night there was a knifing when drunk men got into fights. So they gave a bad reputation to the good apples.

"They took the same mentality when they moved to the other side of Saginaw Street. Same stuff, fights every Saturday night, robberies, shooting, killing.

"People who had children and raised them strictly to go to church and be something, those were the kids who amounted to something. But they were interspersed with those whose parents did all that drinking and fighting. Not all of them, some of them rose above their circumstances."

But like the proverbial greener grass on the other side of the fence, St. John's rough-and-tumble ways held a certain attraction for south-side residents.

"I had the best of both worlds," Audrey Wilson said. She lived on the south side but had an aunt who lived on St. John, in the middle of the block between State and Leith.

"When we stayed with her, we'd lay up in bed in the front bedroom and watch all the action across the street – the fights and the dancing.

"St. John was an active street. That block had The Hut, the Columbia Theater, the Frozen Custard restaurant my dad ran, a grocery store, the Red Dog restaurant and a pool hall."

On her aunt's side of the street was a five-and-dime variety store, a black newspaper office, a black insurance company and another residence.

"We saw people coming out of everywhere. So it was like a floor show for us. In the summer time, it was extra busy, because everybody would be out trying to catch the breeze," Wilson said.

Freddie Williams lived in St. John from the late 1930s through the 1950s. He knew the neighborhood at its worst but savors its best.

"There was prostitutes and gambling," he said. "This was pretty much after the Hungarians and those had moved out. There would be (police) raids down there. Our parents were strict and kept us away.

"There was a time when we all thought we wanted to get away from that but now that we've moved away, we miss it. Now when we have the St. John reunion every year, it's crowded, because everybody wants to see their old friends and rekindle that close-knittedness."

The St. John reunion attracts an array of black success stories. Some are doctors, lawyers and CEOs. One grew up to become the mayor of Flint.

Woodrow Stanley, Flint's second black elected mayor, speaks reverently of his childhood in St. John in the 1960s.

"There was a sense of community, of people looking out for each other," he said. "People were respectful. Even a drunk guy would not curse in front of old people.

"Some people would say that the St. John neighborhood was the toughest neighborhood in Flint, but people knew each other. Before it became predominantly black, it was where most of the Eastern Europeans lived. For a long time, many of them still owned businesses there after they moved out.

"I never saw it as a ghetto, slum or whatever. It was an experience that made me the person I am. You have to have a little bit of grit, I think, to do well in politics. (St. John) was my proving ground.

"I loved St. John Street – the good, the bad and the ugly."

SOUTH SIDE:
"Most of the houses ... in that area were built by blacks."

From an integration battlefront of the 1960s, a show of patriotism fronts one of the modern, upscale homes in the Evergreen Estates and Evergreen Valley subdivisions built in the mid-1950s and early 1960s, east of Averill between E. Court and Lippincott.

St. John had the actual Easy Street but the south side claimed bragging rights to the lifestyle.

A south-side address connoted status. Like owning a Cadillac or a mink coat or wearing a white shirt to work and not getting your hands dirty. All of those dreams were quicker to come true for many south-side blacks.

How sweet it was in the late 1940s-1960s when blacks could first afford to build homes in the south-side subdivision nicknamed Sugar Hill and in this area along the southern edge of Woodlawn Park.

Flint's first black homeowners were south-siders. Before the early 1900s, blacks mostly lived in an area northwest of Thread Lake known as Floral Park.

Typically, Floral Park started out as an interracial neighborhood. Much of it was razed in the 1960s when the I-475 and I-69 freeway interchange was built.

Some well-remembered black-owned businesses that served the area at various times included Walker's Department Store on S. Saginaw near 12th Street, Reed's Drugstore at Kennelworth and 11th Street, Waller's Drugstore at the corner of Eighth and Lapeer, and Brooks confectionary on 11th Street.

Annalea Raymond Bannister's father owned Raymond's barber shop on Kennelworth Avenue in the 1930s.

"It wasn't hard for a black man to get land in those days – it was hard to get money," she said. Her dad's business occupied the ground floor and the family lived in an apartment on the upper level. Her grandparents sent her dad $1,000 to help with the down payment.

Maxie Brandon spent part of his childhood in the area during the 1930s. Most blacks lived between the railroad tracks and Ninth Street, from south to north, and Harrison and Lapeer Road, west to east. Wellington, Clifford, Fay, Stanford and 12th are some of the streets in the area, Brandon said. The southern part of Fay, Ferris and Stanford streets crossed over into the Elm Park neighborhood, which was all-white then.

Many black families uprooted from the dying St. John community relocated to this west Flint subdivision of newer homes. The first to move on their street got mixed receptions from neighbors. Now the neighborhood is predominantly black.

Elm Park is just southeast of Floral Park, between Pingree Street and Lippincott Boulevard.

By the end of World War II, black homeownership had spread from Floral Park to Elm Park to Oakwood Park (a portion of Sugar Hill). The area called Sugar Hill is roughly east of Howard Avenue between Lapeer Road and Lippincott Boulevard.

By 1955, blacks were moving across Lapeer Road and Dort Highway and out to the city limits at Center Road. Those neighborhoods are predominantly black now.

Sugar Hill, Evergreen Valley and Evergreen Valley Estates were brand-new neighborhoods built after World War II. Affluent blacks also built homes along the southern edge of Woodlawn Park, an established all-white neighborhood that is said to have barred blacks until the 1960s.

As the black population spread out, its community fixtures dissipated. Floral Park had been a social and recreational hub. The oldest black churches were there. So were the first black nightclubs – The Golden Leaf on Harrison at Kennelworth and the Sportsman's Club on Clifford at Lippincott.

The Clifford Street Center in Floral Park was sort of the Berston Field House of the south side. The center opened about 1937 and closed in 1962 when it was deemed beyond repair. Before the center opened, area blacks sometimes held street dances for entertainment.

The playground at Clark School was another south-side gathering spot.

Clark School was built in 1913. By the 1990s, it was a desolate, plywood-covered relic overlooking the freeway that gutted the neighborhood it served.

Across the street is the legendary Golden Leaf Club, a popular night spot since 1935. Crowds still pack the narrow dance floor on Saturday nights.

"Basically, we were happy, we had our own little neighborhood, we had our playground and our church activities," Ruth Scott said. She grew up in Floral Park in the 1930s.

"Our parents made it enjoyable for us. We didn't look outside the neighborhood for things to do.

"On the street where we lived, there were two black families. There were (mostly) white children. Everybody on the street was real nice to us. We were at their house and they at ours."

But, in the early 1940s, Scott found out about racial prejudice.

"On the block in front of us were some teen-age girls," she said. "There was an empty lot in front of them and they decided they wanted to have a play lot. They went from house to house delivering invitations to the kids. We were waiting for ours. It didn't come.

"I remember saying to my mother they must have ran out (of invitations). She said it was because we were colored. I still couldn't figure it out because all our (white) friends were there. My mother explained that everybody isn't the same.

"We were so hurt. They had Kool-Aid and they were running and playing, so my mother took us out in the back yard and made Kool-Aid and sandwiches to make us feel better. That was my first experience with racism. It was a shock."

The racial composition of the neighborhood had changed by 1942 when Eloise Caldwell, a cooking instructor, and her husband moved to Elm Park. Their nearest neighbors were black.

"When we first moved out here, this street and Howard Street were the only two that were paved and whites lived out here," Caldwell said.

The Caldwells paid $2,750 for their home; their payments were $27 a month. It was the first time Eloise Caldwell had lived in a house with an upstairs and downstairs, she said. It's been their home for 50 years. They decided not to move when a lot was offered to them in nearby Sugar Hill.

Sugar Hill was the first subdivision to offer blacks new homes. Bertha Simms, a black real estate developer, sold many of the lots in that area.

When Dolores Ennis bought her lot in 1958, "there were no houses here, this was all pure, undeveloped land," she said. "A group of us got together and purchased the land. We bought our own plots and then looked for a builder."

Layton Galloway, a postal worker, knew a good deal when he saw one.

"The last month I rented an apartment, in 1959, the rent was $85 a week. The house (note) was $110. At that time, you could buy a house for like $10 down.

"It just so happened I had bought a lot from Connie Childress (another black real estate agent). I had paid like $900 for that lot. We had the house built there. I paid (the builder) $10 and put the lot up for collateral.

"It didn't cost anything to build the house but you really had to put your nose to the grindstone to get things in the house.

"We didn't have furniture for quite a while. People's Furniture on Eighth and Liberty was a good place to get furniture."

As Sugar Hill filled up, prospective black homeowners looked for new neighborhoods. Some found out that exclusive meant more than just expensive.

Marion Coates-Williams with her husband T. Wendell Williams filed a civil rights suit in the early 1960s after they were denied the purchase of a house in the Woodlawn Park subdivision, off E. Court Street.

She was Flint's first black classroom teacher and he was a physician and the first black elected to the Flint Board of Education. Williams Elementary School on Flint's east side is named for him.

"We wanted to buy a house in the Court Street area and the owners objected and they didn't want to sell to us, so we had a civil rights case," Coates-Williams said.

"The owners wouldn't show the house. The thing about it was that the owner was a colleague of my husband; they worked together at the hospital. My daughter lives on that street now not too far from the house we wanted. Blacks live all over now."

Many blacks who were turned away from Woodlawn Park proper resolved the problem by building homes on vacant land to its immediate south and east, Edith Spencer said.

"Dr. (Clarence) Kimbrough couldn't buy a home in the area he wanted so he built his home on Brookside," she said. "There weren't any blacks living in Woodlawn Park then. None at all." Kimbrough became the first black president of the Flint Board of Education in 1968 and also served on the board of directors at Citizens Bank.

Helen Harris, the first black woman elected to the Flint school board and its first female president, built a home there. So did C. Frederick Robinson, a civil rights attorney. Most of the houses built since then in that area were built by blacks, Spencer said.

Dr. William Simms, a dentist, and his wife, Bertha, were the first blacks to move into that area, Spencer said.

Alexander Jones, a factory worker, was third, after the Simmses and the

Mitchells. Jones said the neighborhood was mostly white in 1953 when he bought his house just east of Lapeer Road.

Minnie Simpson and her family moved in about the same time. Her white neighbors were receptive; one even introduced himself, she said. But neighborly relations soured after some rowdy teens crashed a party at the Simpsons, she said.

Even after Flint's open-occupancy ordinance passed in 1968, Henry Horton said he needed tacit approval from whites to move into Woodlawn Park. He is a former Flint public housing director and county government official.

"When I moved here, there was two other black families. One was Pastor (Robert) Turpin and the other was Dr. Mildred Smith," Horton said.

"The house was empty. I used a broker whose name was Connie Childress and the house was owned by Eldon Auker, ... a Grand Blanc land developer. Connie spoke to Eldon and, I don't know this first-hand, but Connie told me that Eldon talked to the neighbors and they said it was OK."

The Evergreen Estates and Evergreen Valley subdivisions were further testing grounds for integration. Those homes are east of Averill between E. Court and Lippincott.

Development began in 1955 on Evergreen Valley, south of Lapeer Road. Evergreen Estates, north of Lapeer Road, was sold off from the original 400-acre parcel and the first five model homes were built in 1962. With 700 lots, it was one of the last large, undeveloped tracts in Flint to be zoned residential.

"We had a friend, Connie Childress. He was trying to integrate this area," said Annalea Bannister, who moved there in 1971.

"So with us being the color we were (fair-skinned), he asked us to be the ones to tear down the barrier," Bannister said.

"How it works is once blacks move in, the whites move out. I remember when that happened on Lapeer Road and really raised a ruckus."

But Bannister refused to be a guinea pig.

"A friend of mine who was the first black to move out here really caught it. She was a single woman, too. I didn't want to subject my kids to that. It wasn't worth it." Bannister waited. She moved into the area later.

By the 1970s, housing discrimination was more subtle. Real estate agents were accused of intentionally not showing prospective black home buyers houses in certain neighborhoods. Lending institutions were accused of imposing stricter criteria on mortgage applications from blacks.

Some blacks fought back with a subtle tactic of their own. They would get white friends to buy the house, then sell it to them.

Lois Holt looks back with suspicion on obstacles she and her husband Edgar encountered when they tried to build a 30-unit apartment complex near Central High School in the early 1980s. City officials rejected their plans several times even after they downsized it, she said. No local bank would finance it.

Edgar Holt had made enemies as an outspoken Flint NAACP leader.

The Holts eventually built a three-unit house. Not long after that, their builder, who was white, obtained permission from the city to build a 23-unit complex a block away, Holt said, incredulously.

INTEGRATION:
"Would you live some place you weren't wanted?"

Floyd J. McCree refused "to live an equal-opportunity lie."

Instead, Flint's first black mayor threatened to resign from the Flint City Commission (now council) if it wouldn't pass a fair housing ordinance it had been dragging its feet on for months. Several other black leaders supported him and also threatened to withdraw from prominent civic posts.

The summer of 1967 was too volatile a time to provoke racial controversy. Riots were touching down like tornadoes in major cities across the country. Flint, too, had reached a critical crossroad in social unrest. Housing discrimination was a major complaint.

"It was quite prevalent at the time," said Henry Horton, who co-chaired the Fair Housing Committee with the Rev. Earle R. Ramsdell of the Greater Flint Council of Churches.

"In this community, as in others, I'm sure, blacks had a difficult time moving into certain areas, even when they could afford them," Horton said.

"At (that) point, the other side of Detroit Street had no black folks," said Melvin McCree, the mayor's son. "And later when blacks moved across Dupont, it was a major achievement and certainly to get up near Clio Road, that was all white then (1967).

"And on the east side of Flint, the blacks who tried to move there had crosses burned on their lawn. Everything on the other side of the river is east side, predominantly white people who have come from the south," McCree said.

McCree's cousin, Woody Etherly, who played a prominent role in getting the fair housing ordinance passed, has similar memories.

"When I was a kid growing up, you could only go to (no farther than the east side of) Saginaw Street, if you lived on the north side," he said. "When you crossed Saginaw Street, you crossed into a whole 'nother world

Civil rights activism brought demands for change to the doorstep of Flint's largely segregated neighborhoods in the late 1960s. Marches like this one at Flint City Hall preceded a successful drive for an open-housing law. Flint voters were the first in the nation to approve a fair-housing referendum, although by a very narrow margin.

---

and you were subject to get chased back across Saginaw Street."

Black and white leaders formed an interracial committee to push passage of the fair housing ordinance. The controversy created major tension in Mayor McCree's household.

"Riots were happening in other parts of the country," Melvin McCree said. "Police wanted to put security on my father, but he didn't want it. He was getting death threats."

Faced with Mayor McCree's threat to resign and the role he had played in defusing a potential riot, the City Commission passed the open-occupancy ordinance in October of 1967. Immediately, a group that included politicians and real estate agents demanded that the issue be decided by voters.

Some 40,000 residents turned out for the referendum in February of 1968. It passed by merely 38 votes. It was the first ballot-box victory in the country that kept a fair housing ordinance from being shot down. But the ordinance did not magically wipe out discrimination.

As black and white neighbors got to know each other, familiarity usually bred friendships. But in the long run, racially mixed neighborhoods became all- or mostly black. There was a long-established precedent.

In the 1930s, James Todd's family had been one of the first to move to Winans Avenue, off Lippincott Boulevard, on the south side.

"Winans was a nice area, right off Thread Lake," said Todd, who had 10 siblings. "For a while, there was a period where they (whites) called us names and such. We had to go to school in bunches (for protection) but eventually things settled down and integrated and we became good friends."

Todd again got a cool reception in 1963 when he moved into the East Village area, off E. Court Street.

"Neighbors weren't hostile, they just wouldn't talk to you," he said. "This fellow next door here, I remember a year after I got here, he had a big police dog. Every time I went in the back yard, the dog would come out of his house and I'd pet him. My neighbor hated that. He'd say (to the dog), 'Get back here.' Later, after we became friends, he told me, 'The dog had more sense than I did. I wish you'd lived here long ago.'

"There was a Jewish family who came right over as soon as I moved in and welcomed me to the neighborhood. They offered to do anything they could to help. They still live here and we are still as friendly as ever."

Todd's neighborhood is now evenly mixed racially.

Norm Bryant's father bought their first home on Maines Street in north Flint in 1944, he said. During that time, there weren't many blacks west of Industrial. The Bryants were among the first blacks on their block.

Years later, when Norm Bryant bought his first home in the 400 block of E. Genesee Street, he was the second black resident. Later, he moved across Detroit Street, near Welch Boulevard, and integrated that block, too.

'See this here was the elite neighborhood," Bryant said. "My aunt used to do day work in here. We were very limited as to what (houses) we could buy. They listed in the paper, 'This is for colored.' You could maybe get a white person to intercede for you in some cases."

Maxie Brandon, a World War II veteran, got the runaround when he tried to buy his first home in 1947.

"I'd just gotten back from the service and my wife and I had got married and were trying to buy a home," he said. "One of the first places we went to was two brick houses right at the corner of Moore (near N. Saginaw). One is real beautiful. So we went there and tried to buy that house, but the lady told us they weren't ready to sell, but they had a for-sale sign up.

"It was a white family and they didn't want to sell to us. We went down to another house on Maines Street, I'll never forget the address, it was

3818, and this white woman wanted to sell us the house, but her son and husband came home from work and they told her that she couldn't, they wouldn't sell the house to us. They also had a for-sale sign.

"Then we were going to buy another house on Industrial, across from the present fire station." The house was promised to the Brandons but sold to another black family willing to pay $1,000 more.

The Brandons eventually bought a house in that area that has been their home nearly 50 years. The neighborhood is all black now but they were one of few black families for many years.

The pattern continued around the city.

In 1972, Katie Ellis Harper was the third black to move onto her street in northwest Flint. Now only a few whites remain, she said, but they are good neighbors.

Integrating a neighborhood was frightening for some. John Rhodes was relieved to see a black neighbor shoveling snow after he moved into a mostly white neighborhood near the old Northern High School in 1962.

"I was afraid when I first moved up there because I didn't own a gun," Rhodes said. "My next-door neighbor was a clerk at Buick. From my house to Detroit Street were bankers, teachers, salespeople. ... That's who lived up there."

Some welcomed black neighbors and some did not. Bessie Owens Brooks recalled the negative attitude of a white woman she worked for on Adams Avenue. The woman informed Brooks that a "colored" family was moving in down the street.

"I said, 'So what?' She said, 'Would you live some place you weren't wanted?' That lowered my estimation of her right there," Brooks said.

Ruth Scott found no vocal resentment when she integrated a Beecher neighborhood in the 1960s but felt it was there.

"We didn't know the neighbors were upset about blacks moving into the area but the police would circle our block for the first few weeks," she said. "Then, in the summer, (neighbors) would stare when I took my daughter out for a walk. But they accepted us."

Bill Williams recalls he was outright harassed when he moved to northwest Flint in 1968.

"I had two cars," he said. "One I left home with my wife and one I drove to work. I have a one-car garage so I'd park the good one in the garage and the work car in the driveway. I'd come out in the morning and find eggs all over the car and garage. The tree in the yard, we had decorated for Christmas; I came out and the lights had been stolen and it had been decorated with toilet paper."

Four other black families lived on the street. Williams doesn't know if they were getting the same treatment. The harassment subsided after a few years when neighbors saw that Williams had one of the best-kept houses in the neighborhood, he said.

About five years later, when Ruby Turner Noble moved into that area, white flight was well under way.

"We bought from whites but other blacks had moved in previously. Other whites in the neighborhood started selling and (soon) it was St. John Street all over again," Turner Noble said. She had relocated from St. John under urban renewal clearance.

Karen Aldridge witnessed more "pure racism" when her parents built a home on Detroit Street.

"You could see the for-sale signs going up while my parents were watching the construction," she said. "Over the course of years, (the neighborhood) turned black." The same thing happened in their previous neighborhood on Marengo in north central Flint.

Audrey Wilson lives on the south side in the Evergreen Valley subdivision. Her house was built in 1955. When she moved there in 1969, the neighborhood was racially mixed.

"Now I think we're about 95 percent black," she said. "Usually the ones who have stayed are senior citizens."

Integrated neighborhoods are not an issue for some blacks. They prefer predominantly black areas, can't afford to move or believe predominantly white areas are off limits.

Discrimination was the downside of open housing. In some cases, blacks said they were quoted prices for houses three times more than they were worth.

Lena Pridgeon is the mother of three and lives in the Cook School area. She said she "never had a desire to want to move into a predominantly white area because I didn't want that for my kids. I probably wouldn't mind looking at one in Grand Blanc now because a lot of blacks are out there now, but years ago, uh-uh."

Eloise Caldwell likes her predominantly black neighborhood, too.

"I don't mind interracial," she said. "I have white friends. I go to their house and have lunch and they come to mine. But I'm comfortable with my people. I'm proud of my race and I taught my daughter to be."

Audrey Wilson believes open housing harmed the black community in some ways.

'It was good, but it also diluted our strength," she said. "We fought for open housing but when you see some of the consequences, you pay for those advances and wonder if it was worth it."

PUBLIC HOUSING:
"It's not what you have, it's how you keep what you've got."

Flowers that Betty Travis planted around her front porch steps bloom each year in a riot of color. Two trees she planted as saplings years ago tower over her roof.

Inside, her home is immaculate and tastefully decorated. No rats or roaches reside here. The worst she can say about her home is that the basement floods sometimes and the bathtub could stand reglazing. The sound of gunfire some nights does not unduly disturb her.

Most of her neighbors are black and have low incomes. Many are unemployed or on welfare.

Travis lives at Atherton East, one of four Flint Housing Commission family apartment complexes. She was one of the first tenants to move in 27 years ago and has no regrets.

Travis defies stereotypes about public housing tenants.

Critics predicted that public housing would become a ghetto in six months, when it was first proposed after World War II. It took longer but many of the worst fears materialized.

Rampant crime and perpetual disrepair have dogged Flint's public housing for at least 20 years.

Henry Horton, Flint public housing director from 1975 to 1981, sees it as a good but short-sighted concept.

"I think one of the worst things it did was it congregated folks who were all needy, who were all basically not very skillful. It congregated these people who had problems together," said Horton.

"The philosophy and the idea of having housing of last resort is a good, humane idea that we ought to continue to find a way to have. But I think that we ought to build into the system maybe some time limits for how long people can stay or maybe some skill development programs for while they are there, to help people move from there to the next step."

The City Commission listened to detractors in the 1940s and rejected a public housing proposal. It came up again in 1950 and was shot down by a referendum. But the idea finally sold in 1964 when plans to build the I-69 and I-475 freeways created a need to relocate about 3,000 families. Most of them were low-income and black.

The Flint Housing Commission now operates six complexes for elderly and disabled tenants, four family housing complexes and about 130 single-family homes referred to as scattered sites.

Atherton East is the oldest and largest family complex. It is located in south Flint, east of Dort Highway and north of Atherton Road. The first tenants moved in in May 1968. By January 1969, 141 of the 188 families living there were black, 43 were white, three Hispanic and one Native American.

Howard Estates, a 96-unit family complex off Lapeer Road on the south side, opened in July 1968. River Park, 180 units off Carpenter Road in northeast Flint, opened in March 1969. And Aldridge Place, the newest family complex, off Selby Street in north Flint, opened in December 1984. It has 93 units.

Most residents now living in family complexes are black, said Reggie Richardson, public housing director. The buildings for the elderly are racially mixed.

Betty Travis moved into her two-bedroom unit at Atherton East in September 1967.

"I wanted to move here," she said. "I had a son and I was working in the shop and I couldn't pay anyplace else and live as comfortable as I wanted in a nice, clean place. It's not what you have, it's how you keep what you've got. I've always wanted to have a nice, clean place."

She had been living in a substandard rental house in a neighborhood that was razed for freeway construction.

Mary Jamieson moved into a three-bedroom townhouse at River Park in 1978 to escape a dilapidated, roach-infested rental house on Mason Street.

"I wanted something clean and easier for me to keep clean with my girls because I had been used to living in a cleaner place," Jamieson said. She was unemployed at the time and on welfare.

Like Travis, Jamieson refutes the popular image of public housing as dirty, raggedy and roach-infested. For one thing, it is affordable. For another, there is a strong sense of community among public housing residents that is often missing nowadays in the private sector, she said.

Living in public housing also helped Jamieson develop grassroots leadership skills. She was president of the River Park Tenant Council for eight years.

"It built my self-esteem way up," she said. "At the end of 15 years, I had learned a lot. I had learned about people. I had learned a few things about city government, a few things about the state. I became interested in politics."

She worked hard to upgrade the complex but concedes that no amount of organization or money can offset the destructiveness of some tenants.

"That's a major problem. Some people don't take care of their yard. They don't clean up in front of their door and they let their curtains hang out of the window. Bad housekeepers.

"We had people who would come in and just go through it and scuff walls, tear out cabinets, break windows, tear out doors, tear off refrigerator door handles, set fires and trash the whole apartment.

"That was always a big hassle for us, trying to find ways to convince these people that they need to keep their apartment up."

Public housing is more than cheap, temporary housing to tenants like Jamieson and Travis. They see it as a viable neighborhood.

Travis is a building captain for the Atherton East Tenants Council. She acts as a liaison between residents and management.

Tenant councils play the role that block clubs do in regular neighborhoods. They promote upkeep and host fund-raisers, self-help and social programs such as youth activities and Christmas parties.

Atherton East's tenant council members got management to cover windows of vacant units with window guards instead of unsightly plywood. They lobbied for new playground equipment, office space, a day-care center and better police protection.

Before getting involved with the River Park Tenant Council, Jamieson had planned to move as soon as she could save enough money to buy a house.

"When I first moved in I was pleased with the apartment inside but disappointed with the upkeep on the outside, the yard and recreation area," she said.

"I took it upon myself to do my yard. Put in flowers and kept it up well around there. And you know in doing that, most of the neighbors began to catch on and they would come out and do theirs. Eventually, we had our area looking really nice. We did the parking lots and everything.

"Then when I started to work, I would come off third shift and I would get home in the morning and first thing I would do was start picking up paper out of that parking lot."

Working through the tenant council, she got management to supply grass and flower bulbs to tenants and to enforce rules to get lax tenants to clean up and stop vandalizing the units.

Jamieson "had it fixed up just like I wanted," when she moved to a senior citizens complex in 1993.

After 27 years, Travis has no plans to move. She shrugs at the mention of crime and blight.

"That's everywhere. You can't just say it's out here. But you know I can say they never come around in front of my house and do that stuff. Never.

"I feel very safe here. Yes I do. And they have protection. They have policing out here."

Private police patrols at public housing complexes started in 1989. It helped but they are not there 24 hours, Jamieson said. It was not unusual to hear gunshots at night.

"It had got so bad one while that some drug dealers from Detroit had moved into River Park and occupied an apartment," she said. "They just moved in with somebody they knew and took over their apartment."

In occasional upgrades, management installed security windows and doors, painted and replaced broken fixtures.

Basements flood periodically but that is a structural problem that can't be fixed, Travis said. Maintenance is slow because of understaffing. Sometimes the grass gets pretty high before it's cut but snow removal is prompt so children can walk to school.

Jamieson and Travis compare the strong sense of community in public housing to the camaraderie of the old St. John neighborhood. Unlike the isolated, distrustful environment in many neighborhoods, Travis knows her neighbors' names and they know hers.

Strangers are more likely to find trouble at River Park than people who live there, Jamieson said.

"If people from across town come out there at night, these are the people that get jumped. But now the people who live in there, they don't get jumped. Now they might have their regular little arguments, you know, if somebody don't get along. But if I go out to my car, it could be a bunch of teen-agers standing there, they could be drinking beer, but they know who I am and they know who the next lady is and they're going to say, 'Hi, Ms. Such and Such,' and that's all. And they're going to steady drink their beer or whatever they're doing.

"But if somebody comes from across town, those same boys that waved at me, they're gonna approach this person from across town and nine times out of 10, they're gonna beat him up. Now that's one thing I couldn't stand, but they'll do that. They don't care whether you're a little bitty boy or a big-sized boy, they'll jump you."

That sense of community is slowly being lost. Jamieson could name only five families that have lived at River Park for 10 years or more. Travis sees the same pattern at Atherton East.

"It seems like now they move in and out, in and out," she said. "Then they board up the places. It seems like when they move out they destroy

Atherton East is the oldest and largest family complex operated by the Flint Housing Commission.

---

the places so bad they they can't hardly move people back in untill they fix them up. And that just makes the neighborhood look so bad with the boards up."

Public housing's bad reputation extends to other programs managed by the U.S. Department of Housing and Urban Development.

HUD houses were unwelcome in stable neighborhoods when Angela Sawyer was growing up in the early 1970s.

"My father didn't like the concept of HUD houses," Sawyer said.

"He used to call them 235 houses because he said it only cost $2.35 to build one. He knew those houses would attract a certain element of people."

Sawyer's father once organized a neighborhood protest to prevent HUD from taking over a vacant house next door to them because he thought it would be better sold to a private owner.

"Now when I drive through town, I see the HUD houses," Sawyer said. "They're not well-kept. If you blow on them too hard, they'd fall down. I know the intent was good, but they're not stable."

Blame it partly on lax, racist enforcement of building codes, said former Flint Mayor James Sharp. He explained that 235 was a mortgage strategy to provide more low-income housing. Eligible families could buy a 235 house with a down payment of only $200 and the federal government paid the rest. In order for a house to qualify for government reimbursement, it was supposed to be built according to certain standards authorized by the

Federal Home Administration.

"FHA (was) ... the most racist bureaucracy we had in the country," Sharp said.

This was in the late 1960s, immediately after the passage of Flint's open-housing ordinance. Because of urban renewal clearance plans for the St. John and Oak Park communities, affordable housing was needed for relocated families. A lot of folks resented that, Sharp said.

"So they (HUD building inspectors) validated, they inspected, they passed on houses that had pipes leaving the sink going through a wall and leading to nothing. There was no water coming in. The pipe went through the wall and that was it. They accepted that house for occupancy.

"They accepted for occupancy homes that were built 3 feet off the ground with a crawl space and no steps to get up to the door to get into the house. But those homes, I'll bet you, are not standing today. They just were not built (well).

"Flint neighborhoods (today) could have been a lot stronger, if we'd had (a strict code enforcer) watching the store. We let it get away from us."

LIFESTYLES:
"We were poor but we didn't know we were poor."

They were poor but happy.

In the 1920s, childhood was innocent and morality mattered. People made lifelong friendships. Families attended church on Sunday and sat down to meals together.

Everybody knew everybody. An unfamiliar car was a signal that strangers had come to town. If someone was ill, neighbors responded with food and comfort.

There were no expressways. No TV. No disposable diapers. No shopping malls. No McDonald's or other fast-food restaurant chains. And so little crime that a single Saturday-night stabbing was as shocking as a serial murder is today.

It was a treat for children to get a nickel on Saturday to see a movie at one of several theaters downtown. The ultimate Sunday treat was a trip to one of Flint's two amusement parks on the edge of town.

Bliss was when a child could run out to the street with an oversized bowl to be filled at the passing ice cream cart.

"The cart was white and had a striped awning," Ruth Buckner said. She grew up on Flint's south side in the 1920s. "The man wore a boater and the cart was drawn by a horse. For 25 cents you got about a gallon."

Milk bottles were delivered the same way, door to door.

Most streets were dirt and rutted but it didn't matter. Not many people owned cars. Those who did were known by name. Many black families bought their first cars after World War II.

Some of those cars had now obsolete names like the Flint-built Paterson and odd features like a rumble seat, which was ideal for giving thrill rides to children.

Dort Highway, circa 1940, was paved but mostly dirt roads ran from Flint to Frankenmuth. Many residential streets in the densely populated St. John neighborhood were unpaved.

But just because a house sat on a dirt road or didn't have indoor plumbing didn't mean that residents were uncivilized.

"We were renting but we took care of them like they were our own," Katie Ellis Harper said. "At that time (1930s and '40s), people didn't tear up rental properties as they do now. In some places, we didn't have grass but we swept the dirt."

And to hear Ruth Buckner tell it, you haven't known hardship until you've had to use an outdoor toilet in winter.

The Great Depression made difficult times worse. It started in 1929 and lasted most of the 1930s.

"All my friends were in the same shape I was," said Vivian Pugh, born in Flint in 1928. "We were poor but we didn't know we were poor."

Like most children, Pugh longed for a bicycle that she didn't get until she was grown and bought it herself.

"People in my age group, we're used to pinching pennies," she said. "We had one pair of shoes; kids now have a pair to go with every outfit. And clothes, they have a new outfit every week. I don't know where they get the money."

Her parents never owned a car nor did they see two or three parked in one driveway like you do now.

Money was tight but a little bought a lot. A pound of liver cost a penny, bananas 10 cents a bunch and a loaf of bread 5 cents. If the bread was a day old, you could buy an armful for a dime. You had to slice it yourself.

If you could afford a dollar's worth of potatoes, you'd need two or three people to help you carry them home, Alexander Jones said. He was born in Arkansas in 1916 but his family moved to Flint in 1925.

"Back then you worked all the time and you still didn't have anything," he said.

Work was scarce and welfare dreaded. But people stuck together.

"A lot of times, we had neighborhood dinners," Katie Ellis Harper said. "If one person had food, the whole neighborhood had food. We potlucked a lot ... in our neighborhood on Dewey. We'd make a big pot of goulash or something and three or four families would eat together.

"Before World War II, sometimes the men would work five to six months and then be off four to five months," Harper said.

If worst came to worst, they swallowed their pride and went to a building on Hamilton Avenue, where the closed Citizens Bank building is now, across from Buick. That was the dreaded welfare office.

"They had these old, hard shoes you'd try on to get a proper fit," Louise Tarver said. They were issued surplus food – dried beans, beef, staple items to supplement baby-food bland diets.

"When (the government) first started welfare, they'd give you an order, no money," Bill Williams said.

"They'd pay your rent and you would take the order to the grocery store to get food. When (President Franklin D.) Roosevelt came along, he started giving money."

The U.S. government set up the Civilian Conservation Corps in the 1930s to provide jobs for black youth. "They would send young men up north to work in CCC camps, making a dollar a day," Williams said. "They fed and clothed you and kept you in camp and would send $25 (a month) back to your parents and give you $5."

Resourcefulness kept the wolf from the door.

"When I come up we always had plenty of food. We didn't have no luxuries, but I don't know a time when we ever went hungry," said Milton Port, born on Flint's south side in 1912.

"I might not have had the exact food I wanted but back during the Depression, we weren't on welfare. My dad always scuffled around and had something to do to stay off welfare. We ate a lot of beans and potatoes."

Family gardens kept many from going hungry. Wealthy men were buying up farm land to build factories but poor ones could still find plenty of planting land in the back yard or on vacant lots.

"We didn't have farms, we just had a lot of yard," Teresa Crichton said. "The back yard stretched back to the next street. We had all kinds of fruit trees – apple, cherry, peach."

"Everybody had a garden then," Vivian Pugh confirmed. "My mother grew tomatoes, corn and greens. Everybody had a garden behind the St. John center."

Some were fortunate enough to pluck snacks directly from berry bushes and plum and apple trees growing in their yards.

Donn Kersey remembers sneaking onto private property to "steal" his fill from trees loaded with apples, plums and cherries.

"We didn't harm anything," he said. "Most people knew we were doing it. They'd ask us not to throw sticks in the trees to damage the limbs."

Some houses in the St. John area had grape arbors, Maxie Brandon said. He was a Depression-era child, too. "And most of the houses from North Street to Industrial had chickens, ducks or something," he said.

Some families even raised cows and horses. It wasn't against the law then to keep livestock in the city. That went on long after the Depression ended. Selling surplus eggs and chickens was a source of income.

The Rev. Eugene Simpson said his dad raised rabbits. He bought his first car in 1935 with money made from selling 500 rabbits.

Some women took in sewing to help make ends meet. Children helped out with odd jobs like shining shoes, running errands and tending gardens.

Being a child during the Depression could also be a lot of fun.

"We had a lot of playgrounds that were safe for kids to go to," Katie Ellis Harper said. "We walked from one side of town to the other. Our main transportation was foot power."

Community centers provided interesting youth activities on both ends of town. Teens hung out in hamburger joints and soda shops. It was purely social, no loitering or rabble rousing.

"If you did something you had no business, your parents knew about it by the time you got home," Harper said. "Kids got whippings together. Everybody paid the price."

Parents enforced rules such as requiring children to be home by the time the street lights came on, speak courteously to strangers you meet on the street and no sex until you get married.

Few unmarried girls got pregnant. When one did, it was a minor scandal. The unfortunate girl dropped out of sight, sometimes permanently. Extended absences were explained as a long illness or visits with out-of-town relatives.

"We had good times as young people," Audrey Wilson said. She grew up in the 1940s. "We didn't have to worry about walking around late at night. I can remember running down to the Clifford Street Center at night without fear of being bothered. We'd go down to the Garden Theater downtown. The State and Strand (theaters) were side by side in the same block where Michigan National Bank is now (and was then). Also the Capitol Theater. The Rialto. And there was the Nortown up past the Durant Hotel.

"On Halloween, they'd have a midnight special so we'd go down there to the Garden Theater to watch horror movies. After the movies were over, we'd walk home down the middle of street. We were scared to walk on the sidewalk because we were spooked by the movie, but we had a good time.

"We knew nothing about marijuana. The most we ever did was smoke a cigarette. Occasionally, we would buy one jumbo beer and go out by the creek and pass it around, but nobody got drunk because it was too many to go around. We were in our teens then, about 14 to 15.

"We had the Clifford Street Center where we'd go for dances. Just weekend dances open to youth. Mrs. Edith Robinson ran the center at that time."

Church was the main social outlet. Between Christian Endeavor, Baptist Young People's Union (BYPU) and regular and evening service, all day Sunday was spent in church.

In the 1920s, streetcars traveled from one end of the city to the other. You had to catch the streetcar to get to Flint Park amusement park on the north edge of town near Devil's Lake. South-siders walked to Lakeside Park amusement park near Thread Lake. Families would pack picnic lunches and spend the day there.

Radios and record players were the earliest forms of home entertainment.

"The first radio I can remember we had in our house was in 1937," Eugene Simpson said. "It was an old Philco, stood about that high off the floor. Before that we had what was called a Graphonola. They call them record players today. It had a horn on it. You had to crank it up. Had two doors at the bottom where you could store records."

Birthday parties and social clubs filled out the social calendar. Few families could afford vacation travel. Few parents could afford to send their children to college but made sure they got a high school diploma.

"Back then (1920s and '30s), you walked to school and you weren't late either," Alexander Jones said. "No such thing as bad weather. You went. I've seen children walk to school and get there with frozen fingers, ears and noses. You went to school. Now if you got snow forecast and you got buses to take you there, schools are closed and there isn't a drop of snow on the ground.

"And discipline in schools was just about like it was in the service. Oh yes! You did what you were supposed to do or wished like the devil you had."

John Rhodes takes a dim view of other staples of modern lifestyles.

"Since the war, this generation looks for everything to be prepared – like food. I don't like that. I think it's trifling," he said.

"I never bought a Pamper (diaper). We used Pampers in the shop for certain things that needed to be cushioned. I look at a friend of mine. He has two girls always looking for enough money to buy Pampers. That's a waste of money. It would be easier to buy (cloth) diapers and use some elbow grease. With my two boys, I didn't have a washer. You know what I did? I went and bought a rub board and washed them in the tub and hung them in the basement. I didn't buy no Pampers. If I had to do it over again, I'd (still) buy diapers."

Rhodes and his wife worked but still cooked full meals every day instead of depending on fast-food restuarants, he said.

"That's what makes me so thankful for my mother when she used to put me on the back of a chair and make me cook. Some people have forgotten where they came from. I haven't and I never will," he said.

One of Norm Bryant's fondest childhood memories is of playing pickup ball games in the middle of his unpaved street in the 1940s. He lived in the St. John area.

"The whole neighborhood would get together. All the men would come out and play with the kids. Main Street was sort of like a big family. We had some good games out there in the street," Bryant said.

He also remembers Army tanks rolling off Buick's assembly line and being readied for the battlefields of World War II. He had a front-row view from his back yard on Grant Street.

One of Bryant's less wholesome memories happened on his newspaper route. He and his brothers delivered the Detroit Free Press because they couldn't get a Flint Journal route. The Journal is not known to have hired black carriers until the late 1940s, after World War II. Even then, few routes were available and would stay in the same family for years.

Mornings before going to school, the Bryant boys walked their route from Leith to Carton and Industrial to Saginaw. On Sunday mornings, their innocent eyes and ears witnessed the seamy side of life.

"White men would ask us if we knew where they could get black women (prostitutes). They'd been drinking all night. That's what we were exposed to," he said.

Johnnie Wynn Jr. sees a connection between moral decline and the deterioration of families. He also grew up in the 1930s and '40s.

"They talk a lot about one-parent families and that this is where the problem is coming from, but I don't see that," Wynn said.

"When we were growing up, there were one-parent families but those mothers raised their children. What I see as a problem now is these young girls on drugs having babies and there is no one to train their kids and they probably don't know how. Our social programs are being cut out. Churches are not helping out that much.

"Most of the drive-by shootings and the boys and girls getting into trouble have no home life, no love. We didn't have that back then. The girls who were getting in trouble, which were very few, we had a code, you just didn't get pregnant. Morals were taught. My mother instilled that in me, but that seems to be a lost art. Until we get that back together, the morals, our (society) will continue to deteriorate," Wynn said.

That moral code prevailed into the 1960s.

"At that time, you (parents) knew where your child was and didn't have to be overly concerned about your child running around with this or that gang," Sondra Rawls said. Her mother shouldered the responsibility for raising eight children because her father was an alcoholic. Most of them are college graduates, happily married and gainfully employed today, Rawls said.

"Even coming out of a situation where there were that many children in a family, times were not all that easy. We were probably a part of the working poor but didn't realize we were poor because everybody was satisfied and content," Rawls said.

"I can remember getting those Old Newsboys boxes. I have photos of us clutching tightly to white dolls and my brother his guns and holster. That shows how little it took then to content a child. Now they want Nintendos and VCRs for 4-year-olds. But it really took so little in some of things we did for play. In summer, there would always be a baseball or kick ball game going on in the middle of the street. After dark, the game would change to hide-and-seek. We made our own fun.

"That's why I say kids now have no excuse for not doing the right things, for not doing positive things with their lives. I can point to my own life, coming out of that situation. My thing is to not let people categorize your family as dysfunctional.

"It doesn't give my children or any of those coming up now any room for excuses. It doesn't mean that just because you come out of a certain situation, you have to end up a certain way. If you blame your condition on what you came from then you're using that as an excuse."

Social development programs helped instill positive values in the 1960s and 1970s. Black teachers were committed to students learning how to act in public, Debra Taylor said. She was one of the students in a program where they were taken to restaurants to learn how to order from a menu, leave a tip and pass the salt. They started a savings account in first grade to learn about banking.

Parents, ministers and teachers were role models. Taylor's parents started a block club on their south-side street. The club hosted block parties to promote cohesion. The street would be closed off, barbecue grills rolled out for ribs and hot dogs and a disc jockey hired to play the latest dance tunes. Clowns entertained and contests were played on a portable basketball court.

"It was a celebration of community spirit," Taylor said.

Much of that community spirit died when freeways were built, Angela Sawyer said. She grew up in the 1970s.

"You would always see people driving down Saginaw Street because that was the main strip. You don't see that any more because everyone jumps on the freeway now," she said.

"Downtown was a big deal. We'd catch the bus and come down to shop at Smith B's (Smith-Bridgman's department store). I got my ears pierced downtown (where) the college parking lot is now. There were a lot of shops – Connie's Shoes, Baker's Shoes, Stride Rite Shoes, Woolworth's, a hat place, a shoe shine place. One year they tried roller skating, a place to rent the skates. All of that stuff was torn out to make room for Water Street. The downtown area was in decline anyway so I guess they thought this was the renewal project."

Downtown's decline was mirrored in some older neighborhoods where crime and blight were making dramatic changes. Some of it is attributed to folks with bad habits instead of normal wear and tear.

"Everybody here was a transplant," Sherm Mitchell said. The noted musician was born in Scottsville in northern Michigan but moved to Flint as a child during the 1930s.

Flint's automotive industry attracted people from all the country, not just the south, Mitchell said.

"Those people who came here, and this is white, black, came here with one thought: I'm going to work five years and make enough money to go back to a piece of land somewhere else – down south, out east, out west. There's always a piece of land in the family somewhere.

"Most of the people who came here in the late '30s and '40s died here. They didn't get back after five years. They died here; they're buried here. But in the course of their living here, they didn't have any pride or any caring about this area. This was never home to them. This was just a place to work.

"So they dirtied the streets and trashed houses. They threw trash out. Nobody had pride in this town, especially black people.

"Nobody ever said we've made a good living here; let's take care of what we've got. Let's fix up our place; let's try to make this the nicest neighborhood. Let's don't let our city go down. They didn't give a rip.

"You've got a city full of people that have no damn pride because they weren't taught pride by their parents. They have no interest in the history of this city. They don't realize that their mothers and fathers and their mothers and fathers were part of the history that is buried here. They don't have any pride. People with pride do not hurt one another. People with pride care about one another. People with pride take care of whatcha got."

CRIME:
"That would have been big news, somebody getting killed."

The black community was extremely upset when the the body of a young woman was found behind the water plant in the 1940s. The victim was black and the killer was black, Geraldine Smith said.

Murder then was shocking, alarming and rare. The shock value had worn off by 1994 when 59 dead bodies turned up somewhere in Flint. That was up from 47 in 1993 and 52 in 1992. The all-time high was 61 in 1986.

Many of the victims were black; many of them were killed by other blacks. Black-on-black crime is so commonplace now, it is no longer news.

The numbers are steadily rising for other serious crimes – drug trafficking, rape, armed robbery, carjackings, spouse and child abuse. Often, poor black neighborhoods are hardest hit.

Black neighborhoods were close-knit back in the 1940s. But somewhere along the way, trust moved out and fear moved in. Neighborhood crime watches were formed in the 1980s to restore a sense of security but it may never be like it was.

"I can remember a time in Flint when you didn't know what a door key was for, didn't even know where it was," Alexander Jones said. He's lived in Flint since 1925.

Now, not only is the door locked, it is deadbolted, steel-coated and burglar-alarm protected. So are windows.

Minnie Simpson, a resident since 1919, used to leave her doors unlocked while going out of town for several days. When she sold her first home in the 1930s, she searched for days to find the keys. Now, she locks the door when she goes to the mailbox. Mainly from force of habit.

Well into the 1950s, many families slept on the porch during hot weather. Most houses didn't have air conditioning then. Neighbors waved and wished each other good night. Nobody worried about not waking up.

"You could walk the street any time you wanted and no one would bother you," Anna L.V. Howard said. "My mother would leave clothes (outside) on the line while she went downtown or overnight." Her father worked nights but they never worried about intruders. Neighbors kept an eye on them.

A stabbing usually was the worst crime you'd hear about in the 1950s, most likely caused by a gambling dispute or a drunken brawl.

"Knifing was a serious thing then, a man having a switchblade," Audrey Wilson said. "But nobody ever shot anybody. About the most you'd get into was a fist fight.

"That would have been big news, somebody getting killed. We used to joke about it, that (self-preserving) blacks would never rob a bank or commit suicide, it just wasn't a consideration," she said.

World War II initiated a climate of increased criminal behavior, Bessie Brooks said. She was in her teens then and under strict orders from her father to stop walking down familiar streets because of a flood of unsavory newcomers in town.

"Blacks started coming in during the war," Brooks said. "That's when things changed for the worst. There was always fights and things. When I was around 18, my boyfriend and I borrowed dad's car. He asked me where I wanted to go. Dumb me, I said let's go to the north end and see somebody fight. We had it in our minds that people on the north end fought all the time."

A lot of the fighting was isolated around rowdy bars like The Hut tavern in the St. John area, said south-siders Robert and Elnor Pea.

"Even when we went to midnight dances (at the IMA), a fight might break out but nothing like the shootings now. (There was) no stealing or looting, maybe a little shoplifting," Elnor Pea said.

In the 1950s, as more people acquired cars and could move around town easier, crime got worse, she said.

"People began to make more money and others who didn't work would prey on those who did. Then there were a lot of people from the South who migrated here who were not good people. They were fast-talkers, hustlers, pimps. A lot of vices were brought up to us by people who migrated to get away from other things in the South. They came here and figured why work hard for someone else when they could hustle," Pea said.

John Rhodes, a north-side resident since 1962, started locking his doors in the late 1970s after his neighbor's house was burglarized.

"Since then, I've had three break-ins at my house," Rhodes said. "I had an alarm system put in and no more problems. But prior to that, when the neighborhood was all white, we could go anywhere. We would go to Saginaw all day to visit relatives and leave the doors open."

Alexander Jones blames worsening crime on lax child-rearing.

"See, in our day, the children had to respect the elders. Now the elders respect the children. I see it every day. I live with it every day. That home (training), the discipline is not there anymore."

In the 1940s, Flint was like the old African proverb stating that it takes an entire village to raise a child.

"Everybody in a three-block area was my mom and my dad," Sherm Mitchell said. "Any one of them caught me doing something wrong, they'd beat my butt, wipe my nose, take me in the house to iron my clothes, wash my face, depending on what the heck was needed. I had mamas and daddies all over the place. If it got a little dark, (someone would say) you go home, boy. Now if I see you do that again, I'm going to tell your mom."

Geraldine Smith cherishes the freedom she had as a child. She could play outside or roam up and down the street without fearing for her safety. Neighbors watched out for them while their mom was away working.

"Neighbors were our family," she said. "We minded them. Their doors were open. Now you hardly know neighbors. (Back) then you knew neighbors on your street and several streets over."

Minnie Simpson remembers when she would see children fighting and stop to break them up. Not now. She fears becoming a victim herself.

By 1974, crime had become a major problem, said Woody Etherly, who was Flint's Third Ward city councilman then.

"We always had a lot of break-ins, we've had a lot of assaults; murder was not as bad as it is now but the home burglaries, the assaults, prostitution used to be a real bad thing here. When the drug epidemic came the whole nature of things changed," he said.

James Todd blames it on "the dope racket."

"Sometimes it's dangerous for you to walk out of your house," he said. He was one of those people who grew up in the 1930s without locking doors.

"If somebody wanted something from you, they'd knock on the door and ask, 'Can I borrow your lawn mower?' In those days, most of the time, people wanted to help you. Now they want to hurt you."

Desperate people commit desperate acts, Frankie Wynn said. She is a retired school counselor.

"You (drug addicts) got to get the money. You're not mentally functional to do anything except stick-ups. It's not going to change until we start to care about each other. You might live in a neighborhood where there is no problem but if there is a problem in the next neighborhood, sooner or later it will move to yours," she said.

Her husband, Johnnie Wynn Jr., a Flint native, feels sorry for children growing up today. Few constructive activities are provided for them and they can't go to playgrounds for fear of drive-by shootings, he said.

"Drugs have caused a mass destruction of our social world. Back then (late 1940s) it might be one or two of every 600 people on drugs," he said.

They were older people, not children, James Blakely added.

"When I was a kid there was drugs – heroin – but it wasn't widespread," he said. "I had a cousin that was involved in it along with some other guys

I knew but ... now it's small kids and this is what really makes it bad. We didn't hardly find too many kids who even drank back in those days."

The persistent drug epidemic raises questions in some minds that it is a white conspiracy to destroy the black community.

Katie Ellis Harper first heard it rumored after WWII that "if they couldn't get to us through fighting, they would get to us through our young. Drugs have (since) destroyed two generations of young people," she said. "(But) I'm still a firm believer that you're responsible for your actions. Just because they put it (drugs) in your neighborhoods doesn't mean you have to take it."

As a teen-ager, Harper fought prostitution. She still has threatening letters she received from people angry over her efforts to chase johns away from community centers and schools.

"It was the white men accosting women on the street," she said. "Some were bold enough to walk up to houses and knock on doors looking for whores. We couldn't go to school or the center at night because of it. We weren't going to take it. So we went down to city commission meetings and complained."

Areas along St. John Street and Industrial Avenue were known as the red-light districts, the Rev. Albert C. Lee said.

"Those two areas for the evening life are no longer existing; they've been torn down and no new areas established, so (prostitution has) spread all over the city," Lee said.

He came to Flint as a boy in the early 1940s and cherishes his memories of Flint as a low-crime, hard-working community. That had changed when he came back from the service in 1955.

"People were coming into the town by the busloads," he said. "(Crowds) were so tight on Industrial from Wednesday to Sunday night, you couldn't walk down the sidewalk. It was that congested in the area where the bars and nightclubs were and the ladies of the evening worked."

But it was a "big-money era," Lee said. General Motors jobs were plentiful and paid well. When the GM jobs dried up in the early 1980s, drugs became the new industry for those not qualified for, or unwilling to do, anything else.

"As we've gotten into the mainstream that we were fighting to get into, I can see a lot of things that have been detrimental to our race," Audrey Wilson said. "The cohesiveness that we had living next to each other and the extended family (are missing)."

Attorney and civil rights leader C. Frederick Robinson links high crime to the abandonment of the black underclass by successful blacks. That is illustrated by a story he heard the Rev. Jesse Jackson tell on television.

Jackson said he heard footsteps behind him while walking in riot-torn

Los Angeles in 1992 and was relieved when he looked around and saw it was a white person. In contrast, California congresswoman Maxine Waters said she toured the same community and felt no fear, Robinson said.

Robinson feels the same way about his N. Saginaw Street law office in the heart of one of Flint's most deteriorated neighborhoods. Visitors often comment about his unlocked door. That reflects his philosophy on racial equality.

"What is the reason that we are willing sometimes to risk ourselves to confront white folks, but we're unwilling to risk ourselves personally about being involved with blacks," he said. "Is there a big difference, if our aim is to improve the lot of black people? Or have we (successful blacks) completely abandoned that on any kind of collective basis?"

His longtime friend and colleague, A. Glenn Epps, agreed in theory but argued, as lawyers like to do, that Jesse Jackson's attitude is not unfounded.

"Being realistic, we have to face up to the fact that crime is higher in the black community," Epps said. "That's the reason Jesse felt like he did. Every time I pick up a Detroit paper, some black person has killed another black person. I don't think we can ignore that, but how we deal with it is another thing. My whole point, overall, is that we're not dealing with it through the criminal justice system."

The problem is so critical, Epps said, he advocates sending psychologists into schools to literally "brainwash little black children against using drugs."

REINVESTMENT:
"You have to use all the money you can borrow."

Like many Flint natives, Dolores Ennis has a love-hate relationship with its evolution.

"It saddens me to drive up North Saginaw Street," she said. "Same thing in Detroit when I drive down Woodward."

Once impressive buildings are now disfigured beyond recognition. Once prestigious neighborhoods are slums.

Yet, Ennis has never wanted to live anywhere else, she said.

After living in Grand Rapids for five years, Angela Sawyer came home to Flint in 1986 and was shocked by what she saw when she drove through

Without a transfusion of reinvestment funds to keep businesses viable in the St. John Street area, its lifeblood slowly seeped away.

---

her old neighborhood.

"Some of the houses are shacks," she said. "I said, Daddy, when we were living out here, were we poor? He said, heck yeah. I said he must have done a really good job (hiding it) because I didn't know."

Frankie Wynn looks beyond the warts.

"Flint is an excellent city," she said. "The Flint Community Schools and cultural center give it an outstanding way of life. A lot of people want to tear it down. I don't know where all this negative concept comes from.

"There is only a small area of Flint that is really bad and the rest is really good. We don't have any slums. We have shacks that need painting. We have spotted (poor) housing conditions, but not a lot in one area. You might go in a block that's really bad but a few blocks over you're in a nice neighborhood. There is probably about 10 percent of the city that is negative and the whole city of Flint is judged by that small negative part."

Many like Wynn see a city worth fighting for. Several government programs have targeted rehabilitation of declining neighborhoods.

The Flint Neighborhood Improvement and Preservation Project provides loans and grants for home repair in distressed areas. Various mayors have established divisions to work with advisory committees and block clubs on beautification efforts.

In 1968, the Model Cities program pumped a $3.5-million federal grant into neighborhood improvement. Its legacy includes the Spanish Speaking Information Center, The Lazy Leopard day-care center, the

McCree Theater building and Mince Manor, a senior citizens high-rise apartment, said Henry Horton, the program's first director.

In 1988, state Rep. Floyd Clack took up the neighborhood-improvement cause. He formed the Flint Community Coalition for Fair Banking Practices. It forced local banks to honor the Community Reinvestment Act of 1977, which encourages banks to reinvest a percentage of profits into the community.

In most cases, local banks did not have the CRA law posted, as required by law, Clack said. Nor had they maintained a CRA file on loan requests for low-income areas.

Clack filed complaints with the Federal Reserve Board charging that two local banks had "not met the financial needs of low- and moderate-income people in this county." Such complaints can cause costly delays when a bank is sold, merged or investing, Clack said.

"That's your power. That's the only power community groups have," he said.

Clack negotiated two years to hammer out CRA agreements with four local banks. Flint's plan has since drawn praise at CRA conferences nationwide, he said.

"It took them so long to admit that we had rights in the neighborhood," Clack said. "I'll tell you what got them. The law got them. They knew the law but when they found out that Clack was crazy enough to file a complaint against them with the Federal Reserve ... that is the power of the CRA law."

During hearings held before the banks adopted the CRA agreement, local people testified about discriminatory loan practices at banks. One florist testified that banks had rejected his application for a remodeling loan because his business is located in the inner city. The family-owned business had operated at the same location for decades, and the loan likely would have been instantly approved if he had been willing to relocate, Clack said.

"That was a good example of how communities go down, he said. "You take the north end. If you look back at your history of the banks, you literally, in many cases, have not had a business loan up on the north end until recently.

"You think about it. We're not used to seeing a building go up that looks like somebody went to the bank and got a lot of money to build it. We (black entrepreneurs) end up forced into these little buildings. You have to use your credit cards, which cost more than a bank loan. You have to use all the money you can borrow. Sometimes you have to refinance your house. You almost have to go broke to be able to get enough money when, in fact, if you could've gotten a reasonable business loan in the first place, you could have had enough to keep the business going."

Many black entrepreneurs end up losing the business and ruining their credit, Clack said.

The CRA agreement marked a turning point. Clack reported that by 1994, bank lending practices had improved across the board. Banks that had made no loans to blacks four years earlier, had made 60 to 150, he said.

Also, more lending institutions were processing FHA mortgages than before. FHA mortgages are frequently used by first-time home buyers with low-to-moderate incomes because they require low or no down payment. By not making these loans available, the banks were violating the intent of the CRA law, Clack said.

Banks have relaxed other application rules to make it easier for blacks to get loans. If the trend continues, it could help improve the look of black neighborhoods for years to come.

Jobs

The dirty and dangerous work of pouring molten metal would sometimes be too hot to handle for African-American men like these in Buick's die-casting room, circa 1920.

In 1955, Betty Travis hardly had to think twice about moving when she heard about the big bucks Flint factory workers were making. She was earning only $20 a week at a drugstore in Tennessee.

Buick was working around the clock then, Travis said. She got hired right away at Buick's cafeteria and stayed there 18 years.

General Motors jobs in Flint attracted many workers like Travis. Southern blacks migrated north in two major waves. The first, from about 1910 to 1920, accelerated when World War I stopped the flow of foreign immigrants who had been filling Northern industrial jobs.

World War II sparked the second mass migration of blacks in the early 1940s and lasted through the 1950s. By 1960, an estimated 4.3-million southern blacks had moved north, making it one of the largest mass migrations in U.S. history.

"When I came here in '55, they were renting rooms out (by the shift), like first shift, second shift and third shift," Travis said. "They couldn't even find places for you to stay. That's how busy things were then. Anybody could just walk off the street and get a job."

For blacks, they were better jobs, too. Before World War II, the few black men working in the factory did janitorial or other menial labor. Black women were rarely hired until the war created a shortage of men, some said.

Before then, black women did domestic work. They cooked, cleaned house or minded children for white families. A few, if they were light-complexioned, ran elevators at downtown stores or were maids. Others worked in family businesses.

Boys often went to work at a young age to help with family expenses or to earn spending money. Some lied about their age to get hired at GM. Some hustled work anywhere they could find it. They ran errands or shoeshine stands, delivered newspapers, shoveled snow or set pins at the bowling alley.

Many of Flint's first black citizens were self-employed. They were barbers and builders, chauffeurs and handymen.

The first black doctors and lawyers arrived about 1920. The first black teachers were hired in the early 1940s and the first black nurses and other specialists were hired about the same time.

The first black doctor, John W. Moore, came to Flint in 1919. Claude W. Heywood and Dudley Mallory, who are believed to be the first black attorneys in Flint, arrived in 1926.

Moore, Mallory, Jesse Leonidas Leach, a medical doctor, and Roy M. Van Dyne, an attorney, were prominent civic leaders.

Factory workers have always made up the lion's share of Flint's black population.

GM was good to Flint workers but it was like riding a roller coaster. Hard times hit during layoffs lasting as long as six months, during the Great Depression of the 1930s and during wartime when commodities were scarce.

Making matters worse, racial discrimination closed doors to many better job opportunities until the 1960s.

In William Hoskins' view, economic dependency has kept blacks at a disadvantage socially and politically.

"They (whites) are the power. They have all the jobs, all the factories," Hoskins said.

"All the people of our generation came to look for jobs, not to start businesses. Consequently, we don't have many businesses. A lot of it has been politics. We haven't insisted on many of the resources whites used to establish a market place."

Hoskins expressed hope that future generations will develop the foresight, acumen and willingness to work together on amassing resources, starting businesses and creating a vital black economic base.

Toward that end, the Metropolitan Chamber of Commerce was formed in 1985 with a mission to actively promote black entrepreneurship. It has pledged to work with the Flint Area Chamber of Commerce on common business interests.

Massive and permanent GM layoffs in the 1980s took a devastating toll on black factory workers who had enjoyed a middle-class life style. Many found themselves unprepared to do anything else to maintain their standard of living.

GM had been a reliable employer for two or three generations. The old routine had been to graduate from high school and get a job at GM. The new routine was to graduate from high school and become unemployed or leave town to find work elsewhere.

"It's tough now (with fewer GM jobs)," said Ruth Scott, a retired educator.

"Our kids are leaving. My daughter graduated from Southwestern in 1980. She never came back home. She didn't like it here, there was nothing for her to do. She found a life somewhere else.

"Most of her friends left too. She said, 'If you weren't here, Mom, I wouldn't come back.' It's a dead end for young people."

Angela Sawyer, a 1981 Northern High School graduate, left Flint but eventually returned.

"I left Flint for a while because I didn't see a future for me here," Sawyer said. "I was 18. An opportunity came up to go to Grand Rapids to look for work and I didn't come back for five years. I had a very good life there. I'm trying to figure out what I'm doing back here."

That is a sad epitaph for a city that once held a national reputation as a job mecca.

Milton Port, born in Flint in 1912, dropped out of high school to go to work in the shop and never regretted it.

"I made a decent living there," Port said. "I didn't have to leave to go somewhere else to make a living, whereas some can't make a living in their hometown (now), they can do better somewhere else. By not having too much education, I don't think I could have done any better anywhere else (considering) the benefits I got from GM. I know some people who quit, took other jobs (and later) wished they'd stayed with GM for the benefits."

Outside of the shop, black men generally could find work during a normal economy.

Sam Williams went to work at age 13. His first jobs were menial but helped meet the family's expenses, he said.

"They (young people) don't do that today. They don't even want to do nothing around the house."

Modern parents are to to blame for being too lax about discipline, he said.

"Why should you have to fight with (your children) to do this or that and you're giving them whatever they need to survive or for pleasure?" Williams asked. "(Young people) don't even think about it. They think it's what they've got coming and won't realize different until they get out on their own."

Flint Mayor Woodrow Stanley also started work young, at age 14, in 1964.

"I've always had a job from then to now," Stanley said.

His first job was as a gofer at Greene Home for Funerals when it was on St. John Street. After that he worked as a bag carrier at a small grocery store, then as a butcher's helper, a stock person and eventually every job in the store.

Musician Sherm Mitchell, born in 1930, has been a restaurant cook, a truck driver, an auto mechanic, a janitor and "all the things people do who aren't educated," he said. He also worked at GM for 20 years.

Mitchell notes that in his accomplished family, he's the only one without a college degree.

Minnie Simpson's first job in the late 1920s was as a domestic taking care of children. She worked on Saturdays while going to school. Her employer was generous about giving her spending money and cast-off clothing. No other jobs were available for women then, she said.

In 1920, Alexander Jones' father worked at a box factory in Durand. Box-making was booming then because everything was shipped in wooden barrels or boxes, Jones said. He had been a lumberjack in Louisiana and was among about 20 black workers recruited to work at a hoop mill in Durand.

"Then cardboard boxes started coming in and the mill started going down and Buick was going up," Jones said. His dad got a job in Flint and commuted 35 miles each way to work each day from Durand in his Model T Ford. He soon got tired of that and decided to move his family to Flint in 1925.

Beginning in 1929, the Great Depression devastated Flint's job market. To keep the wolf from the door, many took jobs with the Work Projects Administration, a government workfare program established by the Franklin D. Roosevelt administration. It provided work for about 8.5 million needy Americans over an eight-year span. WPA workers built railroads and bridges, produced books, murals and plays and learned marketable skills such as sewing and gardening.

"I tried to get a WPA job but they wouldn't give one to a single person," William Hoskins said. He knew a man who lied to get a job, pretending he was married to a woman who was really his sister. Hoskins didn't want to lie so he ended up taking whatever part-time jobs he could find to stay off welfare.

"In those days, you didn't get taxpayers' money for nothing," Theresa M. Crichton said. "You didn't sit down on welfare then. You had to find your own job to get paid. WPA. The gang leader would write your time down and at the end of the week, you'd go collect your commodities. They created some jobs like street cleaning. Honey, you went (to work) or you didn't eat that week."

Sam Williams was a child during the Depression but remembers that his family struggled like the rest.

"You (talk) about hard times. That hit the whole country. People lost jobs, homes, businesses. The purpose of the WPA was to provide jobs. Everybody got paid pretty much the same thing. I remember my father digging ditches and building roads."

But believe it or not, they were happy, Williams said. Everybody they knew was having a hard time. It was a familiar way of life that lasted long after the Depression was over.

Williams' dad's job in the factory was unsteady.

"You could work six months and be off six months," he said. "I can remember being on welfare when the work was down but the welfare then was that you could go get food, but there was no financial assistance. There was no such thing as money to save your house. Yeah, we saw hard times."

A WPA band employed local musicians, Williams said.

"This was to give people some relief. The WPA band played free at dances, most of them outdoor events. They'd shut off the street, the band would set up and play about four hours. People would dance, congregate."

At one band site on Central Avenue behind the old Fairview School, Williams recalled that "they played swing music. Jitterbug would have been the dance craze at that time."

A WPA project provided work for women who could sew. The mothers of Katie Ellis Harper and Robert Pea worked there.

The WPA sewing project was set up in the old Fisher Building downtown and later in a cafeteria somewhere he couldn't recall, Pea said. He worked for the National Youth Association, a WPA project that provided part-time jobs for youth.

Few people talked about the effect on the black community of Flint's historic Sit-down Strike in 1936-37. That could be because black shop workers held only menial jobs then. But coming at the tail end of the Depression, the strike had to have added to the hardship.

Roscoe VanZandt, the uncle of Lois VanZandt Holt and Ruth VanZandt, had a memorable role in the strike. He is believed to be the only black to remain inside the plant during the protest and was photographed carrying the flag when the victorious workers marched out after a settlement was reached.

Employment was booming again by the time Layton Galloway mustered out of the Army in 1945.

"I had so much money when I came here, I had checks I never cashed," Galloway boasted. "I had a little bank account, but I had so much money I thought I was never going to run out.

"Then in 1947 when I got married, I ... started realizing that you had to have a house, a car, furniture and clothes; my little $2,000 (savings) that I thought was a lot, I didn't have anything."

Money was so tight for Galloway in the early 1950s that he took part-time jobs aside from his regular job at Chevrolet Manufacturing. He delivered jewelry for Flint Wholesale Jewelers, cleaned at Citizens Bank, and taught bridge in a program sponsored by the Mott Foundation.

In 1953, Galloway quit his factory job to go to work at the post office, though it meant taking a 25-cents-an-hour pay cut and no overtime pay. But it was a steady job.

"I left the factory because of the hours; I was laid off more than I was working," Galloway said. He was one of the first black clerks at the post office.

Layoffs and strikes added to the uncertainty of working for GM.

Getting laid off from one plant turned out to be a plus for John Rhodes.

Roscoe VanZandt proudly carries the flag as victorious labor union organizers celebrate the end of the historic Sit-down Strike of 1936-37.

He hired the same day to work at the parts warehouse.

"It was like Christmas (working) in that warehouse because I'd never been off on Saturday and Sunday. In my old jobs, my off days had been during the week. That had interfered with me going to church."

During a factory layoff in about 1956, Woodrow Laws drew only $7 a week in unemployment, he said. It was a raw introduction to hard times. He had heard people talking about standing in soup lines during the Depression, but he didn't know anything about it because he had been living in Mississippi where they grew their own food.

His WPA job down South had been more of a bonus than a necessity.

"We used to have to go out and work out on the road and spread gravel, my brother, my dad and myself," Laws said. "It was fun to us. The more people you had working, the more grocery you'd get, and coal."

Sometimes the government-issued beans and flour would be worm infested, he said. They fed it to their hogs because they didn't need it.

Wartime scarcity was a lot like the hardship during the Depression and long GM layoffs.

During World War II, Ruby Turner-Noble worked at the Office Price Administration (OPA) branch office on North Saginaw near Dayton. The OPA was established at the start of the war to control price increases such as rent and distribution of scarce commodities such as sugar, rice and shoes.

Turner-Noble's first job was parceling out fuel oil but later she rationed shoes.

"All of us were down and out to a point but what we had we'd help one another," she said. "Nobody was hinkty. Nobody had a dollar more than the other fellow."

Katie Ellis Harper remembers going to the OPA office to get rationing stamps during the war.

"You got food stamps. You got stamps for shoes, hose, sugar, cigarettes and everything," she said. "You were allocated so many a month. For some (commodities) like shoes, you only got one per year. All the stores accepted them."

Dolores Ennis remembers standing in line to get stockings for her mother.

People also planted victory gardens and women were active in Blue Star Mothers if they had sons or loved ones at war, she said. Ennis did her part in the war effort by writing encouraging letters to the brothers of friends who were enlisted.

Those who could afford it invested in Defense Stamps that could be cashed in for a profit at maturity. Patriotism was strong and everybody tried to do his or her part to sacrifice for the war effort, she said.

SHOP TALK:
"It took WWII to put black men in the shop on production."

As a teen in the 1940s, Ruth Scott remembers her father coming home complaining about the "Russian" invasion of Flint.

"What Russians?" Scott asked him. He spelled it out for her: rush-ins. Newcomers "rushing in to get a job," he said.

As horrible as war is, World War II was a blessing for black folks. Women got hired in the shop for the first time, black men got better jobs than sweeping floors or sweating in the foundry and workers in general earned wages high enough to get ahead socially.

"That was when most of the blacks came – a noticeable explosion," Scott said. "There aren't many blacks that are native Flint people. A lot of blacks have been here 40 years but there are not a lot like me who were born here."

Buick's bustling assembly line in 1954 operated six days a week cranking out as many as 54,836 cars a month, a record pace.

During and after the wartime "rush-in," work was plentiful and overtime bountiful.

"At that time, people were staying all night on the job," said John Rhodes, who arrived in 1953. "Some guys would go home once a week. Some worked right through."

"Flint was crowded. Plenty of jobs. You could get a job anytime." The rush-in lasted well into the Eisenhower administration (late 1950s), he said.

"Before World II, the only jobs blacks could get in the shop was janitorial or sweepers," Maxie Brandon said. As he recalls, blacks couldn't buy an insurance policy for more than $500, so they had to save for emergencies. Brandon's first job in 1944 was as a sweeper at the Chevrolet plant. He got the job, he said, because a white guy in the personnel office was

Buick welder William G. Washington holds a plum job in 1978, one of the fruits of civil rights campaigns to get more black men into skilled labor.

Cass Campbell, a Buick factory worker, checks under the hood of a 1973 model.

impressed by his reputation as a baseball player.

William Hoskins hired in as a janitor in 1937 at the Buick Retail store on N. Saginaw at Third Avenue. In 1942, he transferred to a janitorial job at AC Spark Plug. Then he was drafted into the Army. When he came home from the service, he was able to get a job at the post office, becoming one of the first black letter carriers.

World War II kept Flint factory workers busy filling government contracts to supply the war effort. Buick made Hellcat tank destroyers (among other war materials) and Chevrolet made machine guns, Eugene Simpson said. The GM plant across from Ron Slivka Buick on S. Saginaw in Grand Blanc is still referred to by some people as the tank plant because it used to produce tanks, he added.

"Out there (on surrounding land) where the deer are was a testing track. Same thing up here on Stewart Avenue. That was a testing field. The tanks would come out of Buick and run around there. We used to walk up there to see the tanks."

WWII was raging when Layton Galloway arrived in Flint at the end of 1942.

"I went out to Plant 3 and went to work the same day," he said. "They needed workers. I started sweeping Plant 3. I did that about four months, then went into production. My first job was putting small parts in bins. I did that until I was drafted into the service."

As more able-bodied men were drafted, factory jobs opened up for women workers.

"I think Buick was the last to hire women in the offices," Marion Quinn said. "I guess so many of the men were gone, they needed someone."

AC hired the most women, Ruth Scott said. "That was really the woman shop. It wasn't heavy manual labor (like) Buick and Chevrolet had. AC (made) spark plugs. They're little."

Annalea Bannister worked at AC from 1943 until her future husband came home from the service in 1946.

" I was the first black girl to work in the office at AC Spark Plug on Dort Highway," Bannister said. "There were people walking past my office in droves trying to see the black girl." She was well accepted there, though.

Eloise Caldwell took a job at AC because of her husband's plan to enlist in the Coast Guard. He didn't want to wait to be drafted because he feared he would automatically be sent to the Army, she said.

"I had all this responsibility so I took a training session and got hired at AC," she said. "I'd never been in a situation like that (work) and I didn't like it too well. I worked two years and nine months."

Caldwell happily quit to take over management of a store her brother owned.

"Women had to more or less do a man's job," Dorothy Parks said. "There was no man in the house, so they had to learn to do plumbing and everything else. I think it made women more independent."

When the war ended, many women were not about to go back to their kitchens.

"I think they thought the women would give up their jobs when they (men) came back, but they didn't," Parks said.

William Hoskins recalled that jobs were plentiful when the men came back from the war because the shops had to reconvert to building automobiles.

And Dolores Ennis added: "There were more jobs than they could fill and no men to take them so they were not going to go back to the way it was before. And those young men who served in the war, they were not going to come back and take less."

Factory work wasn't all blue skies.

"When I first went to AC, they laid us off every year, regular as clockwork," Audrey Wilson said. "I never got a vacation check; it was based on whether or not you were working on a certain date. I wasn't there on that date for the first five years. During the time you were off, there was no supplemental. If you ran out of unemployment you were just out there (on a limb)."

Work rules were a lot different then, too, Wilson said.

"You had to punch in and out for lunch and arriving and leaving," she said. "If you brought lunch, you were not allowed to bring food in, you had to leave it with your coat. You couldn't visit from line to line without permission and you had to ask to use the telephone.

"There was a strict dress code. You did not wear low-cut things. (Women) can wear slacks now, but back then we couldn't wear pants above a certain hem length. You can see their cheeks now they're so short and midriffs and everything. I can't believe some of the outfits I've seen people come in there with. Absolutely no restrictions whatsoever.

"Once you could not leave the shop without getting a (permission) slip. Now there's a steady stream of people coming and going ... to smoke pot, buy lottery tickets, go to the store, whatever. That never occurred when we first started working."

Pay was one of the changes for the better, she said. Hers increased from about $1.89 an hour when she hired in to about $14 an hour by the time she retired in 1991.

"Sometimes I used to say I'd rather have benefits than raises because every time (wages) went up, the price of everything else went up," Wilson said. "So I never could put extra money aside. Sometimes I wasn't always sure that getting a pay raise was the way to go."

Anna L.V. Howard hired in at AC during the war.

"During the war, all the men had gone to the service; they almost dragged you in there."

The exception was pregnant women. A pregnant woman or new mother couldn't get hired until after the baby was weaned but women already working when they got pregnant were allowed to stay, she said.

During the war, many black people got far enough ahead financially to move to nicer neighborhoods, Howard said.

"It took WWII to put black men in the shop on production. Before, they were janitors and did menial work. My husband got a better job. He came out of that foundry and got to be a finisher. That's what he always wanted to be."

Many describe the foundry as hell – dirty, smoky and uncomfortably hot.

Jimmy Jones worked in the foundry 20 grueling years, breaking open molds. The heat was the worst in the summer but it was uncomfortably warm in the winter, too, he said.

"If you were able to climb the stairs at the end of the day, you could go to the shower room to see what you looked like."

A residue mixed with body salt was hard to wash off, he said.

Milton Port's foundry job was pouring molten iron.

"The iron was red hot, running like water," he said. "They tell me now that iron is poured automatically; they don't have people in there. In my day, there was a ladle to pour it from. There was always somebody getting burned. I got burned a few times. If the sand was too wet in the mold, the iron would shoot up in the air or if a mold was bad, the iron would run out of the side.

"The fellow who broke me in told me not to run if the iron broke through. I said, 'You got to be crazy.' He explained that if I ran and that ladle got to swinging, I'd get burned more.

"It was quite an experience. I'm glad I lived through it and glad the people don't have to go through it today like we went through it then."

For all that GM wasn't, when it was up and running, it was a place that provided many blacks a standard of living that they might not have had otherwise.

"I can remember when I got married," Ruth Scott said. "My husband was working in the shop and he was making more money than I was and I was a teacher. For a long time, he made more money than I did. So the shop was paying really good."

Many blacks who built homes behind Stewart School were not professionals, Scott said. "Those were people who worked in the shop. They made good money and could afford to build those nice homes. They had nice cars.

"Then times started changing and people woke up too late. Kids got out of school and there was not an automatic job at GM. In (bygone) days, you could get out of high school and go to work at GM and make an excellent living."

Job discrimination made life in the factory unpleasant for some. There are stories about people being fired just shy of completing their 90-day probation period. Some said whites with less seniority and training were paid more and promoted ahead of them. One of the oldest complaints was that blacks were routinely assigned the worst jobs.

"I learned how to do every job in GM," said Jimmy Jones. "I'd break guys in on the machine and six months later they were foremen. That was an accepted way of life. I never got used to it."

Greg Pridgeon, a GM worker since 1974, added: "I feel there is still a lot going on. I was hired in GM on affirmative action. That's the only reason I'm in there today. Once you get the job, you still can get a job within a job." But in Pridgeon's view, the jobs are given to whites quicker than they are to blacks.

"That seniority don't mean a thing," he said.

Four Flint blacks who believed that GM shortchanged them on pay raises and promotions filed a discrimination suit in 1983. It became a class-action lawsuit representing about 10,000 blacks in Michigan, Indiana and Ohio.

"I was working on salary and we felt like we weren't being promoted," recalled Joan Lewis, a member of the the Pro Minority Action Council (PMAC), which initiated the suit on behalf of managerial, clerical and professional employees.

The Rev. James Kennedy of Mt. Carmel Baptist Church was one of the original plaintiffs and also PMAC president. GM settled the suit out of court in the late 1980s.

Job discrimination was no stranger to rank and file workers either.

"When I first came here, my husband hired in at the Van Slyke plant. They made him like a leader but they wouldn't make him a foreman," Lois Shaw said.

"He was doing the same work the white foremen were doing but without the status or the pay. That's why he left there and went into construction, mostly building churches. It was a white construction company that made him a partner in it and he made more money at that than he did out there at GM."

Betty Travis recalled having a racial confrontation resolved in her favor. She was head cashier in the old Buick cafeteria when a younger white woman decided she should have Travis, sit-down job and Travis should have hers cleaning tables.

"The boss came over and I says, 'No, I'm not doing that. I have seniority not to do that. She does the most undesirable job. Not me. Now if she had the seniority, she's got the right to say the same thing. I'm not cleaning off that table,' " Travis said.

Former Flint City Councilman Woody Etherly said he fought discrimination to get promoted to a welder's job. It started with taking a test for supervisor that Etherly now believes he was never supposed to take. He was one of two blacks among about 54 test takers, he said. After not hearing anything about the test results for a month, Etherly went to the office to inquire.

"They didn't have no record that we ever took the test," Etherly said. "I don't know if it was because they were going by name and maybe my name didn't sound black that I got invited (to take the test) but they never found the papers. We crack jokes about it, that it got filed into File 13 after they found out we were black."

When a welding job opened up, Etherly, who worked on production, applied because it paid 10 cents more an hour than the highest wage on the line. He had enough tenure to be eligible.

A foreman offered him a job as his chauffeur instead, Etherly said.

"I said no, that's not the job I want – I want the job as welder. You can get somebody else to be your driver for you, OK?"

When he saw the job about to be given to a white worker, Etherly said he called the union and the Michigan Civil Rights Commission.

"So they called me back into the shop and told me you got three hours to learn how to put a bead down. When you're welding, you got this electricity that comes through this rod and it melts and you got to be able to lay a bead down without cracking the block. So (the foreman) said he's going to show you one time. So this white (worker) went in there and laid it down one time and left.

"They thought I wasn't going to accept the challenge. Well, I accepted the challenge. I was on my own and had to learn. I messed up a lot of stuff but at the end of three hours when they came back, I had a bead that I could lay up there. And I remember the shop committeeman, he was a brother, Bill Williams, looked at it and said, 'It looks good to me.' " The foreman tried to protest but Williams backed him and Etherly got the job, he said.

John Hightower's mission as a shop committeeman in the early 1950s was to get more blacks in skilled trades jobs. He was working in the foundry but trying to move up to electrician. Every time he asked the personnel director about a promotion, he was put off.

Hightower resorted to political pressure to get appointed to committeeman. He said he was supported by Nathaniel Turner, another committeeman, and State Rep. Roger Townsend.

As a committeeman, Hightower continuously questioned the lack of black skilled trades people and was repeatedly told it was against policy or "not in the contract," he said.

Hightower's reputation as an agitator led to a conflict with a white foreman who called him a nigger, he said.

"I turned and went around the corner and cried and became emotional because I'd just gotten out of the war (WWII) and I said, 'How could this person ... be allowed to call me a nigger?' " He said he complained but a three-month investigation failed to produce enough evidence.

A second incident led to Hightower and the foreman coming to blows. Both men were fired.

Sympathetic co-workers took up a collection of more than $4,000 for Hightower, he said. What most impressed him was that some of the white workers dropping money in the hat were the same ones who had opposed his becoming a committeeman because they had said then the "next thing you know, we'll be overrun with nigger electricians, carpenters, etc."

Hightower sued GM over his dismissal but lost the case. He became a successful businessman and civil rights leader.

Black leadership played an increasingly important role in fair labor practices at GM. Two names often mentioned are Sam Duncan and Sam Carpenter.

Duncan, president of UAW Local 598, was confined to a wheelchair as a result of a war injury. He served 16 years until his death in 1982. A scholarship fund for handicapped students was established in his honor.

Carpenter was the first black vice president of a GM local, the first black supervisor at Chevrolet and a shop superintendent when he retired in 1981. A 1939 Northern High graduate, he started as an hourly employee and worked his way into labor management.

In 1972, Carpenter was handpicked by C.S. Harding Mott, chairman of the Mott Foundation, to become the first full-time director of the National Alliance of Businessmen. It was a job placement service for the hard-to-hire. Carpenter placed some 11,000 workers in 22 months of service.

SELF-EMPLOYED:
"... always looking for a slot he could fill to make money."

"My very first job (was to) haul ice from the ice house," Milton Port said. The year was 1921 and Port was 9. He and his brother used their coaster wagon to deliver ice from house to house, earning 10 cents per packet.

"They had an ice house on the south side," Port said. "You know where the old brewery was on South Saginaw Street, the ice house was a block below it near an old creek. Just as you cross the creek, the ice house was there. They used to get ice right out of Thread Lake at one time. That's before they started making it."

In the 1940s and '50s, Norm Bryant's father created jobs for himself because his religious beliefs forbade working in the automotive factory.

"During World War II, he'd go up North and pick up junk," Bryant recalled. "He sold chickens on the north end and did bump and paint work but he never worked for GM. We didn't go hungry either."

Entrepreneurial spirit like Port's and Bryant's goes back to Flint's first known black resident, barber John Carters who boasted of his superior services in a local newspaper advertisement as early as 1839.

Now an on-going complaint about African-American economic development is that it is limited in scope. It's mostly small, service businesses such as neighborhood mom and pop stores instead of the more lucrative large, manufacturing corporations.

Flint can claim a few black owners of million-dollar corporations. Two are Delbert W. Mullens and William F. Pickard, who made their fortunes in manufacturing automotive supplies. Neither are Flint natives but both lived here many years.

In 1993, Black Enterprise magazine named Mullen's Flint-based Wesley Industries Inc. as the 26th largest black-owned business in the United States. In 1988, Mullens was named Entrepreneur of the Year by the Michigan Department of Commerce.

Pickard grew up in Flint, graduated from Northern in 1959 and Flint Junior College (now Mott Community College) in 1962. He was a social worker for the Flint Urban League and later earned his master's degree and doctorate. He owns Regal Plastics Co. of Owosso and Roseville and several McDonald's franchises in Detroit. Regal Plastics ranked 66th on the

George Artis, circa 1905, was a member of one of Flint's pioneer families and is remembered as a prominent builder.

George Friley, Flint's third black police officer, also owned numerous businesses and houses. Friley's Barber Shop, next door to the popular Papp's drugstore, was among the thriving businesses that once lined Michigan Avenue.

1993 Black Enterprise list.

Black entrepreneurship in Flint declined through the years. By the recession of the early 1980s, many small black businesses folded or never got off the ground.

"Even 20 years ago, which would be the 1970s, there were a lot of black entrepreneurs," Angela Sawyer said. "That could have been because at one time, if you were black you did business with blacks, but by the 1970s, it became more integrated and we've lost that."

A black business directory privately published in 1973 has about 300 listings. Those include florists, accountants, exterminators, real estate agencies, taxi services, construction companies, apartment buildings, moving companies, janitorial services, collision shops, churches, carwashes, clothing stores and many beauty and barber shops.

Black businesses once flourished in the old St. John area where Flint Mayor Woodrow Stanley grew up.

"There is no black-owned hardware store in Flint now, but then (25 years ago) there were two of them within a block of each other," Stanley said.

So was just about every other kind of service you can name. Besides the professional offices of doctors, lawyers and dentists, the spectrum of businesses included funeral homes, insurance and real estate agencies, dry cleaners, restaurants, clothing boutiques, grocery stores, nightclubs, pool halls, shoeshine stands, repair shops and gofer services.

Several black-owned confectionaries have operated. They sold candy, ice cream, sodas and other treats.

Fred Waller had to find private investors and put up his car as collateral to borrow funds to open his pharmacy at Eighth and Lapeer streets.

The Rose Bud Confectionery and Jarrett Bros. Confectionery were on St. John Street. Many old-timers remembered going to Brook's Confectionery on 11th Street in about 1918; Shook's, originally the South Side Confectionery on Clifford Street; and Santee's Confectionery on Clifford.

Some well-remembered dry cleaners include Hayden's on Leith Street, Weaver's on Industrial Avenue and Callaway's and Service Cleaners in the St. John area.

Service Cleaners survives but has relocated. Its original owner, George Lowe, came to Flint in 1939 and worked at other dry cleaners before opening his own in 1947.

Mayor Stanley said he has been a Service Cleaners customer since he was a child.

Before World War II, drugstores included Reed's on Kennelworth and Ferguson's on Kennelworth at Clifford.

In the late 1950s, Fred Waller opened a pharmacy at the corner of Lapeer and Eighth streets.

He had a tough time getting financing. The banks turned him down because he "didn't have enough seasoning." Waller got backing from private sponsors.

"The day I opened the store, I didn't have enough money to make change so I had to go to the bank and borrow $400 with my car as collateral," he said.

"I couldn't understand how I could get money for that and not to open a business."

As far as Waller was concerned, he had seasoning. His uncle, Bruce Dickerson, owned a south-side grocery store. Waller worked there as a young man delivering groceries and running errands.

Black grocers thrived at one time. Elder's on St. John Street was owned by James Elders, who trained many black butchers. Some surviving businesses are Harden's grocery store on North Street and Humpty Dumpty Grocery on Cornelia.

Beauty and barber shops have come and gone but there have always been plenty to go around.

Macks on Industrial at Edmund is one of the oldest black barbershops still in existence. The two-chair shop opened in 1940.

Owner Charles McNeely is retired but visits his shop daily. He sits in a vintage barber chair no longer in use and reminisces with the working barbers and customers about hair trends and old times.

In the 1940s, conks were the rage, McNeely said. The technique required caustic chemicals to straighten the hair. Conks were in fashion with baggy zoot suits worn with long fob chains and two-tone shoes.

Crew cuts came in after World War II, McNeely said. He kept busy cutting as many white heads as blacks, most of them workers from nearby Buick. His shop window overlooks Buick's parking lot.

Raymond's barbershop, 300 Kennelworth, served south-side residents. Annalea Raymond Bannister said her father opened the three-chair shop in 1925 or 1926. Her grandparents had given him $1,000 toward the down payment. Later, her grandfather and uncles moved to Flint from Louisiana to work in the shop.

Donn Kersey's dad ran the Golden Leaf barbershop on the south side. His brother Bill ran a pool room in the same building, he said.

Running black businesses was often a family affair.

In the 1940s, Johnnie Wynn Jr. worked alongside his dad, Wynn Sr., on a milk delivery route for Sprig's Dairy.

"I had to get up early in the morning before I went to school and put them (milk bottles) out," he said. "We would pick it up at the dairy and deliver milk to the doorstep."

Eloise Caldwell helped out at her brother's shop, Santee's Confectionery, from the time she arrived in Flint at age 24 in the late 1930s until she married. It sold ice cream, beer, wine, cigarettes, candy and such, she said.

Audrey Wilson described her dad as "the original entrepreneur because he was always looking for a slot he could fill to make money," she said. He drove a cab, ran a restaurant and sold flowers on Mother's Day.

"We had the St. John Street Frozen Custard next door to the Columbia Theater at St. John and State. I worked there as a young lady (and) had to give up going to football games," she said.

"We sold shrimp dinners, fish and chips, hamburgers; it was like a short-order restaurant. It was a family concern, so we did a bit of it all. I got so tired of cleaning shrimp, I was grown and married before I ate shrimp (again). Same with root beer floats, I had to do so many."

Wilson's dad ran that business about eight years. His sister, Gurthia Waterford, was another born entrepreneur, Wilson said. She owned the Deluxe Gift and Record Shop on St. John, across the street from the Columbia Theater.

Besides the latest records, Waterford sold hats, gifts and hair products – someone said she was the first to sell VO5 hair dressing to blacks.

A baker and a crafts teacher, Waterford baked and sold wedding cakes and dinner rolls.

"She made hats and sold them and taught millinery class at the YWCA," Wilson said. "I remember her teaching at the union hall. She also taught gift wrapping."

Henry Lewis was yet another super-enterprising African-American. Besides working full time at Chevrolet, he owned several businesses, notably Henry's Camera and Jewelry Shop at 1640 S. Saginaw at Twelfth Street.

His daughter, Virginia Lewis Heller, has many memories and mementos from her dad's ventures.

"As a little kid I worked in the store ... stood behind the counter and waited on customers," Heller said. "I would go over (from Clark School) and have my lunch there. My (future) husband learned some of his electrical skills there. He worked in the back room from ... when I was 15 and he was 16 and he worked with my dad after school."

Henry Lewis sold and repaired watches.

"He liked to work with his hands," Heller said. "He had these great big

Entrepreneur Henry Lewis (left) poses with his daughter Virginia and uncle at one of several businesses he owned, circa 1955.

---

huge hands. He would sit there with those big hands and these little pieces that you couldn't see. He'd put those things together."

Lewis started his first business, a photography studio, in 1948. He was a professional photographer and his wife hand-colored photos. She also did oil portraits and sold them all over the city including at Smith-Bridgman's department store downtown, Heller said.

Next, Lewis opened Henry Allen Lewis Realty and became a real estate appraiser. Then he opened Henry's Econo-wash, an automatic laundry on Leith Street in the St. John area, that he equipped with 21 washers, 10 gas dryers and an extractor.

"He ran it for quite a while. I remember being a young girl going over there. But after that, he got interested in flight school. He completed flight

Edith Prunty Spencer and husband J. Merrill Spencer have owned and operated the House of Spencer Mortuary since 1955.

---

school and (practiced) out at Bishop Airport."

Then, with a partner, he opened John's Car Wash on Fifth Avenue, then Henry's Music and Vending. After that, he owned A-OK Construction Corp.

"He had candy machines and cigarette machines," Heller said. "When my kids were born, he used to always bring them Tootsie Rolls and stuff out of the machines. That's how he got called Granddaddy Candy because he always brought the kids Tootsie Rolls."

The House of Spencer Mortuary is another family business that goes back many years. J. Merrill and Edith Spencer opened it in 1955 in the St. John area. It moved a couple times before settling at its present location on W. Third Avenue.

The Spencers moved to Flint in 1950. Merrill worked as a nurse at Hurley Hospital and was one of the first black clerks at the post office before becoming a mortician, his wife said.

Edith Prunty Spencer was a public librarian for 40 years in addition to working in the family business. She acquired her mortuary license in 1962.

Spencer named several black-owned businesses in the St. John area including James Hardware, Callaway Cleaners, Weaver's Cleaners and a coney island restaurant owned by George Friley, an ex-police officer.

The T. Wendell Williams Memorial Building, 4250 N. Saginaw St., is one

The suave and debonair Al Washington left his mark around town in the form of murals and portraits of early Flint civic leaders.

of few remaining landmarks from Flint's black entrepreneurial history. The medical office center was built on the former site of the Nortown Theater and is named for the first black member of the Flint Board of Education.

Promoting black business is a key focus for the Urban League of Flint, the Metropolitan Chamber of Commerce and the Flint Community Development Corp.

FCDC is a nonprofit corporation started in 1972. It provides loans and technical assistance to minority-owned businesses. In about 1984, it launched Flint Industrial Village (now Oak Business Center) on N. Saginaw Street between Taylor and Darmouth streets, where several fledgling businesses are housed under one roof. Low rent keeps overhead costs down while the new business owners get on their feet.

The Metropolitan Chamber of Commerce began in 1985. It provides counseling and sponsors educational conferences, workshops and classes. Its entrepreneurial training classes help prospective business owners develop a business and marketing plan and avoid common pitfalls that cause black businesses to fail.

There were about 260 black-owned businesses in Flint in the mid-1980s, according to the latest data reported by the Metropolitan Chamber.

The Flint Urban League was started in April 1943 by an interracial coalition of local citizens. Its purpose was to help rural blacks migrating from the South adjust to urban life. The League's mission changed to meet the needs of the times such as fair housing, job discrimination, unemployment or assistance for veterans returning from the war.

The Urban League played a leadership role during 1960s civil rights activism but refocused in the 1980s to address education and job training needs.

In 1989, the League opened a training and development center in the former Selby Elementary School, 5005 Cloverlawn, on Flint's north side. The 33,000-square-foot facility houses the League's Employment and Training Service, youth employment and on-the-job-training programs.

Ernest Johnson Jr., a plumbing and heating contractor, got his start in a Flint Urban League training program. He is a member of the Association for Minority Contractors and the Metropolitan Chamber of Commerce.

Ernest "Pete" Johnson Sr. proudly noted that his son reaches back into the minority community to hire and train other blacks. That's important, he said.

Ernest Johnson Jr. credits the example his father set for him.

"When I was growing up, I respected black men doing anything positive," he said. "There were so many who didn't have a chance to do anything positive. My daddy had two jobs. He'd go to work for nine-10 hours, come home and eat and go right back out the door. That's a leader to me, a role model."

PROFESSIONAL GROWTH:
"I had to be twice as good as anyone else."

Attorney C. Frederick Robinson, a native of North Carolina, arrived in Flint in 1956 with a fresh law degree from Howard University and a crusader's attitude.

"My intention was to stay here about five years and go back to North Carolina," Robinson said. "But I found out that black folks were just as bad off here as there, so I'm still here."

Robinson opened an office with a fellow Howard law school graduate and began forming coalitions with other civil rights activists. That thrust him into a key role in many desegregation battles.

"There was no opportunity for blacks," Robinson said. "I am talking about people with master's degrees who were sweeping the floors in the factory."

His good friend and law colleague, A. Glenn Epps, knows that from personal experience.

Dr. Jesse Leonidas Leach (right), was a prominent civic and civil rights leader from the 1920s through 1950s.

"I had my bachelor's degree from U of M (University of Michigan)," said Epps, who grew up in Flint. "I applied for a job at Chevrolet (about 1950). They gave me a job cleaning toilets." He had asked for a job on production.

Epps said he knew another shop worker who had a master's degree from the University of Iowa. He was sweeping floors to save enough money to go to medical school.

"The only thing that did to me was make me more determined," Epps said.

Like Batman and Robin, the dynamic duo of Robinson and Epps teamed up to improve opportunities for blacks in Flint.

Robinson was president of the Community Civic League. Epps was assistant Genesee County prosecutor from 1959 to 1962. The two used the law as an instrument of social change, Epps said.

"We would challenge the constitutionality of existing laws and practices. For instance, when somebody was arrested for so-called loitering, we used law to bring about change in that situation because they weren't doing nothing."

Epps and Robinson handled a successful lawsuit to desegregate Flint cemeteries. Epps represented the NAACP during the fight for fair housing in 1967. In 1972, the Community Civic League mounted a campaign to redraw boundaries for state House of Representatives districts that would improve chances of Genesee County electing a black representative.

The last state representative had been Roger Townsend who served from 1952-64. The first was Flint attorney John F. Young, who served from 1949-51.

In 1961, Flint attorney Otis M. Smith was appointed the first black Michigan Supreme Court justice. He served until 1966. He was an assistant Genesee County prosecutor in 1954. His mentor, Dudley Mallory, was one of Flint's first attorneys. Mallory reportedly encouraged Smith to accept the supreme court post, saying, "You can't do any worse than the rest of those bozos up there."

Epps listed the roster of Flint's first black lawyers. Mallory and Claude W. Heywood started Flint practices the same year – 1926. Then came Roy M. Van Dyne who opened a Flint office in 1927 (he lost a bid to become Flint's first black circuit judge by 24 votes in 1941).

After him, Epps said, came Joseph N. Birch, 1935 (the first black appointed to the staff of the Genesee County prosecutor in 1949); John F. Young, 1944 (he was assistant state attorney general 1937-39); Elisha Scott Jr., 1946; Otis Smith and William S. Price in 1951; Herman Gibson, 1952; and Ollie B. Bivins Jr., 1953, who became Flint's first black circuit judge in 1974.

Then, John H. Thomas, 1955; C. Frederick Robinson, A. Glenn Epps and Kenneth Dones in 1956; and Richard E. McDonald, 1968. Many others came after the 1960s but one worth noting is Edwyna Goodwin Anderson, who was the first black woman admitted to the Genesee County Bar Association in 1974.

Flint's black professional community, in general, grew tremendously as a result of 1960s civil rights efforts. By the mid-1990s, the Flint area had many black doctors, teachers, nurses, police officers, social workers, journalists, business administrators, accountants and more.

Lois Shaw said she became Flint's first black registered nurse in 1947. Several licensed practical nurses but no RNs were working, Shaw said, when she was hired at St. Joseph Hospital.

Shaw worked at St. Joe's for about a year and had been promoted to acting supervisor when a job opened at Hurley Hospital (later Hurley Medical Center).

"Zolton Papp (a white civic leader) was the reason I got hired," Shaw said. "They had an opening but when I applied they told me I was overqualified. Papp was the chairman of the board at Hurley."

After raising a fuss, Papp called Shaw personally to offer her the job. Four years passed before another black RN was hired, Shaw said.

Shaw was closely watched at first.

"They questioned everything I did," she said. "I had to prove everything I did. I had to be twice as good as anyone else. In that first year I had established myself with the doctors and they would ask for me."

Some patients were less receptive. Shaw recalled one seriously ill white man at St. Joe's who frankly told her he did not want a black nurse. A doctor told him there was no one else to attend him. He transferred to Hurley where, she said, he ended up having a black doctor.

Shaw left St. Joe's because a person she trained was promoted over her to the supervisor's job. At Hurley, Shaw found greater success.

As the first black president of the Flint District Nurses Association, Shaw worked on improving professionalism with Elnor Pea, who was the first black president of the Practical Nurses Association.

Flint was a pioneer in organizing the nursing profession in Michigan, Shaw said. She and Pea both served at the state and national level.

"I know I opened a many door for people at Hurley that never would have gotten in," Shaw said. "If I told them, 'This is the person I want,' they hired them, didn't question them. See, we set up criteria. If people couldn't meet it, it didn't matter if they were black or white, they didn't get (hired)."

Louise Tarver, said to be the second black registered nurse at Hurley, was hired in 1951 and stayed until 1968. She felt she was treated well compared to segregated working conditions she'd experienced at a Georgia hospital.

At Hurley, Tarver was promoted to assistant director of nursing in charge of the night shift. It was stressful, she recalled, because she had to try to fill gaps created by staff shortages.

As far as Tarver remembers, patient care was not segregated at Hurley then. Blacks were admitted as needed and there were black doctors on staff. Though some doctors made house calls, black women gave birth in the hospital instead of at home, she said.

One of the black doctors on Hurley's staff was James Hawkins, Tarver said. He practiced at Hurley from 1934 to 1968 and was Flint's first black doctor who had been born here. His sister, Dorothy Hawkins Waller, is married to retired pharmacist Fred Waller.

Vivian M. Lewis was Flint's first black woman doctor. She and her husband Billye, a surgeon, arrived in 1959 to do their medical internships and residencies at Hurley. She also was the first black and first woman presi-

Flint's first black police chief, William Lyght (seated on desk), lends his chair to Flint's first black police officer, Archie Parks (seated right), while Parks' son Leonard looks on.

---

dent of the Genesee County Medical Society.

Blacks in public safety jobs did not make in-roads until the 1960s but Flint's first black police officer, Archie Parks, was hired in May 1931.

The first black fireman, Joe Davis, was hired in 1961. Kenneth W. Burns and Richard Dicks were the first black police officers to make sergeant, both promoted in 1973. Other officers picketed city hall for a week in protest.

William L.D. Lyght Jr., Flint's first black police chief, and Samuel Dixon Jr., the first black fire chief, were hired in 1983 by James Sharp, Flint's first popularly elected black mayor.

Catherine Murphy became the first black female police officer in the mid-1960s during the administration of Floyd McCree, Flint's first black mayor.

Sondra Rawls was among the first group of female police officers assigned to the streets during McCree's term. Some women officers said they were harassed by male officers. It was rough at times, Rawls said, but McCree and city manager Daniel Boggan Jr. worked hard to keep the women motivated not to quit.

"There was so much racism that many of the blacks just never stayed there," said John Blakely, who quit in 1964 after five years on the force. "You deal with the public but when you deal with racism from inside (the office), it's kind of tough."

Flint had 12 black officers then, including Blakely. He had been a military policeman during the Korean War.

Archie Parks, the first black officer, "liked his job (and) was treated well," said Leonard Parks, his son.

Parks died in 1988 at age 84. He had moved away but while back on a visit in 1984, he met and swapped stories with Lyght, Flint's first black police chief. The historic moment was captured in a 1984 photograph, published in The Flint Journal.

Parks had been hand-picked by Mayor William McKeighan and the chief of police as a political favor in return for black voters' support, Archie Parks once told The Journal in an interview. His training consisted of verbal instructions from the police chief and sergeants.

Parks was a tall, heavy-set, friendly man. He began as a patrolman in the St. John Street area, mostly covering his beat on foot. Occasionally, he did detective work but could not get promoted to full-time detective despite several attempts. He was put in charge of the old city jail for five years, before retiring in April 1956.

Parks had been the only black officer during his first four years.

Percy McClellan, a former Central High football star, joined the force in 1935. He resigned in 1939, charged with "conduct unbecoming an officer," but later filed a suit alleging that he was intimidated into quitting, according to Flint Journal files. He was replaced by George Friley, 30, who became a prominent business owner.

The U.S. Postal Service started hiring blacks in Flint in the 1940s. Among the first were William Hoskins, J. Merrill Spencer, Sam Williams, Layton Galloway, Roosevelt Walker, Al Davis, F. Harris and McKinley Waller.

William Hoskins said he was the first black postal employee, hired in April 1946. In those days, only custodial jobs were offered to blacks.

Black postal workers started a union in the early 1950s to push for promotions to clerks and carriers.

"When we went in the post office, the first thing we tried to do was organize the blacks working there so we could get some kind of fair play," said Layton Galloway, a charter member along with Hoskins, Sam Williams, Cleo Rawls, Wendell Galloway (his cousin) and others.

To the best of Galloway's recollection, Al Harris was the first black postal worker to get a job other than janitor. Raphael Metcalfe Sr. is believed to have been the first black mail carrier.

Galloway was one of the first black window clerks and about the fourth to be promoted to supervisor, he said. He was hired in January 1953.

"J. Merrill Spencer, Bernard Greenich and I started at the post office the same day. We did all our scheme studying together, drank our beer," Galloway said.

Sam McClarin, a porter at the Durant Hotel, was one of many prominent black men symbolically elected as the Mayor of Brownsville (black Flint) during the pre-1940s era when blacks held few, if any, political positions.

Floyd McCree, Flint's first black mayor, was chosen for the position by a vote of fellow city commission members. He is remembered as an articulate and diplomatic leader.

He earned 25 cents an hour less than at his old job in the shop. Blacks at the post office had no chance of promotion then and worked extra hard to prove themselves.

"At that time, you didn't have any contracts or any rules," Galloway said. "So if your boss said you weren't doing something right, you were out the door and didn't have any recourse. When I started at the post office, there was no such thing as a break. They'd let you go to the bathroom occasionally."

He had to pass a test sorting mail with 98 percent accuracy. If he'd missed three out of 100, he would have failed. Good memorization skills were vital to keep track of thousands of street names and delivery route schemes.

"I had three schemes to learn in the first year," Galloway said. "You had a year of qualification and had to requalify each year. When I first went in there, there was a demerit system. If you got so many demerits, you got fired."

Now, sorters have to process only about 100 pieces in eight minutes, he said. He had to do about 280 in the same amount of time.

Mail carriers had their work cut out, too, before the union won better working conditions.

"When I went in, a carrier had like 750 stops," Galloway said. "In some cases, they would take the bus to a certain stop, then walk. He carried the mail on his back in a satchel that weighed about 45 pounds. Everything was walked out of the post office then. Now the carrier carries all his mail out on his truck."

Regular carriers earned less than substitutes because they were contracted to a 40-hour work week. Substitutes could work as many hours as they could get, Galloway said.

"Can you imagine that? When I started at the post office on substitute, I was working as much as 12 hours a day, sometimes seven days a week," he said. That meant his pay was cut in half when he was promoted to regular employee status.

Galloway was promoted to supervisor in 1962 and later became superintendent of the afternoon shift in charge of dispatch. When he retired in 1980, his annual income was $40,000, compared to $5,000 he earned during his first years.

Sam Williams started work at the post office in 1947. He also took that dreaded 25-cents-an-hour pay cut, down from $1.56-an-hour shop wages. But Williams wasn't complaining.

"In the shop you never knew how long you would work (between layoffs) but with a federal job, once you got settled in, it was regular. You knew how much you'd have coming in."

When Williams retired in 1981, he was manager of the the north-side post office at N. Saginaw Street at Pasadena Avenue.

Teaching and postal jobs opened up for blacks in Flint about the same time. In 1942, Lois Holt was hired as the Flint Board of Education's first professional educator, working outside of the classroom. In 1943, Marion Coates Williams was hired as the first black classroom teacher. And in 1950, Aaron A. Smith became the first black male classroom teacher.

Rules for teachers were stricter when Coates Williams started. For one thing, there was a dress code.

"You had to look like a teacher, what they said a teacher should look like. Modest. You wore dresses," she said.

Another rule applied to maternity leave.

"You had to take a three-year leave (without pay)," Coates Williams said. In between her three pregnancies, she worked as a substitute teacher.

"You could sub but you could not go back to permanent teaching (for three years). I subbed in any number of schools," Coates Williams said.

Coates Williams began her career at the old Fairview Elementary School on Leith Street. After it closed, she went to Parkland Elementary on North Street.

She retired in 1962 at age 40 but went back to work after her husband died in 1966. She retired for good in 1982.

Lois Holt and her sister Ruth VanZandt had earlier battled the Flint Board of Education's early hiring policies.

VanZandt tested the waters in 1937 when she graduated from college. She was bluntly told that Flint schools had no plans to hire a black teacher, she said.

"I was doing it out of pure hellishness," VanZandt recalled with a still-devilish chuckle. She already had a teaching job lined up in Inkster.

Flint finally hired VanZandt in 1944 because assistant superintendent Frank Manley thought so highly of her sister Lois, she said.

Getting hired was one thing and getting promoted another. Blacks could not teach at the secondary level until 1952 when Dolores Ennis went to work at Emerson Junior High School after substitute teaching for a year.

Ruth Buckner became the first female elementary school principal at Oak School in 1963. That same year, Aaron Smith became the first black male principal at Mary Street School (later Kennedy).

Al Renick was named the first black junior high school principal at Bryant in 1968, but the first black high school principal, Shelby J. Cummings, was not appointed until 1972. Dr. Nathel Burtley became the first black assistant superintendent in 1981 and the first black superintendent in 1988.

Black hiring and promotions escalated in 1968 because of heightened social tensions after the assassination of civil rights leader Martin Luther

King Jr., recalled Floyd Clack, a former teacher who was elected a state representative in the early 1980s and has served several terms.

Flint had few black teachers at most high schools in 1968, Clack said. But the numbers shot up then.

Interest was so keen to hire black teachers that Clack was recruited from Texas. He didn't want to come all the way to Flint for an interview so he was allowed to apply by mail.

Clack started at Bryant Junior High but transferred to Northern High after a month.

"My shocker was that (at Northern) there must have been 25-30 black teachers," Clack said. "We all assumed that everybody had been there forever and when we finally got together (and swapped histories) we discovered we were all new."

Clack taught social studies, political science, government, consumer economics, law and, notably, black history. Former students still tell him they remember the black history lessons most.

"It may have been 20 or 25 years ago but they always remember (me) as being their black history teacher," Clack said. "It was new and it was something that they learned about themselves, so they remembered. Now we have to rally these teachers around here. This is what I tell everybody. We ought to insist on it being a part of the curriculum."

Clack taught until 1982 when he was elected to the Legislature. He is a past president of the Flint NAACP and served on the Flint City Council from 1979 to 1982.

More blacks began to move into public administration and political jobs as a result of social progress.

Henry Horton was appointed director of the Model Cities Program in 1968. Model Cities developed social and cultural programs for low-income families.

Horton chuckled dryly as he recalled power struggles during his four years as director.

"People were not accustomed to seeing a black handle that much money, so I got all these people coming at me who wanted to tell me how to do things and what I ought to do," Horton said.

His biggest critics, he said, were his former colleagues-cum-bosses on the Genesee County Board of Supervisors.

"They were not planners, not people of any managerial skills," said Horton, who has a degree in business administration. "I always considered myself a manager, but I hired planners. So these (supervisors) would come to me with all these ideas about who I should hire and so, yes, I made a lot of enemies.

James Sharp, Flint's first popularly elected mayor, carried on the dream for racial equality espoused by late civil rights leader Martin Luther King Jr. by improving opportunities for minorities.

"All my life I've basically ignored that kind of thing (racism). I see it, I hear it, I feel it when it happens but I keep going."

In 1975, Horton ran unsuccessfully for mayor of Flint and was appointed director of the Flint Housing Commission.

Since the revolutionary 1960s, many black politicians have left a mark on Flint history. The list includes Ailene Butler, Flint's first black city councilwoman from 1973-75; Fred Tucker, a five-term city councilman from 1968 to 1979; and Daniel Boggan Jr., Flint's first black city manager, appointed in 1974.

Few blacks worked at city hall and few held supervisory positions when James A. Sharp became Flint's first black elected mayor in 1983, he said.

"The fire department didn't have anyone above the rank of beginner," he said. "The police (department) did have a few. The hospital (Hurley) was probably the most equal in terms of opportunity (for blacks)."

Outside city hall, "we tried to empower more people in the black community to become entrepreneurs in their own right," Sharp said.

His administration provided start-up funding to the Metropolitan Chamber of Commerce, which promotes black business ownership.

Sharp initiated the idea to re-open a major grocery store on Flint's north side. That plan fell through but when a Kessel "superstore" opened at the Hallwood Plaza on W. Pierson at Clio Road in May 1994, it was the first large grocer serving the inner city for several years.

Former NAACP president Edgar Holt made a name for himself as a man to see about getting a job. GM hired many blacks on his recommendation, his widow Lois Holt said. He provided that service for free.

As a civil rights leader, Holt and others led protests to get blacks hired at Sears, Consumers Power, Michigan National Bank, restaurants, bowling alleys and Buick.

John Hightower, another civil rights leader, opened a fast-food restaurant at Saginaw and Leith streets, to help needy blacks. Tower Drive-in provided jobs and gave away meals. A hamburger, carton of milk and order of french fries sold for 25 cents.

"For some who didn't have money, we fed them anyway," Hightower said. "I had a mission to accomplish – that was my mission." He also owned a dress shop, construction company and travel agency. Hightower Construction built many black churches in Flint.

Hightower said it bothers him some that many young blacks today do not seem to respect the sacrifices made by his generation to open doors for them.

"Some of the sad things I see are those who have made the green – blacks who have forgotten where they came from," he said.

But he takes joy from seeing black foremen, carpenters and skilled tradespeople at GM. Hightower said he fought hard to open up those jobs when he was chairman of the Fair Employment Practices Committee at UAW Local 599 at Buick.

Black journalists have multiplied, too. Blacks have co-anchored newscasts at all local major television networks. Flint's first black-owned radio station WDZZ debuted in 1979 and employs numerous blacks.

Darrell R. Tallifairo was the first black anchorman for Channel 12 (WJRT). Edwyna G. Anderson was the first black reporter at The Flint Journal in 1963. Craig Carter was the first black male reporter, hired in 1971. As of 1995, the Flint Journal had six full-time black reporters, one editor and one assistant editor.

Black newspapers have been a strong alternate voice on community issues. One of the first may have been The Brownsville News, which can

Woodrow Stanley (center) celebrates a primary victory on the road to being elected mayor in 1991.

---

be dated to at least the 1930s. It was edited by Henry G. Reynolds.

The North Star, a weekly tabloid, began publishing in 1955. J. Wesley Caldwell was its editor.

The Flint Spokesman was published from 1946 to 1952 and resurfaced briefly in 1971. It was owned by Thomas M. "Count" Terry, a colorful businessman who died in 1991.

The Bronze Reporter, operated by local NAACP president Herman Gibson, published circa 1955. Historian Melvin E. Banner was once an assistant editor.

Still publishing are the CPSA Courier, a church-based newspaper founded in 1981 by the Concerned Pastors for Social Action, and The Flint Enquirer, launched in 1984. The Enquirer briefly merged with the Flint Editorial in 1986 but resumed its original name after a legal battle. The Flint Editorial began as the Thursday Luncheon Business Journal in 1982. It has since folded.

Jobs in the entertainment field offered another avenue for talented blacks. But a professional musician's life can be "Far Fom Tranquil," according to Sherm Mitchell, who gave that title to his first jazz album in 1988.

"It's not glamorous, it's a job," Mitchell said. "It's a pleasant job if you love what you're doing."

Mitchell started young, first having to overcome his parents' objections. "They didn't think too much of (music as a career)," Mitchell said.

"They didn't fight me on it but they wanted me to be a better student and study other things. I used to practice so much that my mother would have to ask me to stop certain days. Nobody ever had to tell me to practice."

His mother came around when he started earning money and helped ease the family's financial burden.

Mitchell's first professional job was at WFDF radio in 1944. He played in a junior high school orchestra.

"It was decent pay because when I was 15, 16, 17 years old, I could bring money home. I was probably making as much or more than my dad was making because he was just working as a manservant to a private family," he said.

"I'd get out of a (music job) at 10 o'clock at night, go to school the next morning, no problem," he said.

Later, "I worked in the factory for 20 years. I played at night down in Detroit. I'd get off at 2 o'clock in the morning and get home about 4 and had to be at work at 6 (a.m.). I did that for years."

Mitchell began touring in the late 1970s. He traveled to Mexico, South America, the Caribbean and Europe.

He taught himself to play several instruments and reads, writes and arranges music. He's recorded two albums of mostly original songs. He's also recorded with other musicians and played with jazz greats such as Bob James, Sonny Stitt and Dizzy Gillespie.

Though he's not one to harp on racism, Mitchell said that discrimination against blacks was the reason he quit the Flint musicians' union years ago.

"They weren't doing what they needed to do, especially with my musicians," Mitchell said. "We needed more help than anyone else." Nor did he appreciate never being offered free-lance work, he said.

"All the years that they had shows in this town – Shrine Circus and the Ice Capades and stuff – I never ever got called, not once," he said.

"Most people in this town now, when they think of jazz, my name will come up. I'm not sitting back on my laurels and talking about what I used to be able to do."

Dorothy Patton, another Flint jazz legend, traveled extensively across the Midwest and in Canada in the 1950s and early 1960s. She worked nights, slept days and attended business meetings in between, but she's not complaining.

"I've had the luxury of doing what I like to do most for survival, to make a living, so I don't think I could have been any happier than that," Patton said.

White supper clubs were her bread and butter. She made more money playing jazz different from what black audiences liked to hear, she said.

Jazz fans would also pay to watch the Jazz Workshop. For about 75 cents, they could listen for about 45 minutes. Then the room would be cleared and a new audience would come in.

Patton recorded an album in 1967 that was never released because the company went bankrupt. Working for Motown, she opened a new nightclub in Memphis with the Spinners, she said.

Detroit's Motown in the 1960s was red hot. Two Flint women were part of the history-making excitement. Cousins Norma Barbee Fairhurst and Bertha Barbee McNeal were Velvelettes at the same time The Supremes were making a name for themselves.

Fairhurst was still a student at Southwestern High School when she signed with Motown in the 1960s. It was her first professional job.

"My schoolmates never knew I had signed a contract with Motown and was touring on weekends," she said. "I wasn't hiding it, it was just something I did."

The Velvelettes started at Western Michigan University. Bertha Barbee and Mildred Arbor were students there. Arbor's sister Cal, another member of the group, was in junior high school in Kalamazoo. Fairhurst would visit her cousin Bertha and the young women decided to form a group.

They won a campus talent show and attracted the attention of the nephew of Berry Gordy, Motown's founder. A few months later the Velvelettes signed a Motown contract.

"I'd do my homework Friday night and catch the bus to Detroit on Saturday morning," Fairhurst said. "The others would take the bus from Kalamazoo. We synchronized our arrival times to take a cab together to Motown to record, then stayed overnight with Mildred and Cal's aunt in Detroit."

It was sweet revenge for Fairhurst, who had proved an elementary school teacher wrong.

"I tried out for a choir and this teacher told me I didn't have talent. I was on the radio when I was 5 singing 'Yes, Jesus Loves Me.' I sang first soprano and I had a heckuva range, which made the group unique," Fairhurst said.

"I grew up around music. A lot of my family members sing. My uncle Simon Barbee sings. And my cousin Bertha Barbee sang in a group called The Barbees long before the Velvelettes," Fairhurst said.

Like Mitchell and Patton, The Velvelettes can talk about the dark side of show business. There was little time for parties or nightclubs unless the group was working there, Fairhurst said.

"That was very depressing for us because a lot of times we'd have to go in through the back (door). The majority of the time, it didn't seem like work because we enjoyed it, but it got to a point where we had to be a certain place. It was almost like they owned us."

The group always traveled with a chaperone, was not allowed to shop or eat alone and had to take a nap before performances.

"It was sort of a caged-up feeling," said Fairhurst, who was the first to leave the group.

"I welcomed the chance to get out, to lead what I thought was a normal life."

Her advice to aspiring musicians is to develop business management skills along with musical skills. Learn how to read a contract, write a press release and work with an attorney and accountant, she said.

"It's not all glamour and glitz; that's about 5 percent. The rest is hard work."

THIS AND THAT:
"You can't keep a good, determined person down."

When one of his white co-workers didn't show up for work one day, young Woody Etherly Jr. saw his chance.

He was working for the Flint Department of Public Works in the early 1960s. His job shoveling asphalt into low spots in the road was one of the hottest, nastiest jobs to have. The white workers "had the good easy jobs," he said.

So when no one else spoke up when the crew boss asked who knew how to drive a truck, Etherly raised his hand.

"I'd never driven a stick shift in my life but I knew it was better than what I was doing," he said.

Etherly retells the story with great humor. He said it shaped his life's philosophy.

"They took me down to the yard on 12th Street and gave me this great big truck," Etherly said. "It had a high-low and I think something like six forward gears. I didn't even know how to make it move."

He was left alone after being told to drive the truck over to the job site. What followed was a comedy of errors as he pressed different levers and pedals trying to get the big truck started and to keep it moving.

"You should have seen me. I was driving and the truck was jumping down the street. When I got to the job and parked the truck up there ... do you know how you grind gears? If you don't get the clutch down and you try to shift, it'll make a grinding noise. Well, I didn't know all that so I was messing up good, but I got it there.

"And the old foreman, now I have to give this white man credit, he was nice. He looked at me and laughed and (asked), 'How long you been driving?' I said: 'For a little while.' So he gave me a few pointers. There were some white folks who would help you.

"That first week, I burned out the clutch but he let me stay and I got off the shovel and started driving trucks – the first black person to drive a city truck. It was funny, I didn't know a bit more about how to drive than the man in the moon."

The moral of his story: "I often say you can't keep a good, determined person down. You can only throw a roadblock in the way. But if they're determined to be successful, they'll find a way around it and keep on going. And that has been my philosophy."

Other determined black workers in Flint have done a bit of everything – they've been elevator operators, disc jockeys, retail clerks, shoe shiners, seamstresses, government workers, real estate agents, librarians and social workers, to name a few.

Sondra Rawls schemed a bit at age 17 to land her "first real" job downtown at J.C. Penney. She was busing tables at the restaurant at Smith-Bridgman's department store. On the spur of the moment, during her lunch break, she decided to fill out an application at Penney's. She had to lie about her age.

Penney's called her to work the same day, and she stayed for 10 years. She is now director of the Flint Human Relations Commission.

In 1964, Geraldine Smith's volunteer work led to a paying job. She was hired as a teacher's aide for a program called Better Tomorrow for the Urban Child at Parkland Elementary School, where her children were students.

"The principal said to me, 'You're up here so much, we might as well pay you,' " Smith said. She worked a full-time job for six years. In 1970 she went to work for the Flint Public Library as a clerk. When she retired in 1990, she was supervisor of the loan department.

At age 8, Charlotte Williams used to "sneak and sew" on her mother's electric machine on her way to acquiring a marketable skill. It paid off at age 16, when Williams was hired to teach sewing and crafts to children as part of a summer enrichment program sponsored by the Mott Foundation. It paid off again when Williams taught Bishop Sewing classes from the mid-1950s until 1964. At the same time, she was working as a licensed practical nurse at St. Joseph Hospital.

Singing in a band helped launch Sam Williams' broadcast career. The drummer from the band became program director at WBDC on Bristol Road, off Dort Highway. He called Williams when one of the deejays quit.

"I told him I didn't know anything about it," Williams said.

"He asked: 'Do you know how to read?'

"I said: 'Of course I know how to read.'
"He said: 'I can teach you the rest.'"
That was in 1955.
"There were no records programs on the radio (then)," Sam Williams said. "They had stories. It was just segmented-type radio but not continuous music."

There were no black radio stations then and little black-oriented music being played. Then Dick Carter, who was Jewish, bought a two-hour block of air time on WBDC and hired a black deejay to play music, Williams said. Ernie Durham and Earl West were two of the earliest black deejays working for Carter.

After the format expanded to four hours, the station wouldn't sell Carter more time, so he started his own station – WAAM (now WFLT), Williams said.

Williams went to work part time at WAAM when it went on the air about 1960. That was on top of his full-time job at the post office. His shift at the radio station ran from 5 p.m. until sign-off at sundown.

"When I started in radio, I wasn't playing just black music, I was playing everything – contemporary and country and Western," Williams said.

He went to WDZZ-FM when it debuted in 1979. It is Flint's first black-owned station. He still hosts its Sunday morning religious program.

African missionary work seasoned Karen Aldridge's work ethic. She is now a financial program officer at the Mott Foundation.

After a couple of summers working in Liberia, West Africa, as a teen, Aldridge went back there to live from 1974 to 1977 after graduating from college. She worked for the National Baptist Convention managing a K-9 school in a small village where there was no electricity or running water.

"I loved the experience," Aldridge said. "It grew me up. Lots of things became less significant. Over there they deal with basics (like) food."

She was budget director for the city of Flint from 1988 to 1992 and worked for the state Office of Management and Budget before joining the Mott Foundation in 1994.

Elnor Pea saw the need to find jobs for youth in 1955. She and a group of women organized a program to get black carryout boys hired at Hamady's Bros. grocery stores. They also approached downtown stores and churches about creating youth jobs.

A real estate license was Henry Horton's ticket off the Chevrolet production line, where he had not seen much chance for advancement. Horton was the only black working for Connie Benson Realty. Benson used Horton's photograph in ads to attract black clients. Horton later held various public service jobs before becoming a minister.

One of Ailene Butler's earliest jobs was as a seamstress. She did alterations and made draperies and home decorations. She also catered.

In 1940, she enrolled in a mortuary science course at Wayne State University. She ran Butler's Funeral Home from the early 1940s to 1986. As Flint's first black city councilwoman, elected in 1973, she represented the First Ward.

Charles Hamilton went to work at age 11 at a shoeshine parlor on Industrial Avenue between Jamieson and McClellan streets. That was in 1939. At 14, he got a job setting bowling pins.

They didn't have automatic pin-setters in those days, Hamilton said. They didn't allow blacks to bowl then but the owner would let the pin-setters roll a few balls before customers came in, he said. Hamilton eventually settled on a career as a factory worker.

Eugene Simpson started work in 1940 at age 13 at Papp's drugstore on St. John Street. Later, he worked in the Buick foundry and other jobs, retiring in 1980. Before his death in January 1994, he was pastor of Mt. Tabor Baptist Church.

The Flint Public Library was spread out over three locations when Edith Spencer went to work there in 1951. The reference and circulation department was downtown where UM-Flint is now, she said. The children's department was in the basement of Walker School on E. Second Street where the YMCA is now. And a storage building and offices were on Eighth at Harrison, behind Flint City Hall.

Spencer was a cataloger responsible for filing cards in all three places before the main library on Kearsley was built in 1957, she said. She retired in 1987.

DISCRIMINATION:
"They said the job was filled."

Suddenly, the job was no longer open but that's not what Gladys Dawkins had been told over the telephone.

"I was given the OK to come in for the interview but the minute they saw my face, that I was black, they said the job was filled," she said. That happened to her more than once.

Some black women couldn't get hired because their skin wasn't light enough.

"A really big thing when I was young (1940s) was when the banks started hiring women to run the elevators," Ruth Scott said. "But they only hired light-skinned black women. I remember saying to my mother when I was really little, I thought this lady (elevator operator) was so pretty. I said I wanted to do that and my mother said I couldn't. She explained to me that I wasn't light enough and besides she said, 'I don't want you to do that.'"

The job wasn't all peaches and cream for women who did that. When Bessie Brooks ran the elevator at the Durant Hotel about 1929, she liked her job but had to deal with harassment.

"White guys would pick on you but you couldn't complain," she said. "The men would flirt."

"In those days, they didn't have automatic elevators. You had to lower it to the floor level by hand; you better get it right even, too, or the guys would complain to the manager (that) they had to step down or up. I had nightmares working that job. I would dream of holding on to the dresser, trying to get it level, especially when the bell rang on the top level. The big shot up there always pinched me. I didn't dare complain. Negro men did a lot of that, too."

Her fair skin may have helped Annalea Bannister get inside the door at the Genesee County building in 1946 but it didn't get her restroom privileges.

"When I first went there, they didn't want blacks to use a restroom. There was one in my office and later I found out it was because the other women didn't want to use the same restroom a black used. You know, that was really ridiculous."

Simply being black could get you fired, too. Mary Jamieson believes she lost her cashier's job at a Yankee department store in the 1950s because her white co-workers were intimidated by her boyfriend.

The store was located in an area where blacks didn't live or shop. Jamieson was the only black employee.

One night, her boyfriend came to pick her up after work. He came inside the store to wait, and Jamieson immediately knew she was in trouble.

"Their eyes (co-workers) got this big," she said, making an egg-sized circle with her hand. "He was standing there with his coat on and he was just looking but he didn't buy anything and I said, 'Oh my god,' and I knew it was because they were all white and didn't no black people go into that store, so they were afraid."

Jamieson was responsible for counting the money in the drawer at the end of each day. On the night in question, the woman who was training Jamieson told her to go ahead and leave and she'd close out the register for her. The next day, Jamieson was fired. The reason they gave was that the money in her cash drawer came up short the night before.

Lois Holt, Flint's first black teacher, sometimes experienced repercussions on her job because of her husband Edgar's activities as president of the NAACP. One principal accused her of participating in a political survey, then claimed he had no work for her to do, she said.

Flint public schools would not hire J. Merrill Spencer to teach high school in the early 1950s, said his wife, Edith.

He applied four years in a row. At one point, they told him the Flint Board of Education did not hire man and wife. Edith Spencer, a librarian, did some research and came up with names of several couples employed by the school board. The next excuse was that they didn't hire man and wife at the same time.

J. Merrill Spencer worked as a substitute teacher for a while and at the post office before starting a funeral home.

As executive director of multicultural affairs at Mott Community College, Lennetta Coney's job was to make sure that kind of thing didn't happen. She planned programs for MCC faculty and staff and in the Flint community to promote diversity and good human relations.

Melvin McCree, Genesee County Register of Deeds, has an optimistic outlook of Flint's employment future.

Job discrimination persists but in his lifetime alone, McCree notes improvement in job opportunities and practices.

"Blacks are in a lot of jobs that they weren't when I grew up," he said.

And the silver lining in the economic cloud that drove many job seekers out of Flint is that some of them gain perspective to bring back to the city.

"If you're thinking about becoming a business person, you may see a business (elsewhere) that we need in Flint. If you never (went) out there, you'd never have the sense of that vision that, 'Hey, they did that there. Maybe I can do it with this, this or this (here).' "

Education

A 1940s view of student fashions and faces at Lowell Junior High School.

Sherm Mitchell's illustrious music career started with lessons at Clark Elementary School in the 1930s.

"They taught us keyboard, bass clef, treble clef," he said. "That was part of the education before you left the sixth grade. You had to learn that." Sixty years and two albums later, Mitchell has entertained around the world.

Clark School, 1519 Harrison Street, laid a solid educational foundation for thousands of children like Mitchell.

"Oh, you couldn't beat the teachers we had at Clark School," said Anna L.V. Howard, a student there in the late 1920s. "They'd sit there as long as a kid wanted to learn. Their husbands would be sitting out there in the parking lot and we'd be inside having fun with those teachers.

"And when you passed from grade to grade, you knew it (lessons). They didn't care how tall or how old you were. If you didn't know it, you didn't pass."

Howard remembers teachers making house calls to check up on students. And parents wore a path from homes to schools attending PTA meetings and keeping tabs on their children's progress.

Clark School was praised as the finest building in town when it was built in 1912. It is the oldest Flint school building still standing. But the brownish-brick relic, overlooking the I-475 freeway ramp, has been closed since 1971.

Weathered boards now cover its windows and doors, tiles are missing from the faded red roof and grass has grown over the front concrete walkway. Posted "For Sale" and "For Lease" signs have attracted no takers.

Only memories keep it alive. Its playground is a legend in its own right, judging by the stories told. Children overran it during the day and adults congregated there after hours.

Memories of Clark, along with the north side's Roosevelt, Fairview and Parkland elementary schools, are like postcards from a bygone era.

In the old days, if students misbehaved, teachers had authority to spank them. School prayers were allowed. Lessons took young minds beyond reading, writing and arithmetic to an understanding of self-discipline and wholesome values.

Education was highly valued, second only to religion among black cultural traditions, partly because it had been denied for so many years and also because it was considered a one-way ticket to a better life.

Parents who had not gone beyond third grade, for whatever reason, pushed their children to do better. Grade-schoolers in the 1920s routinely did homework. So did those in the 1930s, '40s and to some degree the

A typical class in 1924 like this one at Clark School was integrated but predominantly white.

The final dismissal at the revered Clark Elementary School, which was built in 1912 and closed in June 1971.

1950s and '60s. Some of them willingly walked miles to the library and read books no teacher had assigned. They set goals, minded their manners and respected their elders.

They graduated from high school prepared to work hard, excel and to challenge barriers that had stood for centuries.

Oh, you may hear some complain about having no black teachers or black history lessons, but few complain about the overall quality of education before World II. Many of them are anguished by what passes for education nowadays. Mounting drop-out rates, mediocre achievement scores and diminished ambitions are distressing signals that many young people today do not value education as much as their grandparents did.

The perceived deterioration came about gradually. In some cases, it may be more a case of overromanticizing the past than reality. Many young blacks are excellent students who are achieving in the classroom and beyond at levels never dreamed of by their grandparents. For those who are not achieving (black or white), the causes have been attributed to everything from a lack of personal motivation to an array of societal distractions – racism, poverty, dysfunctional families, drugs, teen pregnancy, changes in the demands of the labor market and more.

Some critics with 20/20 hindsight cite remedies intended to improve education, such as busing, as being detrimental to many black students in the long run. They blame busing for uprooting youngsters from their neighborhoods and placing them in an unfamiliar and sometimes unfriendly learning environment.

Flint classrooms were integrated long before 1954 when a landmark U.S. Supreme Court ruling outlawed segregated schools in Brown vs. the Board of Education. But black enrollment was very low in early Flint schools. Black students mostly enjoyed the same learning opportunities as white children but still experienced discriminatory treatment at school.

Black students in the 1920s and '30s could not dance in the gym, swim in the pool or join school clubs. And there were some white teachers and counselors who had low expectations for black students, so they did not encourage them to aspire to professional jobs or to go to college.

Some of Flint's first black teachers still draw high praise from former students for the depths of understanding and rapport they brought to schooling. There were no black teachers in classrooms until 1943 and after that progress in black hiring was slow. No blacks taught above elementary school level until the early 1950s. The first black member of the school board was not elected until 1963. The first black superintendent was not appointed until 1988.

By the 1993-94 school year, about 67 percent of the district's students were black. Two-thirds of 32 elementary schools were more than 50 percent black and middle schools and high schools about 71 percent black.

Black teachers and administrators are plentiful now. The school board president and majority of members are black. A multicultural curriculum has been developed to address all students' interests.

In-school violence, drop-out rates and standardized test scores still are major concerns, but innovative methods are making inroads toward providing a quality education for all students.

EARLY DAYS:
"They'd tell the black girls they'd make good hairdressers."

Black students are now a majority at most Flint Schools, but they were a definite minority before World War II.

"In a classroom of about 35 people, there might be three blacks in there and the rest white," said Bill Williams, who attended Fairview and Roosevelt elementary schools in the late 1920s and early 1930s. "If you had seven (blacks) in a class, you had something."

Williams did not see much diversity in junior high or high school either. He recalls only four blacks – two boys and two girls – in his freshman class at Lowell Junior High. Lowell is now about 60 percent black.

Williams graduated from old Northern High in 1939 when black enrollment was less than 10 percent. Now it is just the opposite. In the 1993-94 school year, Northern's white enrollment was less than 10 percent.

Williams would find a similar role reversal if he enrolled today at one of Flint's 32 elementary schools. Black enrollment exceeded 90 percent at 11 schools, as of 1993-94. Wilkins Elementary was the highest at 99.4 percent black. Dort and King schools had 99.1; Gundry, 98.0; Brownell, 98.6 and Bunche, 97.4 percent.

Prior to the 1940s war boom, school enrollment figures reflected the city's population.

In 1916, when Fairview Elementary opened on Leith Street, Flint's population of about 90,000 included only about 1,700 blacks. Fairview's enrollment was predominantly black by the time the school closed in June 1971. It was torn down in 1976 after General Motors bought the property.

Black enrollment was also high at Roosevelt Elementary on Thetford

Like a postcard from the past, this view and good memories are all that remain of the old Fairview Elementary School on Leith Street, which closed in 1971 and was torn down five years later.

A breakfast program at Fairview School in 1960 made sure that low-income students did not start the school day hungry.

Road, which served the north side of Flint from 1925 to 1969. It was torn down to make way for the construction of I-475.

Parkland School on North Street, opened in 1914, also served an increasingly black student body. It was closed in 1976 and has been boarded up since about 1978.

On the south side, blacks attended Clark School. It was so overcrowded at times that auxiliary sites were needed. In the late 1920s, Elm Park School consisted of two- to four-room temporary buildings set up near Ferris and Dwight avenues.

Black and white children with disabilities attended Hazelton School near W. Second Street. It operated from 1903 to 1966.

Flint had only one high school until January 1928 when Northern on McClellan Avenue opened. Then, Flint High School on Crapo Street was renamed Central. The original Flint High School was on S. Saginaw at Third Street. It opened in 1875 and was torn down in 1938.

Bessie Brooks was among the first students to transfer from the old site to the new Flint High School in 1923. The only other black students were two girls and one boy, she said.

Brooks had completed eighth grade at Clark Elementary School on Harrison Street because there were no junior high schools then, she said. Whittier Junior High opened next door to Flint High School in 1925.

All teachers were white then, Milton Port said. He said he thought most of them tried to be fair. But he dropped out of Flint High in the late 1920s because, he said, he didn't get the encouragement he needed.

"Schoolteachers disillusioned me about how I couldn't get a job doing this, that or the other," he said. "I wanted to go in for a mechanic and a teacher told me there was no point because no one would hire me. They'd tell the black girls they'd make good hairdressers."

Black students had to put up with more discrimination in school activities. They could not swim in Central's pool until the 1940s. But Minnie Simpson said she and the few other black girls there were happy to be excluded from swim class because they didn't want to bother with having to press their hair after getting it wet.

"We didn't feel that something was being taken away from us," Simpson said. "We appreciated that we didn't have to swim."

At any rate, the separate treatment ended when she transferred to Northern in 1928 – it didn't have a pool until 1956.

But blacks could and did participate in school sports. Houston McKell at Central and James McCrary and Al Washington at Northern were gridiron rivals in the late 1920s.

What Minnie Simpson remembers most about the first Northern vs.

Central football game is being uncomfortably cold because she was not accustomed to attending outdoor games.

Simpson was a member of old Northern's first graduating class in 1930. Six blacks were in her class and two went on to college, she said.

Donn Kersey estimates there were still no more than about 30 blacks at Central when he graduated in 1936.

Annalea Bannister said her 1943 graduating class from Central included only about 25 blacks.

"When we were in school, we were in the minority and they let us know it," Bannister said. "If I never saw some of those people (again) it wouldn't bother me. We (blacks) were just there. We were students. If you were friends with whites in elementary school, by the time you got to junior high, they didn't even want to acknowledge in the halls that they knew you."

Sam Williams graduated from Northern in 1943. He estimates there were about 60 blacks in his graduating class of 400.

Consulting his yearbook, Charles Hamilton counted 27 blacks among the 600 students in his 1946 graduating class from Northern.

"There were only two schools, really, Northern and Central that blacks predominantly went to," Hamilton said. "There was Flint Tech, but I can't remember any blacks going there. And there was St. Matthew's, St. John Vianney, ... but I don't know of any (blacks) that went to Catholic Schools during my time." Flint Technical High School on Avenue A opened in 1939 as a prep school for students interested in business and industrial careers. It closed in 1959.

An influx of black students after World War II pushed enrollment so high at elementary and high schools that temporary buildings had to be opened to accommodate them.

FIRSTS:
"They were advertising for teachers and I couldn't get (hired), so I went to work at Chevrolet."

Charles Hamilton graduated from Northern High in 1946 and from Tennessee State University in 1951. A secondary education major, his specialty was health and physical education.

But the Flint Board of Education would not hire him.

The first ladies of Flint public school teaching – Lois E. VanZandt Holt (right) and Marion Coates-Williams were hired in 1942 and 1943, respectively.

"I think that was the lowest ebb in my life when I wasn't able to get a job as a teacher," Hamilton said. "They were advertising for teachers and I couldn't get one, so I went to work at Chevrolet."

Likewise, J. Merrill Spencer was certified to teach high school sociology when he moved to Flint in 1950. He did substitute teaching for a while but quit after four years of being turned down for a full-time job. He worked at the post office before starting a successful funeral business.

That was years after Flint's first black professional teacher, Lois E. VanZandt (Holt), was hired in 1942 and Marion Coates-Williams, the first black classroom teacher, was hired in 1943.

Teaching is one of the oldest black professions in America, dating back to the 1800s and earlier. But in Flint, many were qualified long before they could get hired.

Ruth VanZandt, Lois' sister, had tried to hire into Flint Schools in 1937 after graduating from Michigan State Normal teachers college (now Eastern Michigan University).

"I went to the superintendent's office and asked for an application and they told me right out they had no intention of ever hiring any blacks," VanZandt recalled.

Helen Harris, the first black woman elected to the Flint Board of Education in 1971, became its first female president in 1973.

"I had a job already. I was hired by the Inkster superintendent (during) the last semester of my schooling, but I wanted to see what they'd say if I applied in Flint."

Five years later, the answer was still no when her sister applied. Despite her degree and teaching credentials from Wilberforce University, Lois VanZandt Holt had to take a temporary job as a maid.

"When I applied, all the employment agencies in Flint, they weren't taking applications for blacks to work in the educational system here," Holt said.

It took support from several influential people, including the school personnel director, for Lois VanZandt Holt to become Flint's first black teacher in 1942.

Still, she had to overcome several objections raised by people who did not want her to get the job. They complained about her hearing loss, though it had been corrected with a hearing aid. Someone started a rumor that she had tuberculosis because she was small, so she had to provide a

In 1963, Ruth H. Buckner became the first black female elementary school principal at Oak.

---

clean bill of health. They said she didn't have a car. Her sister loaned hers.

Lois VanZandt Holt's position as a visiting teacher was outside of the school buildings, making house calls.

In 1943, Marion Coates-Williams became the first black classroom teacher at Fairview Elementary School.

"It was the right time and I was qualified," she said. Still, her hiring came only after more pressure was put on the Board of Education from several community leaders and the NAACP, she said.

During her first few days on the job, one supervisor stayed in her room all day monitoring her, she said.

"It was a lot of pressure, but I survived it and until she died she (the vigilant supervisor) was one of the best friends I had," Coates-Williams said.

Being the only black made Coates-Williams stand out at teachers meetings, but she was generally accepted and treated well, she said.

Aaron A. Smith was the first black male classroom teacher, hired in 1950, and the first black male elementary school principal in 1963.

Civil rights gains in the early 1960s led to more black "firsts" through the 1970s and 1980s.

T. Wendell Williams, a physician, became the first black elected to the Flint Board of Education in 1963, and another physician, Clarence B. Kimbrough, was the board's first black elected president (1968). Helen Harris was the first black woman elected to the board (1971) and its first

In 1988, Nathel Burtley became the first black superintendent of Flint public schools, after serving seven years as deputy superintendent.

As the first black chancellor of the University of Michigan-Flint, 1984 to 1994, Clinton B. Jones oversaw steady growth of the hometown branch, which started in 1956.

female president (1973).

Ruth H. Buckner became the first black female elementary school principal in 1963. Shelby J. Cummings became the first black high school principal in 1972. Al Renick was the first black junior high principal (Bryant) in 1968.

Dolores Ennis was the first black secondary-level teacher in 1952. Her specialty was Latin and French, but she took what was offered to her.

In 1981, Dr. Nathel Burtley became the first black deputy superintendent of the Flint School District, and, in 1988, the first black superintendent.

In higher education, Edwynna G. Anderson was the first black elected to the Mott Community College Board of Trustees (1975). Jesse Thompson was the first black male elected (1981).

In 1962, Alvin D. Loving became the first black professor granted tenure at the University of Michigan-Flint. In 1984, Clinton Jones became its first black chancellor.

On paper, the list of "firsts" sounds effortless but almost always came after a struggle.

Dolores Ennis filled out an application before graduating from college in the spring of 1951. But five months later, she hadn't been called. So she went to work at the post office and was getting ready to take the civil service exam for a permanent position. That's when an Urban League official, familiar with her qualifications, recommended her to Emerson Junior High School's principal, who was also the League's president. She was called the next day.

The school personnel director first tried to get her to take an elementary school position. He also asked if she would consider secretarial work.

At that time, there were no black teachers at the secondary level. Ennis' major in Latin and French and minor in English were high school subjects, but she wanted a job in education badly enough to take what was offered, she said.

"I substituted every day after that and when I went to Whittier (junior high), the principal liked me and he said, 'I really want you on this staff,' " Ennis said. "And so I think somebody got ill in that building and I was there for a whole semester."

She was offered a position teaching art, not her specialty, but she learned to do it because she wanted the job.

"And so I got a contract for the fall of '52, but I had substituted that whole semester. If somebody hadn't gone in there and interceded, there's no telling when I would have got a call."

Even with hiring barriers down, the welcome mats rolled out slowly.

Ruth Scott chalks up the lukewarm reception she got at Dewey Elementary in the mid-1950s to professional envy. She had a bachelor's degree while several of the white teachers she worked with had only a two-year certificate, she said.

"I can remember there were four first-grade teachers," she said. "Two of them were older women. I remembered them because they were teaching when I was in elementary school. They were standoffish, but then there was this white teacher on the other end. She was a Quaker or something. She was very nice to me."

The older teachers would stand in Scott's door watching her suspiciously because of her innovative teaching methods.

"When I look back on it, I could have been very insecure, but I had all the confidence in the world," Scott said. "I knew what I was doing. I have to give credit to my principal who said, 'I have faith in you.' When I went to him a few times with problems, he said, 'Unless I say something to you, don't worry about it.'"

Eventually, Scott and the suspicious teachers became friends.

By the early 1960s, getting hired was a cinch for Dorothy Laws who worked at Stevenson Elementary near Hurley, but she had no black students for several of the 21 years she taught there, she said.

QUALITY RATING:
"At least when we came out of school, we could read and write, which a lot of them can't do now."

Before World War II, the Flint schools' report card rated high marks.

Then came segregation, which necessitated busing, tracking, steering and other undesirable practices. As black student enrollment increased, the overall quality of instruction declined.

In the "good, old days," a school day was eight hours long, not four or five. Nobody graduated from high school unable to read and write.

Marion Wright Quinn gives her parents much of the credit for her academic success. She attended Roosevelt Elementary, Lowell Junior High and Northern in the 1920s and '30s.

"We had to study at home every night," Quinn said. "After dinner, we'd clear the table in the breakfast room and my mother would go around and help all of us. If you claimed you didn't have homework, she'd find something to study anyway, usually math and spelling. She'd call off the words or the problems. Study was regular with us. We expected it."

Parents and others concerned that school policies steered black students away from college-preparatory courses organized protests like this one in 1965.

Parents were strict disciplinarians back then, too.

"If a child sassed a teacher, the teacher would call the parent and the parent would come to the school and whip that student right in front of the class," said Johnnie Wynn Jr., who started first grade in the mid-1930s.

"I've seen that. The parent would make the kid apologize to the teacher. It was an embarrassment for him and he wouldn't do that any more."

High standards like those were still being enforced in the 1940s.

"The high school education we got was just as good as college today," said Sam Williams, who graduated from Northern in 1943.

"How many kids do you know today (who) care about current events? Back when I was 18, kids were older than they are now, not in knowledge but in responsibility. You did your work. Teachers gave good grades if you earned them. We had homework.

"I see my granddaughter. What could she be learning if she tells me she had enough time to do homework at school? They're not getting it."

Vivian Pugh, who graduated from Central in 1943, said, "Yeah, back then, at least when we came out of school, we could read and write, which a lot of them can't do now."

So what's the matter with schools today?

"When the schools became predominantly black, that's when they were lost" is Ruth Owens Buckner's opinion. She said her 1920s elementary school education was as good as high school now.

Buckner first noticed the change decades later while taking classes at Mott Community College. A much-younger fellow student asked Buckner to critique a paper she had written.

"There wasn't a sentence in the entire paper that was right," Buckner said. "Bad spelling. Poor grammar. I was amazed."

Some say that's because predominantly black schools don't get the quality of teachers, textbooks, equipment and programs that black students have when they attend predominantly white schools.

The negative effect of that shift in demographics was cited by Central graduates Dorothy Waller, class of 1940; Annalea Bannister, class of 1943; and Ruth Scott, class of 1948.

"Central is where the people who had money sent their kids," Scott said. "That's why I think we got a good education – because good teachers were there. If something was needed, it got there."

Flint schools started getting more segregated in the 1950s. They partially desegregated in the 1970s under a federally monitored plan but were resegregated by the 1980s as the number of white students continued to decline. By 1993, total black enrollment approached 70 percent and in several buildings was 90 percent or higher.

Now there are about 300 times more black teachers than 50 years ago, more black counselors and school administrators and more black culture being taught.

But students face different obstacles than students did 50 years ago, Susie Duckett Skipper said. When she was in school in the early 1940s, she had selected a complete plan of study by ninth grade. All her classes were held in one building.

"Now you have to go every semester and fight for the classes you want," she said. Plus, she knows a student who had to go to three different buildings in a day (including the Genesee Area Skill Center in the out-county) to complete her course schedule.

Flint's two main high schools got so overcrowded in the late 1940s that attendance schedules had to be staggered and classes moved to other buildings. Some attended classes from 10 a.m. to 4 p.m. and others from 8 a.m. to 3 p.m.

Overcrowding eased in 1959 when Southwestern opened.

About that time, Annalea Bannister had noticed a sharp decline in the quality of instruction. So she decided to send her children to parochial school through ninth grade to give them an academic head start.

"I don't think too (highly) of the schools now. They leave a lot to be desired," Bannister said. "The schools are not preparing kids to get a job. When I left Central (1943), I was prepared to go and take a test in typing and shorthand and get a job."

Some said that education suffered because of practices such as busing and tracking and because society, at large, was in turmoil.

By the time school social worker Ruth Scott retired in 1992, she was seeing drastic social changes affecting children's ability to come to school ready to learn. Some of them come to school hungry, half-dressed and dirty, she said. Some have been home alone all night and responsible for seeing themselves off to school. Some don't come to school at all.

Attendance and test scores are down and parents won't come to parent-teacher conferences, she said.

"If you get a (home) telephone number today, tomorrow it's disconnected or they don't have a telephone," Scott said. "It's getting to the point where some of the workers won't be able to make home calls. It's getting too dangerous.

"Yet you can't give up. It's not the child's fault he was born in a certain situation. Some of them, they really try, but with where they come from and what they have to deal with, I don't know how they make it.

"I've had more little kids in my office, crying because their hands and feet were cold. They had no socks, no mittens and their coats were pinned closed."

Back in the 1970s, busing was the culprit for uprooting black children from familiar surroundings and transporting them into an environment where some did not feel comfortable or were encouraged to achieve.

Officials were blamed for excluding black students from better-equipped schools by drawing the boundary lines outside their neighborhoods. As a result, some black students had to walk or ride the bus farther than white students.

Tracking earned a bad rap for tagging black children for underachievement. Few students were chosen for college preparatory courses. Most were steered into a general course of study, preparing them to become factory or service workers. The practice ended in the 1970s when parents organized a protest.

Geraldine Smith went to bat for her youngest son Steve, a 1975 Northern graduate. He wanted to get involved in theater but his counselor discouraged it. Smith switched her son to a black counselor who supported his career interests.

"From that he went on to work with the lights and settings at Northern," she said. "That's how he got started in his field." After earning a master's degree, he worked off-Broadway for a while before becoming the production and tour manager for entertainer Harry Belafonte.

Likewise, Charlotte Williams said her nephew protested when counselors tried to place him in mechanics courses. He is a chemical engineer now.

Woody Etherly Jr., a 1962 Northern graduate and former Flint city councilman, believes he got sidetracked by the system.

"Most black folks they put on the track system," he said. "They'd train you to be able to go into General Motors but not to be able to go to college. That's the kind of system they had you on, taking home economics and gym.

"All they wanted to do is push you through; they didn't care if you learned or not. Most of the teachers were white. They did not want to be (in the schools) where they were and so they just sent you through.

"When I graduated from high school and went over to the college to get enrolled, I had to take some high school (subjects) because they (Northern teachers) didn't give me what I needed, what I was supposed to be taking. My parents didn't know what I was supposed to be taking. They thought the school was doing what it was supposed to.

"When I found out in my senior year what was going on, when I understood the system, then I asked for algebra and some other classes but they told me they were too hard for me."

Etherly said he took them anyway and earned A's and B's.

White teachers and counselors were indifferent, Freddie Williams agreed. He graduated from Flint Northern in 1951.

"There wasn't any incentive to do but what they steered you in the direction of doing, which was general courses," he said. "There was no personality between counselors and students. Now we have black counselors who get more personal with students."

Athletes were the exception; they got special treatment, he said.

"They didn't want you for your brains, they wanted you for your physical ability. They used you up. Once your four-year eligibility was up, it didn't matter if you had enough credits to graduate, you were out. My term for that was glorified gladiator. (The athlete was) glorified in the press but the next day couldn't get a job."

Shirley Williams, his wife, added that blacks had to rely on other blacks to find out about scholarships and other educational opportunities. Her sister went to college because Odell Broadway, a black counselor, helped her find scholarships. After graduation, Williams said, her sister still couldn't get a teaching job at a Flint high school, so she had to go to Detroit.

Flint's first black teacher, Lois VanZandt Holt, believes the quality of her education was compromised by insensitive teachers.

"As an elementary child, I tried to tell the teacher I couldn't hear and she told me to put my hand down," Holt said. "As a result, I went through school without anyone realizing I had a hearing loss."

Woody Etherly credits black teachers Ruth VanZandt and Cassie Thomas for giving him the extra attention he needed to achieve.

"I learned to do math because of Ms. VanZandt," he said. "She was the only one who acted like she cared about what happened to black students. She went out of her way to take time with you and explain. I never will forget what she told me. She said, 'Woody, these teachers don't care if you get it or you don't get it because they're going to get paid anyway. So they're glad to see you sit there and do nothing, say nothing and don't participate.'

"So I started putting forth an effort. She paid a girl to help me learn my times table; she told the girl she was going to buy her a new bicycle if I could do them at the end."

Lennetta Coney, a 1973 Southwestern High graduate, yearbook editor and cheerleader, said black teachers and counselors definitely enhanced her education. Her parents' generation had gone from kindergarten through graduation with no black teachers, she said. Coney had black teachers in elementary, middle and high school.

Mayor Woodrow Stanley, a 1969 Northern graduate, liked all his teachers. One English teacher in particular, a Mrs. Gould, made a lasting impression.

"On the last day of school, I can recall her giving me a letter and telling me I could leave early," Stanley said. "I kept that letter a long time. It was encouraging me to go to school and to try to achieve. She had taken a special interest in me and we developed a real good friendship, which is one reason I generally accept all speaking engagements at schools."

Melvin McCree, a 1971 Northern graduate, said that self-motivation was the only thing blocking his academic achievement.

"There's no question that I could have achieved a lot more if I had wanted to apply myself, but the opportunities were certainly there," McCree said. "Northern, when I went there, was known for its football teams and wrestling, but it also was known for its debate teams. People lose track of that. I was in the choir and the choirs were A-number-one," he boasted.

"All the schools I went to, as far as I can remember, had opportunities for you to be (as) knowledgeable and involved as you chose to strive to be. Looking back, I wish I had chosen to seize more than I did."

One way to motivate contemporary youth is to turn off the TV and turn on family time, said Karen Aldridge, also a Northern (1970) alumnus.

"I don't think kids now read as much as we read," she said. "We didn't have 90 channels on the TV. (You'd) sit down and talk to your grandma and she'd tell you about the old times."

Aldridge wonders if young blacks are learning about Nat Turner who led a slave revolt in 1831, or Crispus Attucks who was first to die in the American Revolutionary War, or about blacks who fought in the Civil War or about the

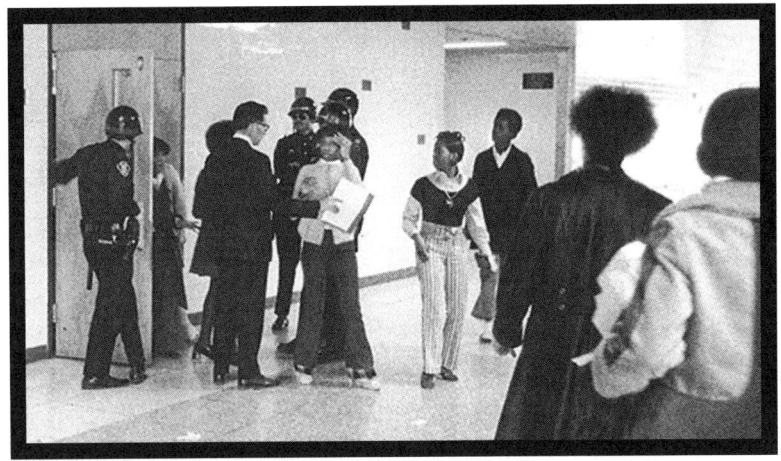
Police monitored halls at several high schools after racially motivated fighting erupted between black and white students in the early 1970s.

Buffalo Soldiers and black cowboys who pioneered the Old West.

And from Michigan history, she asked, how many know about stations of the Underground Railroad or about blacks involved in the logging industry up north? "Kids (today) know so much less than we know," Aldridge said. "It's almost like we have to give up our culture. We have to assimilate. No other group has had to give up who they were. If the churches or other groups don't do it (teach black history), it will be lost."

Not getting enough black history is Pete Johnson's only complaint about his Flint schooling. He graduated from Central in 1945.

"I've learned more since I've been out of school," Johnson said. "They still aren't bringing it out in schools like they should."

Katie Ellis Harper said she may have launched black history lessons in Flint schools. She had learned it from black teachers while attending Detroit public schools.

"The first time we had a black history observance in Flint was at Northern High School in 1944," Harper said. She and Eugene Miller, the student council president, got permission from the principal to do a black history presentation over the public address system. She can't recall the content but remembers that white students showed no reaction.

Flint's first black classroom teacher, Marion Coates-Williams, was among many who had no black teachers growing up. She graduated from Flint Northern in 1939 with a "good basic education" and attended Flint Junior College (now Mott Community College) for two years before going to Michigan State Normal in Ypsilanti to earn her teaching certificate.

She wanted to be a social worker but chose teaching because a counselor at Flint Junior College advised her that it would be easier to get a teaching job.

Teacher Ruth Scott had no black teachers. That didn't much matter to her in elementary school where the white teachers were devoted. But high school was a different story.

"No one really counseled you. I just blundered through and took the right courses in junior high, but in high school we ran into problems," she said.

There were no blacks in the Drama Club or the school band. Sports was the only activity open to blacks. It caused a big stir when Sherm Mitchell was chosen drum major for the marching band in about 1948, she said.

On the other hand, Audrey Wilson, a 1952 Central graduate, never had a black teacher either but praises the teachers she had.

"I can truly say that I had teachers, white or not, who pushed you to learn," Wilson said. "I had teachers that encouraged me, especially in English, that was my strongest subject, and history was another one. When I look back, I think about some of the white teachers we had then, and some of the black teachers we have now who know how hard it is to get by if you don't have a good education, who aren't on the students to learn as hard as they should be."

But black teachers are often praised for acting as advisers, opening the door to extracurricular activities for black students who, before, had not even been able to have dances in the school gym. Boy Scouts and Hi Y Clubs, sponsored by the YMCA, provided after-school activities for black boys.

At Parkland Elementary School in the late 1940s, Ruth VanZandt organized a musical featuring black students.

"It was the first time anyone had seen black students do anything besides athletics," VanZandt said. The show was so good, other teachers were invited to bring their classes to see it. Later, VanZandt took the performance to other buildings.

Bridging the cultural gap often required diplomacy and sometimes confrontation.

Katie Ellis Harper had to set a teacher straight about not giving her son the grades he had earned. She would compare his work to a Chinese student and give that student the edge.

When confronted, "the teacher said that if she takes a little away from him it made him work harder," Harper said. "I told the teacher, 'You give him what he's got coming and stop comparing him to (the Chinese student).'"

Charlotte Williams acted as trouble-shooter in a cultural conflict at Cook School in the 1960s. Black students had recently integrated the school. An art teacher complained about one black girl who was a good student but had a bad attitude.

Williams talked to the girl and got her to open up. The girl told Williams that the teacher slighted her.

"She said no matter how well she did on her projects, the teacher would never touch her, but she had noticed that she'd touch the white students," Williams said. "She felt it was because she was black."

Williams shared that with the teacher who changed her behavior and the problem student's attitude cleared up.

Nerves were raw in schools all over Flint because of civil rights activism.

In 1971, at Southwestern High School, Debra Taylor was part of a black student movement on the cutting edge of school integration. The student body was about 70 percent white and 30 percent black, but there was a black assistant principal.

"Basically, we had a situation where students were not accustomed to interacting with each other socially," Taylor said. "The comfort level wasn't there."

The black students got active in student government and raising cultural awareness. There was no Black History Month observance then, only Black History Week, Taylor said.

Racial tension in the school mounted until it erupted in a student brawl. Several students were injured and police had to be called to restore order.

School administrators and Genesee County Prosecutor Robert Leonard organized a student council on race relations. They identified black and white students who had leadership potential and invited them to several Saturday sessions to discuss racial accord, Taylor said.

Over donuts and juice, the interracial group discussed community pride and mutual respect. Race relations improved and in some cases blossomed into friendships, Taylor said.

Before civil rights activism raised consciousness levels, blacks in Flint schools had mostly endured insults and indignities in silence.

C. Frederick Robinson, a leading civil rights lawyer in the 1960s, said he found a mentality in Flint that was 30 years behind the times when he moved here in 1956 from his native North Carolina.

"Black folks were afraid to challenge white folks about anything and they were satisfied with the state of things," he said. "Many of them who came to Flint after the war from rural areas in Mississippi, Alabama and Arkansas could barely read and write. That put them at a disadvantage."

When A. Glenn Epps came to Flint from Marshall, Texas, in 1943, an assistant principal at Central High told him blacks from the South were routinely put back one grade. But Epps, who was 14, was not demoted.

Epps, who became an attorney, credits that to the quality of his Texas teachers. Robinson said his former teachers in North Carolina held advanced degrees and that the influence of about a dozen black colleges there established a tradition for blacks going to college.

Robinson observed that the Flint school system went to the other extreme – it discouraged black students. One way to discriminate was to draw school boundary lines.

It is not a coincidence that most of Flint's high schools are located at the city limits, Robinson said.

"They didn't want the white folks to walk through all these black folks, so they built them on the city limits so the blacks would have to walk through the white neighborhoods to get to school," he said. "The only one they didn't bother was Central and they tried to keep that as white as possible by drawing the boundary lines. That was a political decision, not a legal one."

Former teacher Ruth Scott added: "They drew boundaries around houses, down the middle of the street, especially when blacks started moving on the south side and started moving across Lapeer Road. When blacks moved onto a street, they would change the (school) boundaries.

"All the way through Central (circa 1940-43), there were not a lot of blacks in my classes," Scott said. "Sometimes I was the only black in my class. I had friends but as far as going to class and having a lot of friends in there, uh-uh."

About the same time, Minnie Simpson realized that children who lived on the same street were attending different schools. The white children were sent to Pierce Elementary and the black children to Clark, she said. There were no school buses then, so black children had to walk far outside of their neighborhood to get to school.

One example, she said, is the former Walker School on East Kearsley Street. It was closer to home for some black children but out of bounds for them until the 1960s, except for summer school.

Looking back, Virginia Heller now sees the evidence of racial steering more clearly than when she lived through it. She lived on the borderline of Central and Southwestern but chose to attend Central because her mother had gone there.

"They built Southwestern with the intention that they would not get black children," Heller said. "That was supposed to be a predominantly white school. But the Flint Board or somebody split those borders up so that it wasn't."

Later, about 1963, the boundaries were challenged, she said. That happened because black students found out they lived within Southwestern's boundaries and were eligible to go there.

Yet Flint schools compared favorably to many others.

In the mid-1930s, Louise Tarver found a big difference when her family moved back to Georgia. She had been in an accelerated program in Flint.

"When we went to Georgia, it was a setback because the schools for blacks were inferior and segregated," she said.

The equipment, books, football uniforms and virtually everything else were hand-me-downs from the white high school. The saving grace was that the teachers, all black, were extremely dedicated, she said.

Angela Sawyer saw a world of difference, too, when she transferred from Beecher High to Flint Northern as a 10th-grader in the late 1970s.

"I thought I was smart," she said. "I was an A and B student in Beecher. I transferred mid-semester. They looked at my transcript and put me in advanced algebra and I didn't recognize anything. So what I had to do was go back and get refresher courses so I could be where I was supposed to be. That said to me that the Beecher district was behind. The ninth grade at Beecher was more like the eighth grade in Flint."

But the 1990s brought a redoubled emphasis on school improvement and quality education.

One of the generals at the helm of many efforts is Lenore Croudy, coordinator of language arts and humanities for the Flint School District. She is perhaps better known in her high-profile role as a tireless organizer and fund-raiser. Her influence and advocacy spans from kindergarten through college and beyond.

In 1995, she was elected chairperson of the Mott Community College Board of Trustees, for which she has served as a trustee since 1987. She chairs the annual United Negro College Fund campaign in mid-Michigan and the Youth Leadership Institute to train minority youth. She also godmothered youth journalism-training programs at The Flint Journal and Channel 12 (WJRT) and spearheaded scholarship fund-raisers and educational programs through her sorority (Delta Sigma Theta), the Urban League of Flint and many more.

SUCCESS STORIES:
"No such thing as I can't."

John Hightower is known for his civil rights leadership in the 1960s and for starting an electrical contracting and construction business that made him a millionaire.

A driving force in his life, he said, is a painful childhood memory of his grade-school classmates laughing at him because he misspelled cat.

"I could not spell and I could not pronounce words, so they put me in the dumb room (in St. Louis, Mo.)," Hightower said. "I thought that if I couldn't read or write or do arithmetic, then my life was over."

He only needed one teacher's influence to turn his thinking around. She kept him after school one day and patiently explained to him that not trying was much worse than failing.

"The man who couldn't spell cat became a millionaire," Hightower said, his narrative taking on the emotional cadence of a Baptist sermon.

"The man who couldn't spell cat changed the lives of people. The man who couldn't spell cat built some of the best churches (in Flint). So ... we should not put so much emphasis on a formal education because we've got many, many other Hightowers out there who couldn't spell cat."

Hightower had a hard time getting an apprenticeship after completing an electrical-contracting program at Mott Community College. There was only one black contractor in town, Roosevelt Ridgeway.

"Ridgeway was the father of (black) electricians," Hightower said. "Most all of us went through him (to earn a journeyman's license)."

Eventually, Hightower became one of only four black electricians in town, earning about $200,000 a year.

"Education is fine," he said. "I have nothing against education, but today where a black man is going to make it is in skilled trades."

If racial segregation and discrimination had not limited chances for blacks to learn a skilled trade, there would not be a labor shortage today, he said.

"Now she (America) wants to welcome us, but she didn't give us a chance then to take mathematics such as algebra, geometry, trigonometry," he said.

Hightower said his business sense began to take shape after another boyhood experience. He was helping his father clean a Jewish synagogue when he noticed that day's lessons still printed on a blackboard, stressing the importance of banking and saving money. Hightower studied it and thus shaped up more than a building that day.

Ruth Scott knows about coming up the hard way, too. She was 12 when her mother died, leaving her and two siblings to be raised by their father. She said he pushed them hard to make something of themselves.

Role models were few. Most of the women who lived on Scott's street did domestic work, the main type of work available to undereducated black women.

"It was always, 'You are going to graduate from college.' It was never anything in my mind but what am I going to be?" said Scott, who became a teacher and later a school social worker.

Lois Shaw became Flint's first registered nurse in 1947.

"When I was coming up, my folks said, 'You better get an education or else,'" Shaw said. "So you had to go to school and you had to achieve or else. They just made you do it."

A winner's mind-set is common among people from her native Texas, Shaw said.

"It wasn't like it is here. We had black teachers (in Texas) and they didn't want the black children to grow up and not be able to read and write. My aunt and mother were teachers and they were not going to have their kids be ignorant."

Shaw's Texan tenacity didn't end when she completed her education.

"My children got from me and my sister that you are going to school, regardless. If they came home with some bad grades, I was up there."

Audrey Wilson, an AC Rochester retiree, had a tough taskmaster in her father who attended only a few years of college before he married.

"He built a love of vocabulary in our lives," Wilson said. "When we were coming up, we had to pick out a new word each week. We had to learn to spell it, know the definition of it and work it into our conversation at the dinner table."

Profanity was strictly forbidden.

"He taught us that we could express ourselves on a higher level," she said.

Wilson read a lot as a child. One inspiration was her grandmother's collection of books by black authors such as Langston Hughes and Paul Laurence Dunbar.

"Education was always stressed as a ticket to a better life," she said. "Can't was not a word in our parents' vocabulary. I'm serious. We were taught not to say that. They wanted more for us than they had for themselves."

A strong entrepreneurial spirit ran in the family. Her dad and his sister ran a variety of businesses, always striving to have more. Her grandparents bought houses, renovated and rented them.

"There was a desire to want a home with grass in front of your house, though we were taught to sweep dirt, if need be, to make it look good. Your lack had nothing to do with your inside. Where you stayed didn't make you a lesser person. You always wanted to do better."

Wilson earned a real estate license while working full time at AC.

"I'm one of those people who gravitates to the positive, so I don't think all our young people are going to the dogs," Wilson said. "My father always used to tell us (about peer pressure), 'Don't let them change you, you change them.'"

Growing up in the 1970s after civil rights gains had torn down the worst barriers to black success, Sheila Miller-Graham could see in her own life how much can improve in a single generation.

"When I went to school and learned to speak properly, I came home and tried to correct my dad," she said. "He'd say, 'Stop correcting me, you went to school, I didn't.'

"I found myself not utilizing words I'd learned at school, at home. My father never went past third grade. He had to work the fields." That made him doubly determined that his four children would get an education.

"As a child, I never perceived my father as not educated," Miller-Graham said. "He would take me through my spelling words and I never knew if he really knew those words or faked it. It's nice for kids to have parents who can sit down and work with them."

Something debilitating happened to the black community during or after the 1970s. The urge to excel seemed less urgent. Drug use and abuse escalated. One theory is that poor educational preparation made it harder for young blacks to compete in the changing work force.

"It's really a puzzle how these kids get so tangled up in drugs," said Layton Galloway, a retired postal worker.

"We've lost a whole generation and a half. I have about 50 nieces and nephews and only one or two of them are doing something with themselves."

Angela Sawyer, a UM-Flint public relations secretary and 1981 Northern graduate, attributes the changes to a sense of hopelessness that seized her generation after Vietnam.

"The drug thing got big," she said. "The guys came back from Vietnam thinking there would be more opportunities and they found it wasn't, so they started drugging and a lot of them started dying.

"I guess I haven't sat down and thought about all this mess, but one of the things we didn't have then was (trouble) with guns. We had fights. Whoever lost was ostracized and the way to regain face was to kick somebody's butt, but you didn't kill people.

"In schools, you didn't have out-and-out defiance the way you do now like, 'I'm not going to school and if you make me go, I'm not going to learn.' "

Sawyer's role model was her mother who, at age 36 with five children, went back to college to earn a nursing degree.

"There is a state exam you have to take," Sawyer said. "She flunked the first time, repeated some classes and passed the next time. She became an R.N. and we were so excited because our mother had initials behind her name."

Many people found it necessary to further their education when auto jobs began to disappear in the early 1980s and an increasingly technical job market demanded more highly skilled workers.

Sherm Mitchell went back to school in 1993, at age 63, to take his first formal music lessons at the University of Michigan-Flint. His goal was self-improvement.

Mitchell plays the flute, trombone, saxophone, oboe and some percussion and string instruments. He reads and writes music and does arrangements for himself and for other musicians.

He been cited in "Who's Who" music directories, worked with famous jazz musicians and garnered honorary plaques from governors and senators.

But "I don't have a great education," Mitchell said. "I taught myself to play. I had what you call natural ability, but you can only ride that so far.

"If you study anything 40 to 50 years, you have to have some measure of proficiency at it. (But) your progress hinges on your ability to improve at what you're doing. That's not because you're black. It's because you're a human being and you have the ability to learn and improve. To improve yourself is to improve the area around you. Every time you (do that), you make it better for somebody else."

Mitchell is now retired from everything but playing music, but over the course of his life he held a variety of jobs from restaurant cook to truck driver, auto mechanic, janitor and autoworker at GM for 20 years.

"I did all the things that people do who aren't educated," he said. "One of the reasons I play music has nothing to do with me getting famous. My whole idea was that I can do it with just a high school education. I was/am an alcoholic (but) haven't drank in 20 years. Nobody had to beat me, throw me in jail or anything else to make me realize that music is God's gift, and you've got to return it."

Yet Mitchell is modest when he compares his success to that of his brothers and sisters who have more advanced educations.

"I'm the least educated of my whole family," he said. "My sister was a Russian interpreter at the United Nations for many years. My brother was a physicist who graduated from M.I.T. and was a vice president of Detroit Edison. My other sister has multiple degrees, traveled the world as an educator."

Mitchell's successful siblings are a good example of outstanding blacks from Flint who have moved away, said A. Glenn Epps, a Flint attorney.

Flint's higher-education record seems weak because many success stories are untold, Epps said. He named a Detroit judge and a prominent Seattle minister as two examples.

"They are exceptions to the rule," argued C. Frederick Robinson, Epps' longtime friend and former law partner.

"When I got here (late 1950s) there were few blacks on the whole who were going to college," Robinson said. "I doubt if Flint turned out three (black) college graduates a year (back then). Contrast that to my (North Carolina) high school class of 30 – 28 went to college of some sort."

Epps blamed the low levels on Flint schools' "tracking" system that condemned so many black students to general studies. When they finished high school, they were not prepared to go to college, Epps said. He said he got into a college-prep curriculum only because he insisted.

James Blakely confirmed that most of his peers "went straight to the shop." He graduated from Northern in 1951 but went to college on a sports scholarship.

Affirmative action programs in the late 1960s generated greater interest and financing for college. Scholarships increased.

At least one UM-Flint student has been awarded the Edgar Holt Scholarship each year since 1987. Holt's widow, Lois, said the endowment fund has reached about $60,000 of a $100,000 goal.

Mott Community College also has an Edgar Holt scholarship. And Wilberforce University of Ohio, Lois VanZandt Holt's alma mater, organized a third fund in her husband's name when he died in 1984.

UM-Flint also administers three other scholarships for black students in the names of deceased black civic leaders Odell Broadway, Sylvester Broome Jr. and Floyd J. McCree.

Retired teacher Ruth VanZandt takes great pleasure in counting the successes of former pupils.

"Every birthday for the past 30 years, I've received a dozen red roses from Dr. Douglas Wright (dentist). I straightened him out," she chuckled.

Dentists Oscar L. Wright and Orlando Roberts were her students. So were Willa Hawkins, a Genesee county commissioner, and Sandra Epps, a principal.

"Dr. Oscar Wright used to almost live at our house," VanZandt recalled. "I always told my students, 'I don't care what you are, but be something. I don't care if you're a garbage collector. There would be pestilence in everything in the city if you didn't. So be the best you can be. Even if you're a ditch digger, be the best you can be.'"

As testimony to her influence, more than 700 of VanZandt's former students from across the country returned to Flint in 1992 to attend a tribute for her.

Bill Williams, a Buick retiree, pointed out that "success" stories are often not an individual achievement.

"I know lots of people who have jobs now who are no more qualified for that job than (a stick of furniture)," he said. "They were just in the right place at the right time.

"Anybody can reach a goal if it's sitting there waiting for you, but when you got to make your own way, it takes more doing."

Williams made a name for himself as a shop committeeman and chairman at Buick. His work with the Fair Employment Practices Committee spilled over into helping to desegregate local businesses. He has a photo of himself and other committee members outside the Blue Bird Bar, which once banned blacks. They are pointing to a large sign announcing that the bar is "under new management, everyone is welcome."

Williams said he wound up in the hospital getting glass picked out of his eye after getting involved in protecting a black family that had moved to Beecher and was being picketed by whites who did not want them there. Williams also was among the planeload of Flint folks who joined the historic March on Washington in 1963.

As community service director of UAW Local 599, Williams organized a jobs fair in 1983 to match laid-off autoworkers with people in the community willing to hire them for particular skills such as home repairs or yardwork.

He likes to tell a story with a moral that involves three ducks getting ready to cross a large body of water. One couldn't swim. So they devised a plan that two would hold a stick in their beaks for the nonswimmer to hold onto and be towed across. As they were crossing over, an observer commented on what a bright idea it was and asked who thought of it. The one being ferried across, piped up, "I did," thus letting go of the stick and drowning.

"That's how it often is," Williams said. "The first one to pipe up and take credit hasn't done the work. Every time someone gets to bragging about what they did, chances are somebody else carried them across."

HIGHER GROUND:
"You didn't pass any black person on campus without speaking."

Raymond Gist, now a dentist, was the first person Woodrow Stanley knew who, as Stanley put it, "actually went to college and graduated." Their families lived on State Street in the old St. John Street neighborhood in the 1950s.

"Ray was one of the big boys in the neighborhood we all looked up to," Stanley said. "Ray was a hero. He was doing something different. He wasn't a sports figure."

Now it is far more common to know someone going away to medical or dental school. But back then, the people he knew weren't going to college, Stanley said. At least, not the men.

A wake-up call for black men came in the 1980s with an alarming statistic: More young black men were in jail than in college. Young black men of college age were labeled "an endangered species" because of a disproportionately high homicide rate, high unemployment and other social prohibitors.

Controversial male-oriented schools were implemented in several cities including Detroit. Flint avoided the boys school approach but started mentor programs. The idea was to expose young black males to positive role models in hope of inspiring them to stay out of trouble and set a goal early in life to attend college.

Attitudes were more laid-back in the 1970s when Melvin McCree, the son of a former Flint mayor, took the scenic route through higher education.

"I've gone to a lot of colleges, goofing off basically," McCree confessed. "I went to Western (Michigan University) right after high school just because they wouldn't let summer students in UM-Flint. I went to both UM-Flint and Mott (Community College), graduated from Mott and probably had enough credits to have graduated from many places. But what really happened, I just goofed off and took the courses I wanted to."

McCree, now Genesee County Register of Deeds, buckled down enough to earn a certificate in real estate from Mott and property management certification from the Institute of Real Estate in Scottsdale, Ariz.

John Wilkinson was one local exception to the black male college drought prior to World War II. His sister, Minnie Simpson, said that as part of his graduation ceremony from Flint Junior College (now Mott), he was asked to sing. He was so good his music teacher wanted to showcase his voice. That was a first and quite an honor, Simpson said. Wilkinson went to Wayne College and studied mortuary science, she said.

Charlotte Williams was among Flint's first black college-educated women. She attended the Flint School of Practical Nursing when it was on Seventh Street. The program was later taken over by Mott College. She trained and worked at St. Joseph Hospital before going into government work.

Williams became Genesee County's second black female county commissioner in 1966. The 68-member panel was called the county Board of Supervisors then. (Read more about her distinguished career in the chapter on politics and race relations.)

Nursing and teaching were two of the few professional careers open to black women before the 1950s. There was the rare exception such as dentist Marie Hackley Wright, who was the first black woman dental student at Meharry Medical College in Nashville, Tenn. Wright never practiced dentistry in Flint but, after World War II, with her husband opened Wright Funeral Home.

Now black women in Flint are dentists, doctors, lawyers, accountants, bankers, engineers and just about any occupation you can name

Quite a few started at Flint Junior College (now MCC). Mott's main campus near downtown Flint now consists of several buildings but it was only one building back in the 1940s.

Flint Community Junior College, founded in 1923, was renamed Genesee County Community College in 1970 and got its current name in 1973 to honor Flint philanthropist Charles Stewart Mott, who died that year.

Ruth Scott studied at Flint Junior College in the late 1940s but said she almost fell into the factory trap. Not many of her peers went to college and, like them, Scott noted the good wages being paid in the shop. She seriously considered working third shift while going to school part time.

"Luckily, I didn't get hired," said Scott, a retired teacher. "A lot of girls who went to Flint Junior College with me were going to school days and working nights and finally they quit and went to the shop (full time) and never finished school."

Ruth VanZandt spent a year and a half at Flint Junior College in the early 1930s, studying pre-law. But she changed her major to education when she got an offer too good to pass up to attend Michigan State Normal, a teachers college in Ypsilanti. It is now Eastern Michigan University.

"We had no money," she said. "My dad made 37 cents an hour. That was before they had unions and, of course, you took what they gave you. But my dad was also a carpenter. He did extra work during the time he would be laid off and kept things going, but we were never on welfare because he didn't believe in that.

"In 1937, when I graduated, I was in the group that was given the last life certificates for teaching," VanZandt said. "That meant you didn't have to go back to school if you didn't want to. That didn't mean anything to me. I've still gone back and done some work at Wayne, UM and MSU."

In her day, Michigan State Normal was a small school with very few blacks.

"There were no dorms; we lived in private homes," VanZandt said.

In 1950, Dolores Ennis found herself one of about 20 blacks among 4,000 students at the University of Michigan in Ann Arbor. She wanted to attend a black college, but her family could not afford out-of-state tuition.

But the few black students at Michigan stuck together, creating the effect of a small black college within the university, Ennis said.

"I was in school with guys who were much older because they were coming back from the war," Ennis said, adding that those were wonderful years.

Paying tuition was such a struggle she had to skip a semester to work at Chevrolet Parts and Service to earn it.

When Sheila Miller-Graham arrived on the Ann Arbor campus in the mid-1970s, her greatest challenge was the academic workload.

"I was floored on the first day of class when the class was told to read the first three chapters and be ready to discuss it by the next class," Miller-Graham said. "That was just for one class."

Coping with that experience persuaded Miller-Graham that high school teachers need to work harder to prepare students for college by giving them heavier reading loads followed by class discussion.

Eventually, Miller-Graham switched majors from mechanical engineering to dance because "the engineering blew my mind. It was so much pressure, plus I didn't like it that well and was surrounded by a bunch of unsociable men."

Karen Aldridge, a UM alumnus (1974), said that "education is what you make it." Solid home training shaped her readiness. "My parents took me to the library every week and there was no such thing as you didn't have homework, it was like 'Well, read a book,' " she said.

A business and finance major, Aldridge said that her Flint education served her well at UM and later in several progressively responsible jobs. She was city of Flint budget director from 1988 to 1992 and worked at the Michigan Office of Management and Budget from 1992 to 1994. She is now a financial program officer at the Mott Foundation.

Despite being 20 years apart, Aldridge and Ennis had similar Ann Arbor experiences. Black student enrollment has consistently been less than 10 percent. In 1971, blacks were only 4.5 percent of the 32,940 student population.

The black student body was a separate community with its own parties, sororities and fraternities, Aldridge said.

"You didn't pass any black person on campus without speaking," she said. "If you were in class together, most of the time you'd automatically introduce yourself because you knew that if you needed help that was the only place you'd get it.

"When we had to form study groups, no one (white) would choose you without knowing anything about your intellectual ability."

Generally, whites on campus treated blacks OK but socially distanced themselves.

Whenever Aldridge "felt lost" she would return home to Flint.

"I wanted to see black people," she said. "I wasn't used to this all-white environment. You'd go to class and be the only black in class. No one would sit near blacks in class until no other seats were left."

Vietnam protests and civil rights activism kept emotional levels high on campus, Aldridge said. Almost daily, activists would be make speeches on The Diag, a popular outdoor gathering spot on central campus.

The Flint College of the University of Michigan was established in the fall of 1956 on E. Court Street, as part of the MCC campus. It moved downtown in 1977.

Dorothy Waller, a retired teacher, was a member of the first UM Flint advisory board. That was before black students were graduating from there, she said.

Early black enrollment figures are unknown, but in fall 1973, UM-Flint counted 355 blacks among 2,555 students overall, according to Flint Journal reports. In the fall of 1971, there were 175 black students.

Black enrollment rose to an estimated 446 in fall 1985, 448 in 1986, 461 in 1987 and 475 in 1988. Student reporting of race was optional.

By fall 1989, black enrollment stood at 425 among a total student body of 6,506. Black male students dropped to 92, down from 116 the year before.

In fall 1990, of 6,593 students registering, 441 indicated they were black. Of those, 109 were black males.

Robert Matthews is part of the black male college revival of the 1990s. In 1994, Matthews, an administrative assistant in the African-American studies department at UM-Flint, was busy completing his master's degree.

Overall, he sees much room for improvement in Flint's educational system from kindergarten to college.

"I really don't think we're preparing students to compete academically on the college level," Matthews said. "We need to do more than prepare people to get by."

Matthews was president of Students for Black Achievement at UM-Flint and has served on the boards of the Urban Coalition and the Flint Urban League.

"People keep asking me, 'When you finish school are you going to stay (in Flint)?' " Matthews said. "Right now, I'm neutral but I really would like to give something back to this community."

Churches

Flint's oldest church, Quinn Chapel AME, was originally housed in this building on Seventh Street.

Once a year, the congregations from all black churches in Flint met at Potter Lake for the Union Picnic.

The time frame could not be pinpointed from memories but apparently dated back to the 1930s and continued until the late 1950s. It was invariably described as the social event of the year for many years.

"That's where I met my wife (circa 1939)," Sam Williams said. "I think I was 14 and she was 13, but we didn't get married until I was 21."

It was a day of fun, food and fellowship, sort of like a family reunion. The church was the social center of the black community in those days.

The picnic took place at the end of July or early in August. Some said it was the only time blacks were allowed to use the park, so they made the most of it.

"The week before, they'd buy maybe two, three hogs and barbecue (them)," Eugene Simpson said. At Potter Lake, the grilled meat would be shared among churches according to their membership size, he said.

Freddie Williams, who was a boy in the 1930s and early 1940s, recalled that "tables would be set up and you could eat all you wanted at any table. That was the great thing about church picnic."

Woodrow Stanley said he has "a vivid memory of fried chicken, and cold pop and potato salad." He remembers getting there on the church bus and having a good time.

Others remember riding out to the picnic grounds on a flatbed truck that went around the neighborhoods picking up passengers.

Sometimes local businesses like McDonald Dairy or Holsum bread company donated goods to help meet expenses.

Many friendships and good memories were made at the Union Picnic.

Some remembered attending the picnics as far back as the 1930s. The annual picnic was said to have ended in about 1957 after a drowning accident. Details are sketchy, but Ruby Turner Noble described it as "the worst sight I've ever seen in my life."

"The undertaker, Mr. Odom, had a boat out there giving kids rides," she said. "I think it was seven boys who got drowned. Mr. Odom died too."

After that, churches held separate picnics closer to home. A few

Fun for all ages like a ladies' nail-pounding contest was part of the eagerly anticipated annual black churches' Union Picnic at Potter Lake.

---

carried on the tradition at Flint Park for a while, but as Flint's black population spread out, joint church picnics died out.

In the early days of the Union Picnic, Flint had only a handful of black churches. Mostly, they were African Methodist Episcopal, Baptist or Catholic. Today there are at least 50 black churches in Flint. They are Episcopal, Seventh-Day Adventist, Muslim, Christian Scientist, Jehovah's Witness and nondenominational congregations.

Black churches have started in homes and in storefronts. Some were built brand new and some purchased from other congregations.

Flint's oldest black churches are Quinn Chapel AME, which organized in 1875, and Mt. Olive Baptist Church, organized in 1910. Galilee Baptist Church on the north side is said to be the oldest original church building still standing, but no dates are available.

Records are hard to come by to pinpoint when other black churches started but many were branches of established churches.

Congregations are not the only thing that's changed. Some religious customs have changed, too. For example, at one time funeral wakes were held at home and baptisms were done in the Flint River.

After preparation for burial, bodies were brought to the residence, Theresa M. Crichton said. A wreath would be placed on the door and people would come from miles around bringing food and sympathy to the bereaved family.

"If they belonged to an organization like the Masons, they'd sit up all night," she said. That was why it was called a wake.

"My mother died in 1939 and they brought her home," Crichton said. "That's the last I remember them bringing a body home."

Funerals lasted longer then, she said.

"If the funeral started at 1 p.m., it was 4:30 p.m. before you got out. Wasn't no morning funeral."

Flint River baptisms took place during the warm months, Ailene Butler remembered.

"When the springtime came and it got warm enough, we'd go down there and get baptized, all the people who had joined during the winter," she said.

"The church was the center of our social life," Minnie Simpson said. She's lived in Flint since 1919. "It was our place to get together and worship. Our lives centered around the churches because there was no place else to go.

"Not very many people had cars. People were closer. Now everybody is going different ways. People are not as friendly. Now you don't know people next door to you or in your church."

John Rhodes doesn't think churches have changed as much as worshipers have, at least in the north.

"I've noticed here in Michigan it seems that the men don't take enough interest in coming to church; whereas down south, it's a lot different," Rhodes said. "Like night and day. I don't know the reasons if it's the environment here that causes them to be as they are.

"I still like down South. Even the services to me there are better than the services here. The people (are) more cordial than here. I like that. I know whenever I go to my home church, it does something to me. I don't want to come back when I'm down there."

The Rev. Alfred L.C. Robbs didn't like Flint's poor church spirit either when he moved here in 1957. He was pastor of Canaan Baptist Church, which later branched off to Christ Fellowship Baptist.

"I have never been to a town where the spiritual ethos was as low as it (was) in Flint, and it is just about there now," Robbs said, shortly before his death in 1994. "It has peaked up at times, and I hope I don't sound braggadocio, but the Lord used me to set a standard for spirituality in this town that helped others become successful."

There is a big difference between going to church and getting involved, he said.

"When I came to Canaan Baptist Church, there was little difference between the church and the Trio Lounge or any other club in town," Robbs said. "There were some people in the church that were saved and they proved it by taking a stand when the Lord used me to lift the church to a higher level and voted out the old regime."

Robbs said he first saw the church in a vision when he was 13 years old, long before it was built.

"I said, 'Lord is that mine?' and he said, 'If you do what I tell you to do.' I didn't do all that he told me to. I let him down. But he has redeemed me, delivered me and forgiven me. I'm all right now," Robbs said, his aging voice cracking with emotion.

Church training for young people also has changed for the worst, Eloise Caldwell said. She learned valuable skills from her elders when she became the youngest member of the Steward's Board at her church, she said.

"It was a learning process. I learned from these older people and learned to do it right. If you didn't do it right, they'd chew you out so you wouldn't make that mistake no more.

"We never used paper cups and plates for a social affair. It had to be nice," she said. "At my house, we eat at the dining room table."

Among bad modern habits, she said, families don't often sit down to eat together or they have meals in front of the television or on the run.

Today's youth have not learned to do things the hard way or to be considerate of others, Caldwell said. Instead, she sees a "don't care" attitude in their dress and social skills.

"People, all they think about is themselves, not what they can do to help someone else," she said. "This is where I think I need to put emphasis with our youth. You don't worry about the person up front that's talking and dominating the talk. Think about the person in the back and try to draw them in. When that person is growing, you grow too."

Caldwell further prescribes for youth the experience of starting at the bottom.

"I look at my daughter and she amazes me because I've never had to tell her to help people. Because I did it, she does it," Caldwell said.

"I don't do as much as I used to because I learned that I can't stand stress, so I have to look out for myself. If I can do something for you, I'll gladly do it, but don't expect it of me and I don't expect anything in return. I've already got it."

Sheila Miller-Graham is glad her "parents raised me in church." It made a difference in her rebellious youth, when she was "getting a bit too big for my breeches."

"You become embarrassed over the things you did, silly stuff like smoking cigarettes in the girls bathroom," Miller-Graham said. "You want to be in with the in-crowd, and it takes getting into those groups to find out that's not where it's at."

Miller-Graham's straight-A average was shaky by the time she got to junior high school and settled down.

"My parents were the type who would not accept grades below what they knew I was capable of," she said.

It is important for young people today to stayed spiritually centered, she said.

"One of the things we do as a people is let Satan conquer us. The oldest trick in the book is divide and conquer. (Instead) try to find out the things we have in common as human beings or women or sisters. Focus on commonalities, not differences."

Values are important, Johnnie Wynn Jr. said. A positive example is the story of former Los Angeles Mayor Tom Bradley, who was a sharecropper's son, so poor he had to patch holes in his shoes with cardboard.

"We need to get our boys and girls to stop thinking that gym shoes and jeans are so important," Wynn said. "If you have money, put it in the bank for college not on your back or in equipment (like) big stereos."

His wife, Frankie Wynn, a former school counselor, added: "My mother used to tell us, "The only handicap in the world is yourself." I don't like to hear our young people talk about prejudice. Sure there is, but climb over it."

The media focuses more on criminals than on successful role models such as Oprah Winfrey, Bill Cosby and Magic Johnson, Frankie Wynn said.

"You don't hear about working-class blacks who go to work every day and send their kids to classes. Don't allow prejudice to suppress you. Rise above it. We have opportunities here. If George Washington Carver did it in his day, why can't we?"

As a counselor, Wynn enjoyed helping young people look past obstacles.

"When you're growing up, you think you know (everything), but you really don't; you have to have someone out there to kind of help you," she said.

"I pray every day that our young people will realize that (using) drugs is not what it's made out to be. It's a trap that will demoralize you into slavery."

ORIGINS:
"All the blacks attended one church."

Mt. Olive Baptist Church, established in 1910, is the oldest black Baptist church in Flint.

Before 1918, there were no black churches on the north end. Northsiders like Ruby Turner Noble had to ride the bus to church.

"When I first came to Flint, we went to Quinn Chapel," she said. "It was the only AME church in Flint." Buses only ran once every hour, so it took a long time to ride to church and back, she said.

Quinn, now located at 2101 Lippincott Blvd., has the oldest black congregation in Flint. The African Methodist Episcopal church denomination started in Philadelphia in 1787, making it almost as old as the United States.

Quinn Chapel was organized in 1875. It started as a prayer service in the home of Nancy West who lived on Mill Street. In 1876, it moved to the first building on Seventh Street, where the Flint City Hall complex is now. A commemorative marker on the lawn of Flint City Hall marks

Old-timers may be able to identify several prominent citizens in the Men's Glee Club at Mt. Olive Baptist Church in the 1930s.

the original site.

The current church was built between 1958 and 1961, as funds became available.

Before 1910, Quinn Chapel was the only black church, Minnie Simpson said. Then, Mt. Olive was organized for black Baptists on the south side and later Galilee Baptist in the St. John area for blacks who lived on the north side. Other Baptist churches sprang up from those, she said.

Mt. Olive Baptist, 426 Kennelworth Ave., started at the home of Sarah F. Howard on Ninth Street.

Johnnie Wynn Jr., who is chairman of the Deacon Board, once lived across the street from the original church. It was a small, wooden building on Ward (12th) Street that was blown down in a storm. In 1915, the church purchased a building at 11th and Pine streets for $4,600.

The sanctuary at E. Kennelworth and Liberty streets was built in 1950 and renovated in 1989. An educational unit was completed in 1957.

"Grace Emmanuel and First Trinity (Baptist churches) both split from Mt. Olive," Theresa M. Crichton said.

That's why there are so many black churches in Flint – because people would get mad and split up, she said.

Vernon Chapel AME started in 1925 when someone suggested that the north side needed an AME church, Turner Noble said. Vernon

Chapel began as a mission of Quinn Chapel. For 10 years, services were held in the basement at St. John Street and Rhode Island Avenue.

In 1954, Vernon Chapel bought a former Catholic church building on North Street. The church moved to its current location at 5802 Dupont St. in 1972 and was dedicated the following year.

Canaan Baptist Church was organized in 1924. Services were held at the Flint Community Center on Dewey Street until a basement church was built at 910 Gillespie Ave. in 1926.

In 1968, the congregation bought a larger building, a former Jewish synagogue, at 317 E. Hamilton Ave. The move caused financial and organizational problems for Canaan.

The banks didn't want to make the church a loan, said the Rev. Alfred L.C. Robbs, who had been pastor since 1957. The asking price was $350,000 but the congregation only had $100,000 in the bank.

"They said to me, 'Oh no, Reverend, we can't let you have that,' " Robbs said. "They said, 'We have never loaned that much money to a black institution.' I said, 'I don't care if you haven't, either you loan it to me or I want every dime of my money (in his account).'

"It was a million-dollar building and I got it for $350,000," Robbs said, noting that he drove a hard bargain to get the original price of $650,000 lowered by playing on the sellers' anxiety about the neighborhood becoming black.

Just before moving in, Robbs renamed the church Christ Fellowship because he said Jesus Christ told him it would give the church a new beginning. But the move divided the congregation and ended up in a lawsuit. When it was resolved, part of the original congregation had split off, keeping the name Canaan Baptist and the former Gillespie Street location.

Black Catholics started their first church in parishioners' homes in 1929. That's when Christ the King Catholic Mission was founded by Father Norman A. Dukette, Flint's first black priest and a legend in his lifetime.

The financially struggling parish rented five facilities in 10 years before it purchased its first building on Clifford Street in 1946. The building was moved from Dort Highway to the Clifford site where it was remodeled.

That building was torn down in 1969 when I-475 freeway was built. The congregation moved into its present home at 1832 Seymour St. in 1972.

Other older black churches in Flint include Shiloh Missionary Baptist Church, organized in 1918, and Bethel United Methodist Church, 1919. Shiloh was originally on St. John Street and is now at 502 Leith St. Bethel is located at 421 E. 12th St., its original site.

LEADERS:
"He took time with all people."

Father Norman A. Dukette, founder and priest of Christ the King, Flint's first black Catholic Church.

Many black clergymen, such as the Rev. Norman A. Dukette, have served as social or political leaders to the black community.

Dukette had a reputation for helping find jobs for blacks migrating to Flint from the South, said Joseph Rawlery, who knew Dukette as a priest and a friend since 1948.

It didn't matter if they weren't members of Christ the King Catholic Church. It didn't matter if they weren't Catholic, though Dukette converted many to the faith, Rawlery said.

"He took time with all people regardless of their creed or color. He had a lot of patience."

Dukette was a meek and humble man, Rawlery said. As a young man, he was short and small but grew heavier as he grew older. He died at age 88 in 1980 after a long illness.

"It was an honor to have his funeral at St. Michael's Roman Catholic Church," Rawlery said. "It was unusual to do that. (Christ the King) was small, so St. Mike was nice enough to provide facilities so it could accommodate the crowd."

When he died, Dukette was the oldest black priest in the United States and had been the only one in the Lansing Diocese for many years.

He was ordained in 1926 in Detroit where he organized St. Benedict the Moor Church. Some said he was sent to Flint as punishment, but that was never confirmed.

Rawlery attended the dedication ceremony when Father Dukette Catholic School was named after the late priest in 1990. A drive to have Dukette canonized started in 1990 but has not been realized.

"I may not live to see it but maybe some young people will," Rawlery said.

Audrey Wilson remembered Dukette as "a quiet, soft-spoken man and very gentle." Children had respect for him and people always said good things about him, she said.

Other black church leaders who made significant contributions to the community as a whole include the Rev. Arthur Davis of Bethel United Methodist Church, the Rev. Robert R. Turpin of Mt. Olive Baptist Church and the Rev. Thomas Courts of Vermont Christian Church.

Davis is remembered as a civic leader and youth role model. He came to Bethel church about 1940 and oversaw construction of its first building.

Turpin pastored Mt. Olive from 1939 to 1972. He died in 1986 and was eulogized as an educator, intelligent speaker and ecumenical leader. He served on several boards including the Urban League of Flint and the Greater Flint Council of Churches. His wife, Annie, was also very active in the community.

Courts was active in the NAACP, participated in the civil rights march from Selma to Montgomery, Ala., and served as president of the Greater Flint Council of Churches. He founded Vermont Church, 2001 Lippincott Blvd., in 1945 and pastored it for 40 years until his retirement in 1985.

Another civic leader, the Rev. Avery Aldridge of Foss Avenue Baptist Church, was elected president of the Wolverine Baptist State Convention in 1991. He is also president of the Concerned Pastors for Social Action, a group he organized in 1969 to address problems in the black community.

Since then, Concerned Pastors has taken a leadership role that includes publishing a weekly newspaper and endorsing political candidates. The group has tackled issues such as a plan to move some courses offered at Mott Community College to its suburban campuses that was seen as detrimental to urban black students who don't have cars. Concerned Pastors supported renaming Detroit Street to Martin Luther King Avenue. It has been active in get-out-the-vote drives and served as a voice for the black community on many controversial issues.

The "calling" to minister happens in many ways.

The Rev. Albert C. Lee of Greater Bible Way Church of God in Christ was called in about 1960 after observing a storefront church at the corner of North and Taylor streets.

"The members of this church had a good sense of serenity and peace and joy about themselves, though they were poor," Lee said. After visiting the church and befriending what he had at first thought were less-privileged people, he felt called by the Lord to minister, he said.

The late Rev. Eugene Simpson, formerly of Mt. Tabor Missionary Baptist Church, traces his religious roots to his family. Simpson taught Sunday school, directed the choir and was a trustee, member of the deacon board and assistant pastor before organizing Mt. Tabor in 1967.

The Rev. Robbs entered the ministry in the early 1940s. He achieved prominence in Flint as a civil rights activist. He led a protest to push for fair housing in 1968. He helped calm tensions in Flint when a riot threatened to erupt in the streets at the same time that other major cities, namely Detroit, were on fire. He marched in Alabama from Selma to Montgomery in the historic protest led by Dr. Martin Luther King Jr.

Robbs raised awareness about political issues through his weekly radio program on Flint's WAMM radio. But the station's management made him stop after there were complaints he was using the worship broadcast to endorse political candidates. Robbs sued, charging that it was a violation of his civil rights, but the case was dismissed. Later, he became WAMM's gospel director.

Robbs also served on the Genesee County Board of Supervisors and Flint Human Relations Commission.

The list of black ministers who have been recognized for civic leadership is too long to list here. A few who are heads of some of Flint's largest black churches are Bishop Odis Floyd of New Jerusalem Baptist, the Rev. Roy I. Greer of Mt. Olive Baptist, the Rev. J.C. Curry of Macedonia and the Rev. LeRoy Shelton of Christ Fellowship.

Also, the Rev. Russell McReynolds, who was pastor of Bethel United Methodist from 1971 to 1991, served on the Flint Board of Education from 1985 to 1991 and was its president in 1987-88.

CHURCH WORK:
"The church could get more involved in problems facing our black youth."

Elaborate Tom Thumb weddings for children, like this one in 1951 at Quinn Chapel AME, were social events almost as big as the real thing.

Everybody loves a wedding. In fact, they loved them so much in the 1950s that mock weddings for children became popular.

They were called Tom Thumb weddings, after either the famous circus performer who was a midget or the dwarfish fairy tale character.

Tom Thumb weddings were elaborate affairs, as detailed as the real thing right down to the pint-sized bridal gowns and tuxedos, music, flowers, a photographer, church ceremony and reception. Invitations were mailed and a menu planned. The key differences were that the entire wedding party was children and the vows weren't legally binding.

Quinn Chapel AME was a frequent setting for Tom Thumb weddings but many other churches also sponsored them, Frankie Wynn said.

The parents of the bride or bridegroom were often prominent in the church or community and could afford to sponsor their child as the star of this expensive spectacle.

Wynn, a retired educator, saw two good purposes for Tom Thumb weddings. One was that they gave children an outlet for self-expression. The other was that it involved them in a church activity.

"I feel the more you get your children involved in wholesome activities, the better off they will be," Wynn said. "If not, they'll be in unwholesome activities."

Wynn, who is a member of Mt. Olive Baptist Church, kept her five children active in a variety of church activities. She and her husband, Johhnie Wynn Jr., believed that exposing their children to plays, parties, recreation and fellowship at church taught them how to have a good time in the right way.

"Luckily when my kids were growing up, there were five or six ladies in our church and we were all working together doing things for our kids," she said.

"I do feel you need to have more black men in the church doing outreach. (Misguided children) are out there and they're looking for someone to reach out to them. They're not really bad kids. They just need someone to give them some direction," Wynn said.

Wynn especially advocates values like teaching young women morals and self-respect. She cites the growing number of teen-age unwed mothers.

Wynn also sees the need to downplay materialism because it is often the mind-set that lures young men into selling drugs or killing each other for gym shoes, jackets and other so-called status symbols.

A good example is a young man at Central High School who came into Wynn's office when when she was a counselor there. The young man was distressed about wearing raggedy clothes. Wynn told him he ought to be more concerned about getting good grades.

Youth dances in the 1940s and 1950s provided wholesome activities for some. Audrey Wilson attended dances at Christ the King Catholic Church that were part of its community outreach. The dances were open to youth from other churches.

There are more black churches now than 30 years ago but seemingly

Among many gifted voices filling Flint's church choirs were those of (from left) Marjorie Robinson, Maude Tyiska, Laura Jean Thompson, Robert Semmes and Harrison McGee.

---

less youth involvement.

Dorothy Parks remembers when the church was the main social outlet for youth. They were involved in groups like Baptist Young People's Union and Christian Endeavor, which provided wholesome activities.

"There are so many things to distract the young people now," Parks said. "I don't think a lot of parents go to church like they used to. This way the children don't go."

Television is the primary distraction, she said. Many children would rather spend Sunday mornings watching TV.

Church programs sowed the seeds of political activism in Woody Etherly, a former Flint city councilman. He earned a reputation for being militant and abrasive.

"They call me everything but what I am and that's a child of the King," Etherly said. "My political endeavors started in the church. I'm a product of the church."

In 1967, at 23, Etherly organized and led the famous youth sleep-in on the lawn of Flint City Hall to push for open housing in Flint.

Earlier, his speaking ability helped get him elected president of the Wolverine State Baptist Convention youth fellowship. One sour note, though, was losing a oratorical contest sponsored by the organization because the judges ruled that he was preaching instead of speaking.

"People were shouting and they were carrying people out of the church," Etherly said. "So they disqualified me and I cried like a baby because I thought I had won." He was 16 or 17 and crushed because he had hoped to go on to the national competition.

Etherly took his passion for persuasive speech into the Flint City Council chambers where he represented the Third Ward from 1970 to 1983. His outspokenness and brash style drew criticism.

"Nobody ever looked at my religious background," Etherly said.

"They can't say that Woody jumped up and he cussed out everybody and he did so and so. All they can say is he beat the gavel on the floor, he disrupted city council meetings, he was argumentative. When you try to do something to hurt black folks, I'm argumentative."

Charlotte Williams, a former county commissioner, traces her early leadership training to her church, Quinn Chapel. When she was about 8, a pastor came to Quinn Chapel who was keen on youth activities because he was raising two granddaughters. By the time he left Quinn Chapel, youth programs were thoroughly entrenched in the church. Williams reaped the benefit as she grew up and afterward. She also was secretary of a youth missionary group.

"My church has been supportive of me in everything I've done down through the years," Williams said.

Young men look back with gratitude to the profound influence of the Rev. Arthur Davis of Bethel United Methodist Church. In the 1940s, Davis ran a boys club that left a positive mark on participants like Maxie Brandon.

Ruth VanZandt worked with the children's choir at Bethel and directed and played for the senior choir for 40 years.

Starting at 13, Marion Coates-Williams was a traveling church pianist. She was a member of Quinn Chapel but played for Baptist churches such as Golden Leaf and Metropolitan.

Coates-Williams met her future husband at church.

The social role of the black church has led to its weekday use as an activities center. Groups and clubs have been formed for fund-raising, tutoring, mentoring, children's recreation and arts and crafts programs, political forums, Bible study, and to plan special events like Women's Day.

At Quinn Chapel, Eloise Caldwell has served on several social committees. She's helped plan church receptions in honor of members who are recent graduates. She created a cookbook to help raise funds to surface the church parking lot. It was a gamble that paid off well.

A Sunday school class in 1957 at Metropolitan Baptist Church on Industrial Avenue. at Myrtle Avenue.

The committee borrowed the money to print the cookbooks hoping and praying they would sell. The first 1,000 books sold like hot cakes and 500 more were printed.

"They're still asking for them," Caldwell said. New members of the church request them, plus there is ample opportunity to sell them at conferences and other outside activities.

Sam Williams has hosted a Sunday morning radio gospel program since 1957.

"I was working for Dick Carter, the Jewish guy who started WAMM," Williams recalled. "They approached Leo Greene (funeral home owner) about doing a program for half an hour. That's all the spiritual time we had on Sunday was a half-hour."

Gospel Time, now on WDZZ-FM, has grown to eight hours and has several sponsors. Several churches now broadcast Sunday morning services on the radio. Canaan Baptist was the first to have a weekly radio broadcast, according to Robbs. At that time, in the late 1950s or early 1960s, Macedonia Baptist Church was on the air but only with singing, he said.

Robbs added preaching and politicking to his broadcast to keep blacks "aware of the issues."

"Things wouldn't be as good as they are if the Lord hadn't sent me here," he said. "I didn't do them (social changes). The Lord did them through me. The Lord was tired of the way blacks were acting, playing (at) church, and the way whites were acting, mistreating blacks."

Dealing with social concerns is the ongoing mission of the Concerned Pastors for Social Action, said the Rev. Albert C. Lee, vice president. CPSA unites the leadership from a cross-section of "Christ-believing" churches, Lee said. Most members are black but some are white.

Collaborative church activities like the Union Picnic are a thing of the past, but some churches still jointly sponsor Good Friday, Easter and Christmas services.

OTHER FAITHS:
She became a Christian Science practitioner – healing through prayer.

John Hightower is a member of Sacred Heart Catholic Church, 719 E. Moore St. So he didn't understand why his priest sent him to Christ the King Catholic Church when he got married in the early 1950s.

"It was strongly suggested," Hightower said.

Christ the King's congregation was predominantly black and its black priest, Dukette, married the Hightowers.

Hightower and Father Dukette became friends, but Hightower continued his membership at Sacred Heart.

Hightower didn't challenge his priest's "suggestion" until years later but resented having to "leave my neighborhood, my parents, to go over to Father Dukette's church," he said.

There was prejudice even in the churches then, Hightower said. Blacks are married all the time now at all Catholic churches, he added.

Blacks are members in churches of many denominations outside of the traditional ones – Baptists, Methodists and Catholics.

Ruth Owens Buckner was raised Methodist at Quinn Chapel AME

but converted to Christian Science in 1934. In 1980, she became a Christian Science practitioner, authorized to heal through prayer.

Illness drew Buckner to Christian Science, she said. She was a young, married woman ready to start a family, but doctors told her that pregnancy would kill her. But Buckner's faith saw her through three pregnancies, including nearly painless childbirth, she said.

"It was the first time I had thought of God being a loving parent," Buckner said. "You know, we'd always thought of God as sitting up there and he'd zap us when we did wrong. After I started studying Christian Science, I understood it better."

A Bible reader since age 17, Buckner said she came to believe that God heals all diseases.

As a practitioner, Buckner said she gets calls from all over the country and from foreign countries requesting her healing prayer.

"It's rewarding work. I learned there's no lack. God supplies us abundantly with whatever we need. Things you didn't think possible happened," she said.

The Rev. Henry Horton also claims a personal relationship with God. He is pastor of the Christian Life Learning Center, 4201 Lippincott Blvd., a nondenominational church.

Horton was raised a Baptist but said he had a sense that there had to be more than he was learning about spirituality.

"I've been a Christian all my life since childhood," Horton said. "Most Southern blacks were raised in the church."

He was called to the ministry on an airplane after a conversation about Christianity and religion with a young man involved in Youth for Christ, he said. After the young man got off the plane, Horton said he clearly understood the call from God to preach the gospel to the black community.

"For me, it was a combination of what I was feeling and what I sensed in my spirit. I don't expect to explain it in a way you can understand. When it happens to you, you know. Now I hear from God often."

Horton's church has about 200 members including children. Services include a family training hour and special weeknight lessons taught by him or his wife.

"It's a growing church, an exciting church," Horton said. "We sing mostly praise songs and upbeat songs. We sing songs that basically are scripture put to music. We sing some of the old Baptist standards when they're scriptural."

Horton teaches a series called "Blacks in the Bible" about biblical figures he believes were black. He challenges the popular image of Jesus Christ with long, flowing blond hair because Middle Eastern people tend to be dark-haired and swarthy, he said.

"In most cases, when you talk about it, people consider you a radical. That's to maintain the status quo. If our children knew what a great heritage they have from the time of the Garden of Eden until right now, they would have a greater sense of self-respect, a greater understanding of who they really are, and I think they would be less likely to get involved in some of the mischievous behavior. I know that's not popular, but that's what I believe," he said.

Social Life

The Zags (Zeta Alpha Gamma), at one of many fund-raisers in the 1950s, are (back row, from left) Edith Bissell, Clotiel Moore-Coney, Esther Simmons; and (front row) Doris James, Otilia Nelson, Anna Lea Bannister, Vivian Edmonds, Jacqueline Weaver, Ozie Grady, Marion Williams and Omogene Spencell Truss.

Comparing Flint entertainment in the 1990s to what it was like from the 1930s to 1960s is like to a weekend carnival to Disneyland. There used to be much more variety.

Judging by some descriptions, Flint after dark offered a choice of black nightclubs. Now, many party animals say that in order to spend an evening nightclub hopping, they have to drive to Detroit.

Now if you want to see a concert by a top act, most of the time you have to drive to the Saginaw Civic Center, or Pine Knob near Pontiac, or Detroit's Joe Louis Arena or Fox Theatre. But in earlier times, Flint's old IMA Auditorium in downtown Flint regularly booked some of the biggest names in entertainment.

Back then, if you wanted to see a movie, you could walk to your nearby neighborhood or downtown theater. Now, you probably have to drive to the outskirts of town to get to suburban complexes.

And until the early 1960s, it didn't take a four-hour drive to the nearest amusement park. Instead, you could walk or take the bus to the edge of town where Flint Park and Lakeside Park amusement parks provided 60 combined years of rides and other attractions right in Flint.

"There was more to do then than now," said Katie Ellis Harper, who was born in Flint in 1928. "We had community centers, ... baseball games all over the city." Berston Field House on N. Saginaw Street had a nice swimming pool and library.

"We had everything at Berston – tennis courts, baseball diamonds – when I was a teen and younger," Ellis Harper said. "We had roller skating clubs."

Blacks were allowed to skate at Flint Park only on Monday nights, but a group of men organized skating trips to nearby cities such as Detroit and Lansing.

"Churches were a big thing in the olden days, as the kids call it," said Minnie Simpson, who came to Flint at age 6 in 1919. "The church was the center of our social life."

Church activities included musical programs, Bible-study groups, picnics and social development programs.

When Flint's first radio station – WFDF – crackled to life in 1922, it added a new form of entertainment.

"We had one of the first radios and people would come and sit on the steps and listen to 'Amos and Andy.' They were two white men acting black. It was a comedy thing," Simpson explained.

As in everything else, discrimination affected entertainment for black people, but that didn't spoil their fun. It meant going to IMA concerts that started at midnight, after whites had used the facility first. It meant sitting in the balcony at the movie theater though you had paid the same admission price as whites. And for a time, it meant being assigned a certain day to visit the amusement park, the skating rink or the municipal swimming pool.

The good times really started to roll after World War II when blacks began earning discretionary income in the factory.

Black nightclubs were so popular they sometimes drew whites, but blacks could not go to white nightclubs unless they were performing there.

During the Big Band Era in the 1930s and 1940s and long afterward, musicians like Sherm Mitchell and Dorothy Patton provided live entertainment at local black and white clubs.

Through the years, Flint has produced some nationally and internationally known black entertainers, such as Motown's The Velvelettes, Tony Award winner Dee Dee Bridgewater, rap artist M.C. Breed, vocal groups Midnight Starr and Ready for the World and many other vocalists.

In cultural affairs, a group of prominent blacks got together in 1960 to pledge $25,000, a full sponsorship, to the development of the Flint Cultural Center on E. Kearsley Street between Crapo Street and Longway Boulevard.

Isaiah Jackson, who is black, was conductor of the Flint Symphony Orchestra from 1982 to 1987. Black concert attendance reportedly increased during his tenure.

Among noted African-American visual artists are Al Washington and Lavarne Ross.

Washington, who took his first art lessons in Carriage Town at age 10, has painted portraits of prominent citizens such as Charles Stewart Mott, Walter Reuther, Frank Manley, Guy Houston and Michigan Gov. G. Mennen Williams. His murals decorate several buildings in Flint and he is a co-founder of the Flint Museum of African American History.

Washington said one of his most treasured memories was meeting Josephine Baker in 1941. He had painted a portrait of the legendary dancer and entertainer and presented it to her during an appearance at Detroit's Fox Theatre.

Among Lavarne Ross' many celebrated works is a series of paintings that preserve images and memories of the former St. John neighborhood. He was commissioned to paint a mural commemorating General Motors' 75th anniversary in 1983 and mural is on display at Delphi Flint East. His work has been displayed at the governor's mansion in Lansing and purchased by art lovers in China.

Another big part of Flint's entertainment calendar is filled with activities sponsored by social or hobby clubs, catering to recreational, religious, cultural and educational interests.

Black sororities and fraternities, which started in Flint in 1940s and '50s, have sponsored theme dances, formal balls and ongoing community service projects.

House parties and cabarets were very popular until the early 1980s.

Other entertainment involved excursions to recreational attractions near and far.

Between 1950 and 1980, but especially during the 1960s, Eloise Caldwell said her family traveled. Her brother and his wife from Kansas City would visit every summer, and they would choose a destination and set out, sometimes driving 500 miles a day, staying at the best hotels and eating at the best restaurants, she said.

Their travels took them to the world's fairs in New York and Montreal. They toured just about everywhere except the Deep South and the New England states.

They went to Jack and Jill conventions in California. Jack and Jill is a family-oriented group that promotes the social, cultural and religious development of the whole child. The Jack and Jill annual weekend at the local YWCA camp was a family affair, Caldwell said.

Parents monitored the various camp activities for children. Then they'd have a family dinner. The adults would sit up until 3 a.m. playing cards and the kids would get up as soon as the sun came up. So the parents would be exhausted by the time they went home, Caldwell said.

Her husband and his male cronies preferred to "rent a cottage and do nothing" at Idlewild, a black resort area near Baldwin in northern Michigan.

Closer to home, they visited Boblo Island every year, riding the theme boat from the dock in downtown Detroit to the amusement park in Canada. A promotion during the last week in August admitted children under 4 years old for free, Caldwell said. There would be dancing on the boat and activities for old and young.

IMA:
"We had to wait until the whites left."

Big Band leader Duke Ellington brought his "A Train" to audiences at Flint's IMA Auditorium. Crooners like Nat King Cole and Johhny Mathis appeared there. And the golden voices of Lena Horne, Marian Anderson and Sam Cooke also have been heard live in Flint.

Teens have swooned over pop idols like The Jackson 5. Comedian Richard Pryor tickled funny bones and James Brown did his famous splits.

For many years, into the 1970s, crowds packed into the old IMA in downtown Flint for concerts by such entertainers as Lionel Hampton, Count Basie and Cab Calloway.

When Detroit's Motown sound took off in the 1960s, Flint's proximity to Detroit meant regular revues by name acts including the Supremes and Stevie Wonder.

The old IMA Auditorium, which later became a part of AutoWorld, was built in 1929 as a social and recreational center for factory workers. Dances, concerts, boxing and wrestling matches, the circus, political speeches and more were staged there.

The spacious auditorium in the $1.2-million facility had 4,000 permanent seats on the three-sided balcony overlooking 2,500 portable seats on the main floor that could be removed to make room for dancing. A decorative 93-foot-high ceiling helped create an elegant feeling.

The stage and orchestra pit had room for a 100-piece ensemble. There were dressing rooms for men and women, offices, club meeting rooms, a first-aid department, candy and tobacco concession booths, and massage and shower rooms.

"They also had what they called the annex (built in 1959) and they had dances in both places," said James Blakely. The size of the crowd determined whether a dance concert would be held in the auditorium or annex, he said.

Audiences were racially segregated during the IMA's early years.

"The most popular thing we did was go to dances at IMA, but we had to wait until the whites left," said James Todd, a ballroom dancing teacher and 1930s-era patron. "We'd dance from midnight to daybreak. The whites danced from 9 to midnight.

"The discrimination bothered us but we knew we had to go along with the flow. You get used to it after a while."

Socializing at the IMA was a popular form of entertainment in the 1950s.

No one remembered when the segregation ended though a good guess would be after World War II when blacks began making social progress in general.

Bessie Brooks was glad to see an end to conditions that blacks put up with at segregated events.

"I liked going to the IMA but the bad part was that it was after the whites left," she said. "The band would be tired, they had about a half-hour to rest. And we went in those dirty restrooms."

Many young women never got to attend the dances at all.

"My dad would have thought I was crazy if I'd asked to go to a dance at 1 a.m.," said Minnie Simpson. At 17 in 1930, she was bound by strict society codes, but later her younger sister, who was only 16, was allowed to attend IMA dances, she said.

Vivian Pugh wasn't so lucky. She was a grown woman (18) when she attended her first concert in the late 1940s, she said.

Annalea Bannister was in college before her father relented and let her attend a midnight dance in the 1940s.

"My dad didn't feel that was a place for his daughters to go," Bannister said. "Everybody wanted to go to the IMA, but we didn't go."

Ruth Scott recalled that those strict parental rules were still in place for many young women in the mid-1950s.

"I couldn't go because I couldn't be out that late," she said. "I cried to go to see The Platters, but I still didn't get to go."

Being treated like second-class citizens at the IMA bothered young Max Brandon for a different reason.

"The IMA, mind you, was built with dollars taken out of the paychecks of our fathers and grandfathers that worked in the foundry and in Buick for years," he said. "They helped build the IMA with their money and yet we were treated in that manner."

Milton Port was one who helped foot that bill.

"When the IMA was built, I was working at the Buick," he said. "They took half a cent or a cent out of every dollar we made to help build it.

"We weren't supposed to pay to attend the affairs there, but eventually, they came around and paid us off, gave back the money we'd spent." That was the end of free admission.

The IMA hosted everything from car and flower shows to political rallies. Former U.S. presidents Richard Nixon and Jimmy Carter spoke there. But the best memory for many people was the "music that would make a preacher pat his foot," chuckled James Wesley.

All the big bands came. Band leaders Noble Sissle, Benny Goodman, Duke Ellington and Jimmy and Tommy Dorsey were among them.

Other memorable performances were given by instrumentalists such as B.B. King, Cannonball Adderley, Earl "Fatha" Hines, Lionel Hampton, Ray Charles and Fletcher Henderson.

Singers playing the IMA have included Billy Eckstine, Mary Wells, Dinah Washington, Ella Fitzgerald, Dionne Warwick and Aretha Franklin. Rock-'n'-roll guitarist Chuck Berry appeared about 1955 on the same bill with Bill Haley and the Comets. James Brown made a lasting impression in a 1971 concert. And Isaac Hayes appeared in 1972.

Motown staged revues featuring acts including Smokey Robinson, the Supremes and Flint's own Velvelettes. Other group appearances were made by Average White Band, the McKinley Cottonpickers, Parliament and gospel singer Andrae Crouch and the Disciples.

Long-time radio personality Sam Williams especially recalled a performance by Bill Doggett.

"He had a song come out about 1955 called 'Honky Tonk,' " Williams said. "They called it the Negro national anthem. When it came on everybody stood up and started dancing."

Angela Sawyer was a preteen in the 1970s when her heartthrobs – The Jackson 5 – were booked for the IMA. Her parents decided she was too young to attend the concert.

"I thought I was going to die," Sawyer recalled. "They were so close. I cried.

I could not believe that I wasn't going, but at the last minute my parents relented. I was way up in the balcony with no binoculars, but I was there."

Afterward, The Jackson 5 spent the night at the Durant Hotel and hysterical teeny-bopper fans stormed the building trying to see them, Sawyer recalled.

"I was so outdone that I couldn't get close to them, but that's a good memory for me."

Few people remembered how much they paid to attend IMA dances and concerts. Some said $1, some said $3 or $5. But it was a bargain at any price, according to James Blakely who remembers some of the summer revues when one ticket covered seven or eight acts.

Melvin McCree said he liked the wrestling matches between favorites like "Leaping" Larry Shayne and Bobo Brazil. That was in the 1960s and early 1970s.

The IMA's decor made it attractive to groups hosting special events like The Sportsman's Club's annual ball. The Sportsman's Club was a black men's social club. They owned a small building on Clifford Street near Lippincott Boulevard but held their invitation-only balls at the IMA. To be invited was a big deal.

"That was a beautiful occasion," recalled James Wesley. "They would hire a well-known orchestra to play. We had a fellow here named Max McClarin, he was the one who booked all the dances for us."

Lennetta Coney, who grew up in the 1970s, has bittersweet memories of being left at home with a baby-sitter while her parents attended the formal balls. Her mom and dad in formal attire looked as regal as a king and queen.

Years later, Coney had her turn to attend the Cotillion Ball, where debutantes in their virginal white gowns were formally presented to society.

Cotillion balls were a social occasion many remembered attending at the IMA in the 1960s and 1970s.

NIGHTCLUBS:
"It was wall-to-wall people."

Envision soft, dim lights casting intimate shadows in a long, narrow, low-ceiling room. A bar counter runs half the length of one wall. Crowded into the back of the room are about 20 tables and chairs and a small parquet dance floor, giving new meaning to the word cozy.

The venerable Golden Leaf Club on Harrison Street is showing its age after 50 years in business but still filling up the dance floor most Saturday nights.

Neon lights in a rainbow of colors race like liquid fire around the perimeter of a portly jukebox. Reflected lamp light twinkles like little stars off a large mirror. Liquor bottles behind the bar and racks of cocktail glasses are lined overhead.

Pack in about 200 people, dressed in their fashionable best. Add a live band or punch up a Top 40 tune from the jukebox. Layer a cottony cloud of smoke overhead and you are there – enjoying the first and last word in Flint's night life in the mid-1930s through '50s.

The Golden Leaf Club, on Harrison Street near Kennelworth Avenue, opened Thanksgiving night in 1935. It was said to be the first legitimate club for blacks and is one of few still around.

Among old clubs once considered main attractions in Flint were The Royal Garden at Dakota Avenue and St. John Street; The Tropacanna, The Four Leaf Clover, The Green Mill Social Club and The Ebony Social Club, all on Industrial Avenue; The Frolic on N. Saginaw Street; The Vehicle City Elks Club and Club 400 on St. John Street; The Fifty Grand and Club Hurricane on North Street; The Unique Social Bridge Club on Leith Street; The Fraternal Club at Dewey Street and Industrial Avenue, The Casablanca, Joe's Place and The Family Grill ...

The Golden Leaf, granddaddy of them all, now sits among vacant lots and a few weathered houses in a faded south-side neighborhood. Clark Elementary School sits gloomily across the street, boarded and vacant for 20 years. The

> **The Golden Leaf Club**
> Desires to extend to
> **Mr. Hondon Hargrove and his President the Season's Greetings**
> and a Successful Career at
> WILBERFORCE UNIVERSITY
>
> After this Meeting and Every Meeting
> Greet your many friends at the palatial
>
> # Golden Leaf Club
> **1522 Harrison St., Flint, Mich.**
> South Side
>
> Sunday Cocktail Hour 6 until 9 P. M.
> Every Other Night Until 1 A. M.
>
> **Regular Meals, Soft and Other Drinks**
>
> Get what you want at the
> **Golden Leaf Club**
>
> **Members and their Guests Only**
>
> R. M. Van Dyne, Pres.
> Magnus Clark, Sec'y
> Dr. C. E, Walden, Treas.

This handbill from the prestigious Golden Leaf Club was typical of its first-class reputation.

---

freeway that wiped out most of the old neighborhood is a stone's throw away.

"When I (drive) through there, a lump comes in my chest," said Bessie Brooks who grew up in the area and attended Clark School through eighth grade. Indeed, a forlorn, sentimental aura seems to hover over the small area where Clark School, the former Clifford Street Community Center building and the Golden Leaf are within sight of each other.

The Golden Leaf is the only one of the old buildings still open for business but is now regarded as "an old people's club," some said. During a brief revival in the 1980s, it became a popular after-hours spot for a young crowd looking to dance until dawn.

North- and south-side residents flocked to the Golden Leaf in its heyday, when it was the only club in town. On weekends and during the week for some, it was THE place to mingle, sip rum and coke, listen to a nice band and wear out the dance floor.

"It was classy; had white tablecloths on the tables," said Alexander Jones. "As far as I can remember, it's the first black club that served liquor by the glass, with a bar and bartender. That was not normal in clubs owned by blacks."

The dress code was fancy on weekends and for special parties during the week, but casual attire was acceptable the rest of the time.

Jones was one of the first to join the club soon after it opened in 1935. As he recalls, it was first owned by black attorney Roy M. Van Dyne and businessman Magnus Clark.

Twenty-one was the legal age minimum, but that didn't stop younger ones from trying to sneak in. Big, strapping guys and poised young women who knew how to behave usually succeeded in gaining admission. But Katie Harper ruefully recalled being turned away at 19 and 20 because the woman on the door knew Harper was the same age as her daughter.

At one time, illegal speak-easies were the only alternative to the Golden Leaf. Those were disreputable after-hours joints where the hard-core party crowd went to "smoke reefer," drink bootleg whiskey, gamble and dance, said Ailene Butler, a prominent businesswoman.

"They had them in houses and on the north side," she said. "People who ran them were called sporting people. Maybe they handled prostitutes or stuff like that. One of the biggest known spots in Flint for prostitutes and pimps started up on Michigan Avenue."

Because of its first-class reputation, the Golden Leaf was a popular spot for local bands and showcased many well-known black entertainers who came to town. Comedian Redd Foxx appeared there one weekend and singer Sammy Davis Jr. reportedly played there during the early years of his career. One longtime patron said there once was a photograph on the wall of Davis and Ola Hughes, the club owner or manager.

"It cost a bit more to get in when the big names were there," said James Todd. "The entertainers were housed at private homes because they couldn't go to (segregated) hotels."

A piano player named Teddy Wilson, who started at the Golden Leaf later joined the Benny Goodman Quartet, Alexander Jones said. Jazz great, Lionel Hampton was a member of the quartet at that time, between 1936 and 1940.

Sherm Mitchell and Dorothy Patton, two of Flint's better-known black jazz musicians, entertained at The Golden Leaf.

Patton said that of all the local clubs she played, the Golden Leaf was "the most exquisite." It was an intimate sort of club with soft lights and nicely decorated, she said.

"It was a place where people met and saw old friends," Charlotte Williams said. "It was a place you could take out-of-town guests and not be ashamed to be seen in there."

The Golden Leaf sometimes doubled as a community center.

Some of Flint's leading women, teachers and the like, have hosted programs there, said Ailene Butler, who came of age in the 1940s.

"We all grew up together. We used to put on style shows, talent shows and programs.

"I loved to dance and was one of those people who could do the splits and come back through my legs and all that. That's probably why my back is messed up today."

But by the time Ruth Scott came of age in the 1950s, the Golden Leaf "was where you didn't go. It was rough over there," she said. Sometimes "nice girls" ignored the warnings and sneaked in to satisfy their curiosity.

Scott remembers it as a small place patronized by mostly older men. At least, they least seemed old to her. Young people didn't go there then, she said.

The place to go then, if you could get an invitation, was The Sportsman's Club, Scott said. That was located around the corner from the Golden Leaf on Clifford Street at Lippincott Boulevard. Scott's uncle was a member.

"It was really nice," she said. "You could have a drink and there was no fighting."

A group of black business and professional men formed The Sportsman's Club in 1938. In 1952, with about 45 members, it built the private clubhouse at 2039 Clifford St. for $17,000. The brick building still stands.

"I can remember when the Sportsman's Ball used to be a big affair at the IMA," said Dolores McGowain. "That was the who's who in the black community. Anybody would attend but it was mostly the elites."

By the mid-1970s, The Vets Club on S. Saginaw Street was the southside hot spot. Officially called The Veterans for the Promotion of Civic Activities, the founding organization was the Korean War veterans in 1953. The nightclub was built in 1974.

Then the after-hours revival at the Golden Leaf in the 1980s brought back a younger crowd.

Angela Sawyer, then in her 20s, heard about "this new club" the in-crowd was going to, but was disappointed when she found out it was the Golden Leaf that people were talking about.

"I said, 'That old juke joint! I'm not going in there.'" But she did ... just once.

"It didn't appeal to me," Sawyer said. "It's small and they played a lot of oldies."

Ken Ross, who is about Sawyer's age, said he went and had a good time.

"It was wall-to-wall people (inside)," Ross said. "We stayed for about an hour and a half, and the whole time we just danced. The whole building was shaking. It was a nice mix of people."

Many marriages and memories were made at the Golden Leaf. People who simply liked to have a good time said they will never forget when the Golden Leaf was the place to have it.

Details about the club's origins and chain of ownership is sketchy. Some said Ola Hughes owned the club; some said she managed it.

Milton Port, a former bartender at the Leaf, said it was originally called the Maple Leaf Club. Ruth Buckner recalled that the Maple Leaf Club was a men's club owned by a man named Kersey. When his wife sold it, it was renamed the Golden Leaf and membership opened up to men and women, she said.

By the late 1940s, several nightclubs had opened on the north side.

"We had the 400 Club, RG (Royal Garden) and The Unique Club on Leith," Sam Williams recalled.

The Tropacanna on Industrial Avenue was built in the same shotgun style as the Golden Leaf. The Royal Garden, popularly called the RG Club, also was similar in size and format to the Golden Leaf. Both had floor shows, live bands, a dress code and a mixed crowd, Williams said.

The Elks, across the street from The RG Club, was probably the largest club on St. John Street. The Hut, a rowdy bar on St. John between Leith and State streets, was the smallest.

Then came The Green Mill, The Fifty Grand on Stewart Avenue and The Subway on Leith Street. The Hurricane Dining Room on North at Taylor streets was a hotel and nightclub. Henry's Place on N. Saginaw Street and Eddie's Lounge brought in live shows six nights a week.

Les' Chicken Shack and The Dew Drop Inn were smaller hangouts where food and liquor were served. Old city directories show that The Dew Drop Inn was first on Stewart Avenue and later moved to St. John Street.

The Guys and Dolls Club on N. Saginaw Street near Wager Avenue later became the popular Jolly Six Club in the 1960s. The original Jolly Six Club was on St. John Street in the 1950s. The Motor City Club occupied the building that became the Hammer Dropper CB Club on N. Saginaw Street between Addison and Tilden streets.

"A lot of social clubs didn't have a facility, but they'd rent a building and hire a band," said Dorothy Patton, who played her organ at most of them.

Patton said she opened The Fraternal Club, the city's first black jazz club, in about 1937. Later, she and her band, The Blue Notes, had a standing engagement at The Casablanca and The Motor City Club but worked from place to place from the late 1930s through the late 1960s.

Patton still chuckles delightedly when recalling one occasion when the Casablanca's owner told her, as she was moving her organ out, not to bring it back. Patton thought she was being fired. When she stopped by the club later to make sure, she found a new organ waiting for her. The owner explained that he was tired of seeing her drag her organ in and out of the building every night.

Indeed, Patton had dragged that organ to clubs all over Flint. Some she played were Club Hurricane, The Frolic, The Four Leaf Clover, Duffy's, The Fifty Grand, The Unique Club, The Royal Garden, Club 400, Joe's Place, The Elks, The Family Grill, Okie's Place and Club Mayfair.

Most of them were owned and operated by blacks, she said. Now the big mystery is where did they all go?

Patton's theory is that nightclubs began to die out in the late 1960s after the civil rights movement desegregated entertainment facilities that had been off-limits to blacks.

"See, there was a time when we couldn't go into the white clubs in Flint," she said. "They could always come to our clubs but we couldn't go to theirs. Then when we could go to theirs, we went there and left the black clubs over here with no support. So they just closed. They didn't have a (clientele) because it had gone the other way. I think that's what happened."

The popularity of live bands died as well, but Flint has continued to have moderate nightclub action through the years.

In the 1970s, a nice, modern club called Poppa's Bag opened on N. Saginaw Street between Baker and Rankin streets.

"At Poppa's Bag, they used to bring in a lot of entertainment. It was kind of our luxury place at the time," Sondra Rawls recalled.

Poppa's Bag doubled as a rental hall, hosting events like Sweet 16 parties, beauty pageants and fashion shows.

Two popular lounges in the 1970s were Harold's Lounge on N. Saginaw near Dayton St. and Mitchell's Lounge on Lapeer Road.

A downtown club, Studio 416 on Harrison Street, was popular in the early 1980s. And Hollywood East Supper Club on Clio Road near Carpenter Road became the premier nightspot in the mid-1980s.

Smaller or semiprivate clubs such as Mr. Lucky's, Club Sobriety, Club Quorum and the Hammer Dropper are sprinkled throughout the city.

Club Retreat, a million-dollar facility on Carpenter Road near N. Saginaw Street, opened briefly in the early 1990s.

Two new hot spots in the early 1990s were The Network Nightclub on S. Dort Highway at Hemphill Road and Beaver's Sports Lounge on Clio Road near Myrtle Avenue.

Many night-life devotees said they regularly drive to Detroit to visit nightclubs.

"I can't say there are any serious dance halls (in Flint) now," said Robert Matthews, of the twenty-something crowd.

"Four or five years ago, I would frequent (downtown) The Copa college night and even on Saturdays when they had things going on. (But) there really are not a whole lot of dance clubs. The (downtown) Hot Rock was off and on."

Matthews said he occasionally dropped by the Weekday Wind-Down, an after-work gathering sponsored by black radio station WDZZ-FM at various downtown locations.

"I go out to be social, but I don't necessarily find tons of enjoyment," he said.

AMUSEMENT PARKS:
"We went separate from the white kids."

Samuel and Susie Skipper have raised a family and successfully navigated nearly 50 years of marriage since this newlywed photo was taken in 1947 at the old Flint Park amusement park.

Jazz vocalist Ella Fitzgerald was one of the well-known artists who once performed at Flint Park, an amusement park in northwest Flint. Her appearance, with the Chick Webb band during the 1930s, was said to be an occasion that drew a large black audience.

Flint Park was one of Flint's two amusement park success stories. The 39-acre park operated between April and Labor Day from 1920 until 1960.

But first came Lakeside Amusement Park on Thread Lake, which opened in 1911. It is uncertain when or why Lakeside closed but it appears to have been a casualty of the Great Depression, which hit in 1929. An old newspaper article listed it as part of the estate of David D. Aitken, a prominent Flint attorney, who died in 1930. And in 1935, it was sold after a foreclosure.

The nine-acre property was sold to the city of Flint in 1939, redeveloped as a recreation center and renamed McKinley Park in 1942.

Both Lakeside and Flint Park were popular for family outings after church on Sunday or for special occasions like the Fourth of July fireworks.

Indoor roller skating rinks at both parks were extremely popular with teens and young adults.

Lakeside's half-mile roller coaster was the longest in the state when it opened in 1916, according to The Flint Journal's files. From its 65-foot-high apex, riders could see over the entire city to surrounding farms.

Hot-air balloon ascensions were another crowd favorite.

"We didn't go up in the air. We'd watch them go up in the air," said Alexander Jones. "But that was fun to watch them blow up the balloons."

Jones would ride the streetcar from his north-side home to Lakeside, paying the 7-cent fare from his shoeshine earnings.

Lakeside also offered canoeing and picnicking at adjacent Thread Lake Park. Other amenities included a dance hall, a miniature auto racetrack, a baseball diamond and spectator stands and concessions buildings. Auto shows were held there.

Some said that the area remained a favorite youth swimming hole long after the park closed permanently.

Across town, Flint Park was billed as a "first-class establishment." It had up to 15 rides in its heyday, including a roller coaster, Ferris wheel, carousel, swing rides, water ride, dodgem cars and loop-the-loop planes.

Kiddie Land had a miniature railroad, golf course and cars, swan boats and live pony rides.

Flint Park's dance pavilion was touted as the largest in the county. The park also had a family-style clubhouse, concert auditorium, sporting grounds and a picnic area.

Roller skating contests and beauty pageants often were held at park facilities.

Park admission was free, but individually priced tickets were sold for rides and some attractions. Free-ride days during the 1930s and 1940s, sponsored by the Mott Foundation and later Hamady Bros. grocery stores, were well-remembered treats.

The Mott Foundation distributed park and bus passes at local playgrounds. So many children participated that they had to be assigned different days to go, determined by where they lived. For example, all children who lived on the south side went on the same day.

James Todd recalled that in 1929 specific days were set aside for blacks to visit the park.

"Sometimes twice a week they'd let the blacks go over there. On (those) days ... the whites stayed home," said Todd, who was about 15 then.

Ruby Turner Noble added: "If I remember correctly, we went separate from the white kids. I think we went late on Friday."

Others recalled designated nights for blacks to use the roller skating rink.

Transportation to the parks sometimes posed a problem, too, depending on where you lived.

"Flint Park was a long ways to walk," said Milton Port, who lived on the south side. "If you weren't fortunate enough to have streetcar fare, most of the time we walked wherever we wanted to go."

Turner Noble walked from the St. John Street neighborhood where she grew up in the 1930s.

"The (Hamady) grocery store would give us (admission) tickets and we'd walk over there because we didn't have money for bus fare," she said.

MOVIES:
"There was a theater on every corner."

In the 1960s, Sondra Rawls recalled: "The Nortown Theater was the hangout for everybody on the north side."

For Ruth Scott and her teen pals in the 1930s, the ritual spot was the Michigan Theater on S. Saginaw Street near 12th Street.

"All of us south-side kids met at the Michigan on Saturday," Scott said.

Neighborhood theaters served as a primary social outlet for several generations of young blacks. Show time was almost every Saturday night or Sunday afternoon.

"That was all there was to do," said Annalea Bannister, a young patron

Many theaters operated throughout Flint until the 1970s. The downtown Capitol Theater, said to be the grandest, is the only one that survives.

in the 1930s. Much has changed since then.

For one thing, blacks no longer have to sit in a "colored only" section in the balcony.

And in earlier times, the show opened with cartoons and newsreels instead of movie previews. And you didn't have to leave when the movie ended. So if you arrived after the movie started, you could stay to watch the part you'd missed.

Fred Waller reeled off the names of some of the downtown movie houses he frequented as a youth – the State, the Strand, the Garden, the Palace, the Rialto and the Capitol.

Also there were the Columbia, Richard and Tilden theaters on the north side.

Some described the era as a time when it seemed like there was a theater on every corner. About 1930, Flint had some 17 theaters, according to The Flint Journal's files. Most of them closed between 1950 and 1965. And the 1980 opening of the Showcase Cinemas complex in Burton dealt the final blow.

Only the Capitol Theater on E. Second Street survives. Though it hasn't screened a movie in nearly 20 years, the stage is used for concerts and variety shows. The building has been designated a historic site.

Going to the Capitol, in earlier times, was a dress-up occasion.

"The Capitol Theater was the premier theater in downtown Flint," said William Hoskins. "Lots of blacks went to the Capitol. They had this beautiful pipe organ. You could hear it outside."

Inside were 1,986 seats surrounded by ornate walls and lavish furnishings. Built in 1927, The Capitol was called an "atmospheric auditorium" because of features such as a painted ceiling that created the illusion of a starry sky and fountains and statues recessed in wall nooks that gave the effect of a Roman garden house.

"That was a first-run theater," said Robert Pea. "When new movies came out, the Capitol had (them) first. We'd walk down on Sunday and ride the trolley back."

The Palace, on E. Kearsley at Clifford streets, also commanded well-dressed audiences. It had a new stage show every week, said Ruth Buckner. Some local stars from those shows later became professional singers, she said.

Cowboy movies were the house specialty at the Strand and State. They stood side by side downtown next door to Michigan National Bank.

At the Columbia on St. John Street and the Richard on Leith Street, mainly black audiences took in second-run and B movies, and talent shows. The Columbia was the only place showing specialty movies such as "Cabin in the Sky," a 1943 musical starring a black cast.

Midnight horror movies at the Richard were favorites of Maxie Brandon and his siblings. Their spooky post-midnight walk home, after watching "Frankenstein" and "Dracula," was part of the thrill, Brandon said. He especially liked teasing his sister by running off and leaving her.

The Rialto featured all-night movies. It was located on S. Saginaw Street where Citizens Bank is now.

The Garden once stood at the corner of E. First and Harrison streets where Genesee Towers is now.

Other well-remembered movie hangouts ranged from the neighborhood Tilden Theater on Tilden Street at Industrial Avenue to the spacious Flint Cinema on S. Dort Highway, built in 1967, which had a 1,000 seats and a screen 60 feet wide and 30 feet tall.

One treasured feature of those old theaters was that they were "right in our neighborhood," said Anna L.V. Howard, who lived near the Michigan on

S. Saginaw Street, where the Sunshine Bible Shop is now located.

Admission was once a nickel for children and 10 cents for adults. The price crept up to at least $1.25 by the time many of the theaters closed.

APPEARING LIVE:
"It's not all glamour and glitz."

Dottie Patton & the Blue Notes in 1952 featured internationally known musicians Patton on the piano (right) and Sherm Mitchell on trombone (seated, second from left). Also shown are, Jordan McCree on bass, Floyd Moreland on tenor sax, Wesley Jones on drums and Matt Garrett on trumpet.

Dorothy Patton struck a few chords on her organ and gospel-flavored music soared and vibrated enchantingly through the room, though she was playing with one ailing hand.

With a trickle of notes, Patton gave a quick history lesson in jazz styles from the progressive jazz era of the early 1930s through the traditional jazz era, be-bop and experimental jazz to the contemporary new wave era.

Speaking through her organ, Patton played a danceable series of upbeat notes she called Dixieland jazz, the style played commercially by Louis Armstrong and Duke Ellington, she said. Next came a brooding series of sustained notes she called black style.

"If I played that in a white supper club, they wouldn't know what I was doing," she said. "That's Jimmy Smith style." She explained that Smith was an internationally known organist but probably unfamiliar to most whites in Flint.

For more than 40 years, Patton's versatility kept her working the Flint nightclub circuit and throughout North America and overseas. She is but one of many successful musicians who calls Flint home.

Sherm Mitchell, a one-time member of Patton's band, has also been making waves in music internationally since the 1930s.

The 1960s launched the Velvelettes, who were said to be the first female group outside Detroit to be signed by Motown. Two of its four members are from Flint.

Actress and singer Dee Dee Bridgewater won a Tony Award in 1975 for her role as Glinda the good witch in "The Wiz," a black version of "The Wizard of Oz." A graduate of Southwestern High School, Bridgewater has released several albums, appeared on television shows and entertained abroad.

An all-male group, Ready for the World, first topped the R&B charts in 1984 with hits like "Oh Sheila."

Three members of the group Midnight Starr are reportedly from Flint.

When the rap era took off in the mid-1980s, Flint contributed (Eric) M.C. Breed, who had cut four albums by the early 1990s.

Vocalist Rhonda Clark, formerly of Mt. Morris, has released two albums. And Vann Johnson sings backup for pop idol Michael Bolton.

There are, no doubt, many others, but those were some of the names mentioned most often in reminiscing.

Taking it from the top, Dorothy Patton's musical career began at age 16 when she opened The Fraternal Club, Flint's first jazz club. She was so young her mother had to ask permission from their church board. Patton had been chosen for the job by Jesse Leach, a prominent Flint physician and civic leader.

"He told me to go to Stevens Moving Co. on Broadway and pick out a piano, and he would pay for it and put it in the club," Patton said. Leach also hired someone to drive her to Detroit to find backup musicians.

The six men Patton chose included Wardell Gray, a saxophone player "who turned out to be the greatest of all of us," she said. He too was only 15 or 16, so his mother had to be persuaded to allow him to come to Flint.

"My mother promised that he could live with us at our house and she would look after him, fix his meals and keep him clean," Patton said.

At age 19, Patton started touring with her band, the Blue Notes. Travels took them as far as Newfoundland and the Azores islands, she said.

Patton first played piano but switched to the organ in the 1950s when big bands became too expensive for small clubs. The organ is "an orchestra by itself," Patton explained.

Among her career highlights were a Canadian USO tour and a Motown booking. There also were occasional lows like the time she had to integrate a nightclub in Chilicothe, Ohio. The doorman refused to allow her black friends to come in to hear her play.

"I said, 'They are my people and if they can't come in then I'm going out. Either they come in or you haven't got a band.'"

Patton said the doorman threatened to charge her with breach of contract, but luckily, the club owner was in his office checking the books that night.

When he heard what was happening, according to Patton, he said to the doorman: "No. 1, you're fired. And No. 2, I don't care if a black chimpanzee comes to the door, if it's got on a white shirt and a tie and a suit, and some money in its pockets, you let it in here because that's what this place is about, making money. And money ain't got no color."

Patton called that her worst experience. She said she was less bothered by knowing that white musicians were paid more or that being a female, a rarity in the jazz industry, often shut out her of jobs that went to men.

As jazz clubs died out in the 1960s and work became harder to find, Patton began spending more time in Flint. But giving up the road meant a drop in earnings. Patton sees Flint as more of a rhythm and blues town than jazz. That made it harder for local jazz clubs to draw a large enough audience six nights a week to stay in business, she said. Larger cities, like Detroit, have a more diverse professional community to generate crowds, she said.

Since 1981, Patton has been teaching children.

"I've got them playing jazz, some playing gospel and some playing classical," she said.

She's saving the rest of her knowledge for a book she plans to write, tentatively titled "The Jazz Heritage of Flint and Vicinity," she said.

Sherm Mitchell, Patton's ex-band mate, worked at most local nightclubs in the 1940s and 1950s. He entertained at balls at the IMA in the 1940s and played at the Durant Hotel.

Mitchell is mostly self-taught and plays the saxophone, trombone, flute, oboe, and some percussion and strings, among other instruments.

In 1944, at age 14, he landed his first professional job at Flint radio station WFDF, as part of a junior high school orchestra.

"There wasn't a lot of live music during the war years," Mitchell said. "Most of the people I used to play with were ... in the military or they had wartime jobs. So I worked a lot as an adult musician. I worked in a lot of adult bands."

The Velvelettes included Flint cousins Norma Barbee Fairhurst and Bertha Barbee McNeal and were Flint's link to Detroit's influential Motown label and sound in the 1960s. Pictured here is the original lineup (from left): Mildred Gill Arbor, Betty Kelly (who later joined Martha and the Vandellas), Bertha Barbee McNeal, Norma Barbee Fairhurst and Cal Gill Street.

In the late 1960s and early 1970s, Mitchell started touring, beginning in Mexico and the Caribbean and later in Europe. He writes his own music and has released two albums, "Far From Tranquil," in 1988, and "Once Upon A Lifetime," in 1992. He's also recorded with other musicians.

"My music has been all over the world," Mitchell said. "I get a lot more performance calls than I take."

There has been a Sherm Mitchell Day in Flint in his honor. His home is decorated with numerous plaques and awards and he has accumulated 25 albums of photographs and thousands of performance tapes and music videos.

"Music is like a marriage," Mitchell said. "There's a lot of give and take. Part of my give and take is that my music doesn't make everybody happy, but it makes me happy."

One reason he has made albums, he said, is to inspire future generations. His message to up-and-coming musicians is: "You make happen what you want done. Music is what you do. You believe in it."

When Detroit's Motown sound exploded in the early 1960s, Flint cousins Norma Barbee Fairhurst and Bertha Barbee McNeal signed on as two-fourths of the Velvelettes. Other members, Mildred Gill Arbor and Cal Gill Street, are sisters from Kalamazoo. The female quartet shared studio time and fellowship with many Motown greats.

"That's where we met Marvin Gaye and Stevie Wonder, Diana Ross and the Miracles, Claudette (Mrs. Smokey) Robinson, the Temptations and others," Fairhurst said. "We were a family. We had corporate picnics and staff meetings."

Fairhurst further argues that the Velvelettes were as good or better singers than the more-celebrated Supremes, which included superstar Diana Ross. To prove her point, she cited a talent show won by her group competing against the Supremes. It was a fund-raiser and promotion staged by Motown owner Berry Gordy Jr. Judging was done by the audience, which gave first place to the Velvelettes, Fairhurst said.

And she noted a second occasion when Dick Clark, host of TV's "American Bandstand" teen dance program, requested the Velvelettes for a tour he was promoting. But Gordy would not send them without the Supremes, Fairhurst said. Both groups went on the tour and later to the renowned Apollo Theater in Harlem, N.Y.

"There is no doubt in my mind that we were the best," Fairhurst asserted. "Our routine was unusual. Our harmony was tight. We were creative, much like En Vogue today. We sang a cappella, did five-part harmony, did jazz chords like Take 6. Nobody else was doing that."

Unlike many other Motown artists of that era, the Velvelettes also could read music and play piano and were going to school, Fairhurst said.

The Velvelettes formed in Kalamazoo where Arbor and McNeal were students at Western Michigan University. Still in high school, Fairhurst would visit her cousin McNeal on campus on weekends. Street was still in junior high school. A temporary fifth Velvelette, Betty Kelly, also was in high school.

The young women competed in a talent show at a campus fraternity party. Berry Gordy's nephew heard them and invited them to audition in Detroit.

Several months later, they signed a contract, Fairhurst said. Actually, their parents signed for them because they were under 21. They did so reluctantly because of Motown's rule against having a lawyer present, Fairhurst said. One stipulation in the contract their parents insisted on was that the girls not be taken out of school.

Thanks to shrewd negotiations, the Velvelettes are one of few Motown groups who own the rights to their name, unlike the Supremes, the Marvelettes and others who were named by Motown, Fairhurst said.

"We thought our sound was smooth like velvet so we came up with the Velvelettes," she said.

Fairhurst said she wrote the group's first release, "There He Goes," but didn't get credit for it because that's how things were done then. Their first hit, "Needle in a Haystack," was written by Norman Whitfield, whose name is associated with many Motown hits. Later, the Velvelettes landed a Top 40 hit with "He Was Really Saying Something."

In the mid-1960s, they performed at Flint's IMA in a Motown Revue that included Stevie Wonder, Marvin Gaye, the Supremes and more.

"That's how we would tour," Fairhurst said. "That's (camaraderie) what made it so fabulous.

"I'd do my homework on Friday night and catch the bus to Detroit on Saturday morning. The others would take the bus from Kalamazoo. We synchronized our arrival times to take a cab together to Motown.

"Sometimes we would be recording late at night. We had to wait our turn. We'd sit there and talk with Marvin Gaye. He was waiting his turn. He'd talk about being careful if we went to the Apollo."

Stevie Wonder called Fairhurst "songbird," she said, because of her high-pitched singing voice.

Fairhurst remembers Diana Ross as hard-working and determined to succeed.

"The majority of the time it didn't seem like work because we enjoyed it," she said. "(But) it got to a point where it seemed like they owned us. It was uncomfortable.

"When traveling, we always had a chaperone. We couldn't go shopping or eating alone. We had to take a nap to get ready for a performance. It was sort of a caged-up feeling. So when I got a chance to come home, it felt free. I welcomed the chance to get out, to lead a normal life."

Besides, making music was a sideline for the Velvelettes, unlike some of the acts for whom Motown was a career, she said.

The Velvelettes all became successful businesswomen. Fairhurst is sales and marketing director for the Radisson Riverfront Hotel in Flint. Arbor is a registered nurse at McLaren Regional Medical Center. McNeal teaches music and in the early 1990s was working on a doctorate. Street works for the Upjohn Co. in Kalamazoo.

Years after their Motown days, Fairhurst said she learned from Berry Gordy's sister, who runs the Motown Museum in Detroit, why the Velvelettes never got a big break.

"She said, 'I used to keep telling Berry back then how good you girls were and to promote you along with the Supremes and he wouldn't. ... He didn't want your attorneys on his back.'"

One of Fairhurst's goals today is to ensure that other artists don't run into such problems.

"We'd like to educate young blacks on things they should know to be in the business – how to read a contract, write a press release, have an attorney and an accountant, the business end," she said. "It's not all glamour and glitz; that's about 5 percent. The rest is hard work. If you're a good business manager, you can go far in this business. A lot of black entertainers have not had people to school them. We didn't."

In the late 1980s, 30 years later, the Velvelettes achieved modest stardom when a London promoter tracked them down through Motown's Los Angeles office.

"Motown nostalgia music was really big in Europe," she said. "We went over (there) and that started things all over again."

A Motown Revue album, that includes two Velvelettes songs, went gold in 1992. A collector's album of their old songs is in the works.

"Needless to say, we never thought we'd be a part of history," Fairhurst said. "Our picture hangs in the Motown museum. It gives a good feeling."

Sondra Rawls noted that singing groups were a big thing in the late 1950s and early 1960s. She never landed a contract but was part of a female trio that won a local talent competition at the Fifty Grand nightclub.

"We were like 14 or 15," she said. "They'd have five or six acts. Every week they'd have a different winner. Now that I think about it, it might have been set up. We didn't really win.

"It seemed like then, everybody and their brother ... like the scriptures say, 'everywhere two or three are gathered,' ... well, wherever two or three gathered, they had a harmonizing group. You had four or five guys on every corner harmonizing. Some of them were quite good."

The Flint Emeralds was one such group, she said.

A group of young men who were her neighbors gained their 15 minutes of fame with a local hit called "Booger Bear." Their processed hair and "high-water" pants gave them a uniform look.

"They had a cement ledge outside of their house," Rawls recalled. "All the neighborhood girls lined up across that ledge while (the boys) were in their house practicing. Sometimes they'd come out on the porch. They had a harmony that would not wait."

The Four Kings were a 1950s-era "doo-wop" group from Flint, according to The Flint Journal's files. The four young men enjoyed brief fame in Michigan and Ohio, opening for headliners such as Miles Davis and Della Reese.

The Kings formed to compete in a talent show at Central High School. Later, they performed at local nightclubs before signing with Detroit's Fortune Records, releasing several singles.

Three of the former Kings – Edward Little, Chester Simmons and Julius Smith – became kingpins on the Flint City Council. Other group members (Simmons was a replacement) were LaVern Rawls and Pete Hartfield, a shop worker who later signed with Motown Records.

The 1980s introduced a new breed of Flint recording artists with rapper Eric M.C. Breed, members of the group Midnight Starr, Ready for the World and a few female vocalists.

Memories and details are sketchy about the Midnight Starr members, but it included three Flint men – Bo Watson, Melvin Gentry and his twin brother, said local promoter Bernard Terry.

The young men started out in the 1970s, at about age 9, performing in a Flint group called Young Generation, Terry said. They entertained at local parks and special events such as the Black Arts Festival. They had left Flint by the time they joined Midnight Starr.

Midnight Starr disbanded and the Gentrys' whereabouts is not known but Terry mentioned that Watson, a keyboard player, did production work on a (singer) Toni Braxton album.

Ready for the World burst onto the national scene in 1984 with two hits, "Tonight" and "Oh Sheila." The album went platinum in 1986, selling more than 1.5 million copies. It spelled overnight success for members of the group – Gregory Potts, keyboards; Melvin Riley Jr., lead vocalist; Gordon Strozier, lead guitar; Willie Triplett Jr., percussion and keyboards; Gerald Valentine, drums and keyboards; and John Eaton, bass player.

RFTW has released several albums and performed benefit concerts in Flint.

In 1989, vocalist Rhonda Clark of Mt. Morris had a Top 10 hit with "State of Attraction" from an album produced by Jimmy Jam and Terry Lewis, a talented team that also has worked with singer Janet Jackson. In the late 1980s, Clark signed with Tabu Records, a CBS subsidiary.

Vann Johnson grew her stage legs as a model and singer in shows in Flint and Detroit before becoming a backup singer for pop artist Michael Bolton's band in 1991. Her first break came in Hollywood in 1989 when she appeared in an Eddie Murphy music video. She is the eldest daughter of Flint City Councilman Matt Taylor.

As of the mid-1990s, rap artist M.C. Breed had made four albums. His first included the hit "Ain't No Future in Yo' Frontin,'" in 1991. A high school dropout and probationer, Breed got his act together, earned his GED from the Flint Academy and got busy musically. He started out with Kidd Blast and the Task Force and went solo in the late 1980s.

CLUB AND SERVICE ORGANIZATIONS:
"We started meeting from house to house."

Working to make Flint a better place to live and work were an abundance of social and service groups like this one.

"I remember you had a certain time to go to bed and a certain way to make up the bed – to crease the corners," said Lennetta Bradley Coney, describing her stay at Hamady House.

The donated mansion was part of a 12-acre estate on Branch Road. Girls, ages 10-14, who were involved in the Stepping Stones program, spent a week there polishing their social skills.

"That's where you learned which spoon to use, which fork, how far to space it from the edge (of the table), using your index fingers," Coney said.

"That's been years now, and I remember it still when I'm setting my table for guests or making up my bed. I think it was an enriching experience that contributed to who I am today."

Stepping Stones, founded in 1938, was sponsored by the Mott Foundation and administered by the Flint Board of Education.

Hamady House provided an opportunity for the races to mix, said Coney, a Stepping Stone member in the late 1960s. The second-floor dormitory could hold about 25 girls at a time.

"The bus would take you to school every day and pick you up and take you back, so you'd get homesick. But it was a great experience.

"There were white girls and black girls there. That was one of the first exposures on both sides. Here you are, sharing a big room full of bunk beds."

Meantime, Coney's future husband, Craig Coney, and other black boys were learning etiquette and social skills in the Bachelor's Club. That was a small group privately sponsored by Johnnie and Frankie Wynn, a black couple.

"I would cook dinner and they would set the table," Frankie Wynn said.

The boys are men now but still talk about those experiences when they meet, Johnnie Wynn said.

Boys also participated in the YMCA-sponsored Gray Y, while in elementary school, and in High Y, as junior high and high school students.

In the early 1940s, Charles Hamilton participated in High Y at Emerson Junior High and at Northern High.

"I guess it was one way of getting the black guys in a club," Hamilton said. "We met right after school. I think it was primarily to keep us off the streets."

Some High Y activities were organized by the Rev. Arthur Davis of Bethel United Methodist Church. He was widely praised as a mentor and role model for black boys.

One president of Viking High Y at Northern grew up to become president of the Flint City Council, Hamilton pointed out. That is Johnnie Tucker, who represents the Third Ward.

Other men who grew up in Flint remembered sharpening their leadership skills in the Police Athletic League boxing club or in the Boy Scouts. Girls were involved in Girl Reserves and Girl Scouts.

One popular children's event during the 1950s was a Tom Thumb wedding. Children, including the bride and groom, made up the wedding party in this make-believe ceremony. It was held in a church and said to be as lavish as adult nuptials, right down to floral arrangements and formal attire.

Elsie Pratt of 'Hats by Elsie' taught millinery classes at the Durant Hotel in the 1940s.

Many south-side residents spoke fondly of Edith Robinson, a church worker, who coordinated youth activities at the Clifford Street Center for 26 years.

North-side youth divided their leisure time, depending on the era, between Berston Field House on N. Saginaw Street, the Flint Community Center on Dewey Street (built in 1925) and the St. John Street Community Center.

Through the years, Flint has offered all sorts of social clubs for men, women and children. Some groups have centered on church and some on such hobbies as golf, bridge, chess or bowling. Others sprang up to satisfy social, political, educational or professional interests.

Men bonded in clubs including the Masons, Elks, Veterans for the Promotion of Civic Affairs, Old Timers and fraternities.

Women's groups included sororities and service organizations such as Zeta Alpha Gamma, The Links and the National Association of Negro Business and Professional Women's Club Inc.

Parents organized a local chapter of Jack and Jill to promote the social, academic and cultural development of children ages 2 to 18. Lifelong friendships were formed for some children who participated in local group workshops and attended national conferences. The group also held an annual ball.

Lavish formal balls are rare nowadays, but for many years, several were hosted by various groups. People looked forward to them and sometimes schemed to get invited.

Some of the best balls were said to be sponsored by The Sportsman's Club, the Community Civic League (African-American Ball), the Unique Social Bridge Club, The Cotillion Club and the Greek-letter organizations.

In 1965, Michigan NAACP President Edgar Holt and his wife, Lois, hosted an African Ball to promote community diversity. Held at Flint's National Guard Armory, the event attracted a standing-room-only crowd of about 1,000, Lois Holt said.

The Holts often hosted visiting African students and helped many re-settle to Flint.

The Flint Chapter of the NAACP, founded about 1922, has long been a key organizer of civic and social activities.

"Of course, everybody belongs to the NAACP," said Marion Coates-Williams. "The first thing you hear, is, 'You know you ought to take out a membership.' " But outside of making a financial contribution, most members are not very active now, she said.

Charles Hamilton joined the NAACP in 1945, at age 17, because of its record for effecting social progress.

"At 17, you know that things aren't right in society; you know that you're segregated," Hamilton said. "You go to school and see all those white kids, and they go down to this neighborhood and you go to that one."

Joan Lewis, a Flint NAACP secretary during the mid-1960s, cherishes the memory of getting a call from the White House. It happened while Whitney M. Young Jr., National Urban League executive director, was visiting here.

Young served on several presidential commissions during the Kennedy and Johnson administrations. Someone at the White House, needing to get in touch with Young, called Lewis' home.

"I was so excited," she said. "President Lyndon Johnson's office called my house. I will probably never forget that."

Civil rights concerns forged groups such as the Urban League of Flint (1943), the Community Civic League (late 1950s), and the Concerned Pastors for Social Action (1969). Briefly, during the 1970s, a small chapter of the militant Black Panther Party was active in Flint.

Over the years, various community centers have sponsored group

A chorus line of black beauties pose for the judges in a 1940s contest sponsored by the Sporstman's Club, a leading social organizer.

---

activities for children and adults. Those have included sports, arts and crafts and dances.

Hobbyists came together to form the Flint Snowbird Ski Club and the Great Lakes Golf Club, later renamed the Vehicle City Golf Club.

Bridge clubs were popular in the 1940s and 1950s. They had descriptive names such as Just Us, Hard Knocks, Smart Set, Jollibums and the Unique Bridge and Social Club.

The Unique Club on Leith Street had the distinction of having its own building and evolving from a private social club into a business.

Ruby Turner Noble recalled that her mother was one of the organizers in the mid-1950s. The group obtained a liquor license and ran the nightclub for quite a while, she said.

Smart Set was a group of black women who met in each other's homes. They only played against each other, not other clubs, Eloise Caldwell said. The 12 members made up three tables of players. New members had to be recommended by an established member and voted in.

"Attorney Joe Birch would come and give us lessons," Caldwell said. "We were not serious bridge players at that time. I think he enjoyed being with the women as much as we enjoyed having him."

Every year, the club sponsored an invitation-only ball at the IMA. About 500 people would attend, Caldwell said. They also held dances at the former Great Lakes Country Club.

Twelve men organized the Hard Knocks Bridge Club in 1948, said Layton Galloway, who joined in 1953 and was active until it folded in 1993.

"The ladies' clubs (met) on the opposite Saturdays than the men, so they would save that baby-sitting money," Galloway said.

"We had one contest at Fairview School with the men and women in competition and the women beat us. I think that was because they paid a little more attention to what they were doing and the men were too busy mouthing (boasting)."

Black bridge players also participated in tournaments at the Durant Hotel, sponsored by the American Bridge Association, he said.

Galloway taught bridge from the late 1950s to early 1960s in a recreation program funded by the Mott Foundation. His students in the two-hour, 10-week session were men and women, blacks and whites, he said.

Bowling is another recreation with a long history in Flint, but black enthusiasts said they were barred from local lanes until after World War II.

Black boys could not bowl at the alleys though they were working there as pin setters (before automation), Katie Ellis Harper said, noting that her uncle was one of them.

She recalled that the Century Bowling Alley, on North Saginaw near the Durant Hotel, closed shortly after blacks were allowed in.

During the 1960s, Harper worked as a cashier at the Duck Pin Bowling Alley on Industrial Avenue at Parkland Street. It was owned by Connie Childress, a black entrepreneur, and a white partner.

"It was mostly a black clientele," Harper said. "The neighborhood was mostly black by then, but some whites came to the bowling alley."

Zeta Alpha Gamma, better known as The Zags, formed in the late 1940s, said Annalea Bannister. Despite the Greek-sounding name, it was a social club, not a sorority. The Zags sponsored skits and musicals to raise money to give scholarships to black youth.

Local chapters of traditional Greek fraternities and sororities started in the early 1950s, Bannister said. Few blacks were enrolled in local colleges then, so graduate chapters were formed by those who had gone to college elsewhere. Sororities included Delta Sigma Theta, Alpha Kappa Alpha and Zeta Phi Beta. Among the fraternities were Kappa Alpha Psi, Omega Psi Phi and Alpha Phi Alpha.

Also, blacks formed chapters of society groups – the Masons, the Elks and Shriners, and the women's auxiliaries, Order of the Eastern Star and the Daughters of Isis.

A men's group called the Old Timers Club started about 1932, said James Wesley, a longtime member.

"The only thing we had back then was the Old Timers," he said. "We used to get together and sit down and talk. The purpose is to reminisce and tell lies, one after the other." Sports and life in general are main topics.

In the mid-1990s, the group was still meeting on the first Tuesday of every month at a local restaurant. Their bond is strong. When a member is hospitalized or has a death in the family, other members arrange to send fruit or flowers, paid for from a fund set up for that purpose.

When members who have moved away from Flint come back for visit, they are drawn to a club meeting to drink beer and catch up, Wesley said.

But their camaraderie has created somewhat of a political problem.

"The women want to get in it, but it's all male," Wesley said. "That burns me up. We don't want them in there. Why can't they organize their own?" He explained that with no women around, the men enjoy freedom of expression, including liberal use of foul language. Otherwise, membership is open to anyone interested, he said.

Alexander Jones, also a member, added that Old Timers should be at least 65 years old in order to be knowledgeable about old times.

The Vets Club has a similar format. It was organized in December 1952, said A. Glenn Epps, a member since 1953.

"At the time we started, we all were Korean War veterans," he said. "We started meeting from house to house. We were all single and had just returned from Korea."

"I named the club, based on the idea of what we wanted to do: Veterans for the Promotion of Civic Affairs. We had ideas in mind other than social. We always used to give to all the fund-raising efforts – the Jerry Lewis Telethon, United Negro College Fund, holiday baskets."

The Vets Club on S. Saginaw Street was built to provide a meeting place for blacks, Epps said. It has garnered a reputation as a social club and is open to the public. Most club members are war veterans.

Similarly, Club 13 was a private social group for Navy veterans, said Sam Williams, a member and World War II veteran. The 13 in the name corresponded to the number of founding members.

Religion brought some groups together.

"There was a center called the Christian Center run by a woman called Rev. Jimmie Johnson," said Marion Coates-Williams.

"She fed children. It was sort of like the social services we're doing now. We got a lot of help from the North Baptist Church on Saginaw Street near Hamilton Avenue. One of the men at that church gave us a lot of things. We were like his project."

Johnson's Christian Center on Pasadena Avenue also was the headquarters of the Women's Christian Temperance Union and Youth Temperance, which she headed. Scout meetings also were held there.

Other young church members were active in the Christian Endeavor League and the Baptist Young People's Union (BYPU).

Forming private clubs was one solution to boredom because "back then, there weren't too many things blacks could do," said Vivian Pugh, born in 1928. She belonged to a teen social club that met once a year in Mt. Morris. She thought it was a big deal because it involved a Greyhound bus ride from Flint.

In the late 1930s, Annalea Bannister's teen group was called 12 Topper because of the number of members. They had met in the Girl Reserves in elementary school and wanted to keep the group together in high school. Twelve Topper hosted house parties and other social activities, she said.

About the same time, Anna L.V. Howard was a member of the Society Debs that met at the Clifford Street Center. Odell Broadway, a noted social and civic leader, taught the Debs poise, flower-making and other social skills, Howard said.

About 1941, Charlotte Williams and friends started a social group called the Ritzy Teens. To distinguish themselves, they wore navy skirts and burgundy sweaters with white letters, she said.

In the mid-1940s, Ruth Scott and friends formed a teen social club called the Charity Girls.

"We held a couple of dances at the Clifford Street Center and charged a quarter to get in," she said. "One of my girlfriend's older sister was our chaperone. She was 20. That's why our parents let us have this club."

In her early 20s, circa 1945, Theresa Crichton became one of the Foxy Foxes. The 12-member social club continued to meet at each other's homes for about 20 years, she said. They hosted dances, fish fries and picnics.

Ruth Buckner belonged to the Community Aidettes service club and the Homemakers Club, which sponsored a three-day family event at Tyrone Hills Camp around Labor Day.

As a young adult, she was active in Flamingo Families Inc., which hosted weekly potlucks at the YWCA. Families took turns providing entertainment such as a black history presentation. Buckner's husband called square dances.

DOWNTOWN AND OTHER SOCIAL VENUES:
"Downtown was beautiful to me."

Downtown (1961) used to be a bustling place where there were several theaters and stores galore.

Downtown Flint was THE social and shopping center until the suburban shopping mall takeover started in 1970.

"Oh yes, we used to walk downtown," said Marion Coates-Williams, who was born in Flint in 1922. "It was fun. All kinds of things going on down there.

"We used to have such a nice downtown. We had Smith B's (department store) and The Vogue and Lerner's and Kresge."

Some popular stores through the years included Neisner Bros., Miller-Wohl and Bush, The Fair, J.C. Penney, Sears and Montgomery Ward.

"I wish we could revitalize our downtown," Coates-Williams said. "We used to have a lot of movies we could go to – the Capitol, the Palace, the Michigan.

An early 1950s Christmas display in the window of the landmark Smith-Bridgman's department store in downtown Flint captured the attention of Jacqueline Weaver (left), shopping with her family. Some blacks said they were welcome to shop at the store but few were hired as clerks in those days.

You were going someplace when you went to the Capitol. It used to have a pipe organ and doves that looked like they were floating around in the alcove, not real doves. It was pretty in there."

Except for a few small shops in the St. John area, downtown was the only place to shop, Gladys Dawkins said. She recalled buying shoes for her children at Drew's and dresses for herself at Betty Richards.

"Downtown was beautiful to me," she said, wistfully.

Joan Lewis fondly recalled walking downtown to buy a hot dog at the Original Coney Island, located where the Radisson Riverfront Hotel is now. She bought candy and peanuts at Schiappacasse's Candy Kitchen on S. Saginaw Street near the Flint River.

Having a vital downtown nearby tempted many Central High School students to play hooky, Fred Waller said.

"All the stores were open," Waller said. "They had Christmas decorations. All the theaters were open. The Durant Hotel was open but you couldn't go there until later." He frequented Kresge's five-and-dime store where he bought sodas and hamburgers.

Downtown parades of the 1950s left a lasting impression.

"I can remember being a kid and seeing the big Chevrolet parades," said Ernest Johnson Jr.

Anna L.V. Howard added: "The streets would be crowded with people. We'd have beautiful parades from Fifth Avenue to the old Durant Hotel."

Several mentioned the fun they had at Playland, a games arcade and magic shop, located about where the University Pavilion is now.

Besides downtown, other entertainment and leisure outlets included listening to the radio, roller skating, bowling and having a picnic in the park.

WAMM-AM (1420), was one of the first radio stations to offer programming for the black community. WAMM debuted in 1955, broadcasting from dawn to dusk from an old house on S. Grand Traverse.

Sam Williams, a radio personality, was WAMM's director of gospel and spiritual music for 20 years. In 1979, he moved to brand-new WDZZ-FM (92.7), Flint's first black-owned radio station.

WAMM is believed to have been the first radio in the state to have a black co-owner, Ernest Durham, a disc jockey, Williams said. The station went out of business in 1981 and became WFLT.

Milton Port, born in 1912, said he didn't have a radio until he made one in high school. It was a crystal set that had to be listened to with earphones. Port used to sit up nights sharing the earphones with his family.

When Port's family bought a battery-operated radio in about 1928, that wasn't exactly easy listening either. The batteries lasted about a week before they had to be recharged, he said. That involved walking down to the gas station to get them recharged for a small fee. You could get a loaner while your battery was being recharged, Port said.

Television sets began trickling into middle-income black households in the early 1950s and were pretty much a standard fixture by the mid-1960s.

Other favorite pastimes such as checkers, billiards, horseback riding, roller skating and softball games filled many leisure hours.

Dances were held almost every weekend. The house party provided a popular dance hall option, though most dances were also held at community centers, in schools or at rental facilities such as the National Guard Armory.

"There were lots of quarter parties at people's houses or waistline parties where admission was based on the size of your waist," said Gregory Pridgeon, who grew up in the 1960s and 1970s. "If your waist size was 20, you paid 20 cents to get in."

Rent parties were held to raise rent money, he said.

Cabarets came to town right after Prohibition ended in 1933, said Alexander Jones. Then, the illegal bootleg joints got liquor licenses and went legitimate, he said.

Good times have always rolled at roller skating rinks. For most of the 20th century, it has been a weekly ritual and youth hangout.

Bessie Brooks, who was born in Flint in 1906, skated at Lakeside and Flint Park amusement parks, a rink on St. John Street and at the Arcadia downtown.

"I was a roller skating fanatic," she said. "Boy, did I love it."

Fanatical skaters in the 1940s and 1950s made their memories at a rink on N. Saginaw at Louisa streets. No one remembered the name but the location was faithfully recited time and time again.

In the 1970s, Skateland Arena in Mt. Morris was the place to be on Monday nights. In the 1980s, the hot spot was Rollettes on N. Saginaw Street near Hamilton Avenue.

Ice skating has had its devotees, too.

"We used to ice skate down off of Seventh Street in that area where city hall is now," said Annalea Bannister. A pond there froze over in winter.

A frozen spot behind Berston Field House on the north side was popular with ice skaters.

"It would be full of people, black and white," said James Todd. "Most of the kids during those days got a lot of outdoor activity. We didn't have no TV. We had radio, but nothing kids were interested in. There was no inside entertainment unless you were going to a house party. (TV) ruined our country, especially our kids."

Mayor Woodrow Stanley pronounced his Flint childhood in the 1950s and 1960s as "fun."

"Folks will probably say, 'But weren't you poor?' " he said. "Yeah, but I don't remember that being an obstacle to anything we wanted. I know that I didn't have everything I wanted but not to the point of creating bad memories."

He and his friends devised ingenious ways to have fun without money. Sometimes they were mischievous but did no harm, he said.

Many structured activities for children who grew up in the 1960s and 1970s were eliminated in the 1980s, when funding dried up. The Mott Foundation was often mentioned as the primary sponsor.

The IMA offered Safetyville, a miniature village of streets and buildings in Kearsley Park, created to teach children about traffic and pedestrian safety rules.

From 1963 until the early 1980s, delighted children drove miniature cars through the streets of Safetyville. The IMA turned ownership of Safetyville over to the Flint parks department in 1978. It was eventually torn down after unsuccessful attempts by other groups to restore it.

"With the socioeconomic plight of broken families (not just here in Flint, but everywhere), I've notice a decaying effect because the funding levels have been reduced, and there's not the same level of activities that I enjoyed as a youngster," said Lennetta Bradley Coney.

"I never felt, as an child or adult, that there was nothing to do in Flint. My parents always made sure there was something to do and I guess that carries over to my adulthood. I'll pick up in a minute and go to Chesaning or Davison or shopping. When people come to visit me, they know I'll give them a good tour of the city and surrounding areas."

Debra Taylor, who reached adulthood in the late 1970s, said she tended to go to Detroit for entertainment and still does.

"Detroit still is the area where the concerts occur, where a lot of the plays of interest to the African-American community are held. There's more to do there, more jazz clubs, more social life," said Taylor who lived in Detroit eight years, after graduating from Michigan State University in 1977.

Many black families take interest in Flint's cultural life. They have taken art classes at the Flint Institute of Arts or attended Flint Symphony Orchestra concerts, recitals at Bower Theater and plays at McCree Theater and enjoyed performances by national artists at Whiting Auditorium.

James Todd teaches ballroom and square dancing to senior citizens at McKinley and Hasselbring community centers and sometimes Berston Field House.

"I've been doing it about 25 years," he said. He learned from Melvin Butler, a black man who gave lessons at the old Clark School for a small donation.

And last but not least on the leisure circuit, the Flint area offers a variety of recreation at nearby parks.

One local favorite was Dewey Woods, now Forest Park, on Flint's north side. Families used to picnic there and enjoy amenities such as a petting zoo. The huge, tree-lined park has been neglected and prone to criminal activity since the 1980s.

Richfield Park was a popular site for picnics and softball games in the 1970s.

Ophelia Bonner Park, formerly Jefferson-Oak Knoll Park, has hosted numerous black community events in the 1990s such as local radio station's WDZZ's Sizzling Summer Cook-off, a barbecue grilling contest and promotion.

The park was named for a tireless civic worker who raised funds to develop it. Bonner also raised 15 foster children, provided college scholarships for needy students and was the founding secretary of the Flint NAACP chapter. She died in 1982 at age 84. Bonner Park is believed to be the first in the state named for a woman, according to Flint Journal files.

Families that had transportation traveled to the Holly Recreation Area, Kensington Park or Detroit's Belle Isle.

Children of Flint's more prosperous black families recalled summer vaca-

Forest Park in north Flint was a popular gathering spot until the early 1980s when crime problems led to barricades being erected to eliminate congested 'cruises' like this one.

---

tions at Idlewild, a black resort area near Baldwin in northern Michigan. Idlewild's peak years were from about 1938 to 1960.

In its heyday, Idlewild attracted as many as 5,000 middle-class blacks per season from throughout the Midwest, according to Flint Journal files. Its Club Paradise featured top entertainers including Duke Ellington, Cab Calloway and Count Basie.

The Idlewild Lot Owners Association in Flint had 17 members. There were also chapters in Chicago, Baldwin, Detroit, Cincinnati and Dayton.

"My parents used to go to Idlewild when I was a little girl," said Virginia Lewis Heller, who was born in 1946. "That was where all the black people used to go in the early '50s.

"They were mostly prominent, like your doctors. They all went up there. From what I understand, they had clubs and stuff up there and they would go up there and socialize and have a good time. They would come back talking about Idlewild. They liked Idlewild. Then it kinda died out."

Some blamed Idlewild's demise on a fire that destroyed its major social club. Some said the community eventually became run-down and lost its allure.

Others said that Idlewild died out because civil rights progress opened other resort areas to black vacationers.

Athletics

Hall-of-famer Ellis Duckett, a member of Northern's 1950 state championship team, guaranteed his spot in the legends book when he scored the winning touchdown in Michigan State's 1954 Rose Bowl victory.

Robert Matthews asserts that Flint has produced more ranking athletes per capita than any other American city. And he is mainly talking about his 1980s-era generation that included outstanding players such as Andre Rison and Carl Banks in football and Jeff Grayer, Glen Rice, Eric Turner and twins Pam and Paula McGee in basketball.

Matthews' view might not be certifiable, but it is no idle boast that Flint is the home of a large number of nationally known athletes, especially African-Americans.

"That's no joke," said James Blakely, who can trace the sports tradition back to the 1950s when he was a softball player of note.

"Whenever they scout for potential athletes, they come to Flint."

Blakely named many of the sports giants from the 1940s, 1950s and 1960s. He knew some of them personally.

Among the football greats he cited were Don Coleman, Bill Hamilton, Leroy Bolden, Art Johnson, Lee Jones, Jesse Thomas and Freddie Williams.

Hamilton, Thomas, Jones, Johnson and Williams also excelled in other sports. Bolden signed with the Cleveland Browns in 1958, probably the first black from Flint to play in the National Football League.

Baseball produced top-flight players such as David Hoskins, who played professionally for the Cleveland Indians in the 1950s.

In basketball, Justus Thigpen Sr. played for the Detroit Pistons in the early 1970s and Floyd Bates Sr. played with the Harlem Globetrotters from about 1942-45.

Some of boxing's knockout kings included Benny McCombs, Auburn Copeland and Floyd Fielder, Blakely said.

Among the top performers in track and field were James Luckado, James R. Johnson and Bates.

"Sports then was different than now," Blakely said. "When I came to Flint (in 1948) as a teen-ager, kids didn't do a lot of things people do now. We didn't have the cars to ride in, ... but now these kids, before they get out of junior high school, they have brand new cars. So they wind up with a lot of other things to do.

"My enjoyment was to get up in the morning and go down to the St. John Street Center and spend the day down there playing ball. If we wanted to go out to Beecher, we'd walk out to Beecher to play softball."

Some say that Flint owes its incredible athletic history to organized sports programs and fine facilities like Berston Field House on N. Saginaw Street.

Some credit might be due to the abundant recreation programs and clubs offering training and competition in dance, golf, tennis, bowling, skiing, figure skating and more.

Those neighborhood playground contests seeded the development of some of Flint's greatest high school athletes. But they had to not only be good athletes but also good students.

Academic standards for athletes have changed since the early 1940s when Charles Hamilton ran track and played varsity basketball at Northern High School. Athletes who were performing poorly in the classroom could not participate in school sports, he said.

Hamilton noticed that only about one in 10 players on the team was black and wondered why, because he knew some of them could play as well as he did.

"What happened (is) a lot of guys weren't eligible academically," Hamilton said. "If they could not get their cards signed every week by the teacher, they couldn't play. During the season, if you had a game, you had to have the card signed. We had to have, if I'm not mistaken, a C average."

Sam Williams remembers that era as a time when there was less incentive for black athletes to pursue sports other than for the love of it.

"When I was a kid there was nobody black playing (major league) basketball or football – not until after WWII (1945)," he said. "Then things started to open up some when guys came home from the service.

"There was nobody (black) playing professional (sports). Basketball hadn't even started as a national (league) sport. There was nobody on the tennis circuit. Sports wasn't integrated.

"Jackie Robinson was the first black guy into baseball on a national level, playing for the Brooklyn Dodgers (1947), but they had a black baseball league and they traveled around, had players better than those (in the major leagues).

"Proof is Satchel Paige, a pitcher for the Cleveland Indians. He didn't come to the (American) League until he was in his late 40s. Nobody knew his age for sure, but he was so good he could pitch until his outfielders would sit down and he'd strike out the team."

Until the 1890s, major league teams had black ballplayers, but segregation laws then banned them from the sport. So Jackie Robinson actually re-integrated major league play after about a 50-year hiatus.

Williams saw Robinson play at Atwood Stadium in 1945. He was playing then for for the Kansas City Monarchs of the Negro National League.

After signing with the Dodgers, Robinson made a guest appearance at Atwood in July 1950 to raise funds for the Boys Baseball Program.

During that visit, The Flint Journal reported Robinson traded quips with David Hoskins, who two years later became Flint's first black major league ballplayer.

Hoskins was pitching that night for the Dayton Indians in the second game of a double-header at Atwood.

Robinson and Hoskins had competed against each other in the Negro League when Robinson played for the Kansas City Monarchs and Hoskins was with the Homestead Grays. Their conversation reportedly went something like this:

"Remember that night in Kansas City when I hit a a home run off you," Robinson teased Hoskins. "It went a mile."

"Yeah, and remember when you came up the next time and I struck you out," Hoskins shot back.

"Sure, I still remember that the pitch which was called a third strike was way inside and you know it, too," Robinson retorted.

"All I know," Hoskins laughed, "is that the umpire said strike three and it was still strike three after you got done arguing."

Robinson visited Flint a third time in 1963 for a program at Quinn Chapel AME Church, celebrating the 100th anniversary of the Emancipation Proclamation.

Several famous African-American athletes have made guest appearances in Flint. Joe Louis, the world heavyweight boxing champion from 1937 to 1949, played softball in Flint many times. And Jesse Owens, gold medalist in track and field in the 1936 Olympics in Berlin, East Germany, came to Flint for an exhibition.

Speaking of famous athletes, many Flint-grown champions have garnered national and international recognition. Male and female athletes have distinguished themselves at the college level, in Olympic competition and in professional sports.

Their names can be found among inductees into the Greater Flint Afro-American Hall of Fame, the Greater Flint Area Sports Hall of Fame or other state, collegiate or national shrines.

To give recognition to the famous and the not-so-famous, Flint's Afro-American Hall was organized in 1984. One of its goals was to preserve the records of overlooked sports standouts from earlier eras.

By the mid-1990s, more than 60 names were enshrined. Five to eight more are added each year.

Plaques honoring them are on permanent display in the lower level of the Flint Public Library's main branch. Each honoree is depicted in uniform with a list of career highlights.

"We've had some tremendous sports heroes in this town," said Maxie Brandon, an AAHF inductee in 1994 and one of its founders.

"Many of them didn't receive the attention they should have because they were black," he said. "The local media tended to mention them minimally, if at all.

"Proof of this was when the Afro-American Hall of Fame started. We were at the library checking in the archives back in the early 1920s and late 1900s. These fellows that were so great, (we) couldn't find hardly any documentation on them. We could find some but not what we should have found on them for the caliber of athletes they were."

Grady Carpenter, for example, was one of Northern's best linemen ever, Brandon said. But the AAHF research committee could not find enough information about him to support an induction.

"Every now and then you'd see (an article) where the coach would call him one of the greatest lineman or (say) if you could play like Grady Carpenter ... but they never gave his statistics. So you can't induct a person into the hall of fame on just that. You've got to have some statistics for children to look at and identify with."

There are untold stories about players like Bill Cavette who inspired what Brandon called one of the first acts of union solidarity in Flint. It led to Cavette of Central becoming the first black black captain of any high school sport. This happened sometime in the 1930s, as best Brandon can recall.

"His teammates voted for him to be captain of the squad (but) the administration and the coach and all those powers-that-be told them there would be no black captains in sports at Central," Brandon recalled. "But his teammates got together and told the administration and faculty that if Bill Cavette couldn't be the captain then they wouldn't play basketball. Now that's what you call brotherhood.

"(The team) was mostly all white. Bill was the only (black) starting and leading his team in scoring and what not. His teammates saw his value to them as a leader (while) his coaches and others couldn't see it."

Among the first former sports heroes to be inducted into the AAHF were Percy McClellan, Houston "Mickey" McKell and James McCrary.

McClellan is believed to have been the first black football player at Central High School. McKell was noted for baseball, football and basketball and Brandon called McCrary "one of the best baseball players this town has ever had."

"He went to Michigan State from Flint Northern (in the early 1930s)," Brandon said. "He really wanted to play baseball because when he was at Northern he batted somewhere in the neighborhood of .500 and hit some of the longest home runs ever hit on a baseball field in high school. (But) when he got to Michigan State, the first thing they told him was 'You go out for the football team (because) no blacks play on the baseball team'. He had to play football and of course, he became one of the greatest fullbacks in the history of Michigan State."

Halls of fame and playground legends teem with stories like McCrary's.

The AAHF ensures that future generations will remember outstanding athletes such as Edward Simmons, a black tennis pioneer in the 1930s, and James Navarro Wardell, who was Flint's first black high school student to letter in golf (1946).

According to Simmons' 1994 induction listing, he was the first black to win Flint's novice tennis title, the first to represent Flint at the state tournament in Detroit and the first to win a state tournament match, all in 1938. From 1935 to '38, Simmons played in three National Negro Tennis Association tournaments.

Wardell won most valuable golfer honors at Northern in 1946 and the most medals in 1946 and 1947. He was a runner-up in the Negro National Tournament in 1947 and the first black to play in the Michigan Junior Amateur Tournament in Lansing in 1948. He was the captain of the state championship team at Flint Junior College in 1950; they placed second in the 1951 state finals.

The AAHF has preserved the memory of the St. John Women's Softball team that was the city champion and state semifinalist in 1940. Stella Williams Robinson, a softball pitcher in the 1940s, is so far the only individual female inductee (1990).

Managers and trainers such as boxing's Clair W. James and Deeyamporte "Dee" Cavette and softball's Harold Johnson and James "Jimmy" Jones have been duly enshrined.

James Wesley, a 1989 inductee for his baseball and bowling record, would like to see more support for the hall of fame from former Flint athletes who have gone on to successful professional careers.

"We write them and ask for donations and don't get a reply," he said. "They've forgotten where they came from."

Many Hall of Famers and former athletic standouts have excelled outside of sports.

Southwestern's former star linebacker Reggie Williams, an Ivy League graduate, was appointed to the Cincinnati City Council in 1988 and won re-election the following year. His community service work would take too many pages to list but earned him the Jackie Robinson Humanitarian Award, presented by the U. S. Sports Academy in 1990.

Northern football great Leroy Bolden advanced to become a doctoral student, admissions director at Stanford University and an electronics consultant in California's Silicon Valley.

Northern football, basketball and track star Al Washington painted portraits of many Flint civic leaders and murals in or on local buildings.

Central track and football star Jesse Thomas played professionally with the

Baltimore Colts and the Miami Dolphins before becoming an assistant professor at Morgan State University in Maryland.

Life after sports carried Central star lineman Don E. Coleman, now a Ph.D., back to his alma mater Michigan State as an associate professor in the College of Osteopathic Medicine and dean of the graduate school.

Golden Gloves champion boxer Herb Odom is a wealthy Chicago dentist and entrepreneur and Jay Watkins is a Flint minister.

And that's just for starters.

PLAYGROUNDS:
"I lived at Berston."

Berston Field House was a home away from home for youth from all over the city who were drawn by assorted recreational activities – swimming, baseball, ice skating, boxing and more.

A painted-on sign shining up from the gym floor of Berston Field House proclaims it the "Home of Champions." Few can argue with the legend or the trophy-filled showcase in the lobby or the memories of thousands of athletes who honed their skills there.

A full range of organized activities at Berston has included swimming, boxing, dance, horseshoes, tennis, basketball, baseball and softball.

In winter long ago, the flooded baseball diamond became an ice-skating rink. Crowds of skaters, black and white, would cruise around the makeshift rink.

Inside, there was a library, an auditorium, meeting rooms, a gym, a kitchen, locker and shower rooms and more.

The venerable, north-side community center was named for Neil J. Berston, whose widow and sons donated the land in the 1920s.

"I lived at Berston," said Jimmy Jones, who came to Flint in 1918 at age 6. "That was the playground. Some of the greatest athletes in Flint came out of Berston. All colors. The history of Berston reads like a who's who in the world of sports."

Maxie Brandon has been at home there since the 1930s. On a guided tour, he can point out all the special features and tell you how each room has been used over the years.

Brandon is among the aging center's loyal fans fighting to preserve it. After a lot of effort, it was finally designated a state historic site in 1994. Brandon is hoping that designation will bring in more funds badly needed for restoration work.

The tan stone exterior of the building looks presentable and all the windows are intact, but waist-high bushes poke through floor cracks in the huge, outdoor pool that closed in 1978.

The multipurpose gym floor, in what was originally the auditorium, was installed in the mid-1980s. So were the lightweight, energy-efficient steel doors that replaced drafty, wooden doors throughout the two-story building.

The original gym on the left side of the building is now an activities room, where senior citizens play cards and checkers. A few fitness buffs walk the planks of a circular track on the second level, overlooking the activities room.

In the basement, debris, grime and a faint smell of urine attest that the shower and locker rooms have not been used for a long time.

Voices echoing throughout the building belong to retirees greeting each other, players ribbing each other on the basketball court, students arriving for dance lessons in the second-floor studio or boxing practice in the basement, and casual visitors.

A stage at one end of the auditorium-cum-gym is used for community events such as talent shows or political rallies.

Berston is one of two community centers serving predominantly black north Flint.

Just about every face in the place now is black, which is just the opposite of the center's early years. When Berston opened, blacks were allowed in on a limited basis such as to use the library, and then only if escorted by a teacher on a class field trip, Brandon said.

For more years than anyone seems to remember, blacks were assigned one day a week to swim in Berston's pool.

"We would always have access to the pool after it had been used by the white community," Brandon said. "And when we finished using the pool, that evening all the water would be drained out. All the splash boxes would be emptied. The next day, the white community would have clean swimming water and clean splash boxes to step in before entering the pool."

Under community pressure, those rules eventually changed and blacks and whites swam together, he said.

Ailene Butler said she thinks that blacks did not gain open access to Berston's pool until the 1950s. By then, whites were moving out of the neighborhood as more blacks moved in and the city recreation department had stopped taking good care of the pool, she said.

Discriminatory practices at Berston didn't stop at the pool.

At one time, blacks were barred from leagues Berston sponsored, Brandon said. Old photos in the center's lobby show some of those all-white teams.

A black basketball team called The Owls was one of the first allowed to play at Berston, Brandon said.

In other discrimination, black athletes sometimes got second-rate equipment.

"When the black children would go to check out bats and balls, the bats would be cracked and had been taped and tacked back together," Brandon said. "The balls were either raggedy or the hide had come off them.

"But we had some white friends in the community we had become close to. When we'd want a good bat and a good ball to play with, we would always tell Tony or Steve to go check out the bats and balls. Then we'd get a good ball and bat to play with."

Young blacks were accustomed to improvising in recreation.

"Back in my day, they didn't have the facilities like they do now," said Alexander Jones, who's lived in Flint since 1925.

"Every vacant lot was a softball diamond. I learned to swim in the Flint River."

Many youngsters broke collar bones and suffered other bruises from playing softball without pads on the hard ground behind Berston, Jimmy Jones said. Back then, home plate bordered Dewey Street and balls would be hit toward Berston, he said.

James Wesley called it "the rock pile."

"It's a nice, beautiful place down there now, but when we played it was rocks and glass and what have you," he said.

Wesley was one of those champions Berston boasts about. Over the years, he played for several outstanding softball teams.

By the 1970s, baseball was a dying sport in Flint. Youth participation was so low that city-sponsored leagues were closing.

Basketball replaced it as the dominant sport at Berston. On some days, more than 100 youth crowded into the gym, waiting for a chance to play.

It marked the end of the sunshine epoch when television, video games and home computers moved youth activities indoors.

"We did all the different games because we didn't have TV," said Susie Duckett-Skipper, who grew up in the 1930s and '40s.

Girls then and in earlier decades enjoyed yard games like hopscotch and hide-and-seek.

Or, they'd rig a board on an old pair of roller skates to make a scooter. In winter, they'd build snow forts and have snowball fights. On occasion, they visited the petting zoo at Dewey Woods, now called Forest Park.

Duckett-Skipper ran track, played softball and swam at Berston three times a day. Some activities took place at the St. John Street Center and later at a recreation center at St. John and Leith streets, she said.

The Y Teens program at the YWCA offered dinners, parties, dances and swimming. Duckett-Skipper learned to swim after falling out of a canoe at Y Camp one summer.

Marion Quinn and Rachel James, who are sisters, would walk 16 blocks to Berston to use its tennis courts. Other times, they went to nearby Buick Park on Selby Street or Richfield Park.

Bessie Brooks liked spectator sports like the baseball games at Athletic Park and neighborhood sandlot games. Athletic Park near the old IMA in downtown Flint was a popular playing field. Atwood Stadium on Third Avenue was another.

In the 1930s and '40s, Charles Hamilton said he and his friends created their playgrounds wherever it was convenient.

"We played baseball in the street," he said. "We played football in the street. Sometimes we'd play on the grass. Sometimes we'd go up to Parkland (School) to play."

Other than house parties, there were few indoor amusements for youth in the 1930s, Sam Williams said.

Most of his recreation centered in the neighborhood or at the St. John Center where there were baseball diamonds, tennis courts and a football field.

The St. John Center had playground equipment and a full range of programs, said Robert Pea, who worked there 22 years.

From the early 1930 to the late 1940s, all races used the center. Everybody got along well and some are still friends now, he said.

In the 1950s, the St. John Center was Woodrow Stanley's main hangout. Berston was off-limits because he wasn't allowed to venture that far from home.

The St. John Center offered almost everything Berston did. The only thing it didn't have was a pool, which is why St. John kids had to go to Berston, Stanley said.

Besides, swimming at Berston cost a quarter, so a popular alternative for Stanley and friends was skinny-dipping in a swimming hole in the Flint River off W. Boulevard Drive.

They had to swim without trunks because those would have alerted their parents to what they were up to. Parents would have been concerned about their safety. The swimming hole was muddy up to their knees but Stanley and pals had fun. Luckily, no one got into trouble or drowned, he said.

A generation earlier, Freddie Williams and his buddies frequented another "illegal" swimming hole dubbed Sandy Bottom, between Massachusetts and Rhode Island avenues, off the right bank of the Flint River.

"It was illegal because our parents didn't want us down there," he said. "We went so much we wore a path through there. As soon as you passed the (swimming) test over at Berston, the older guys would let the younger ones come." They were around 10-12 years old.

Neighborhood parks were heavily utilized in those days.

Avid basketball players, Stanley and his pals, when they were older, shot hoops in just about every park in the city, he said. He would ride around with a basketball and his gym shoes handy at all times.

That's where many local legends were born. People like Rodney Young, who played football, and Richard Dicks, a boxer, were neighborhood heroes, Stanley said.

"We didn't have TV and the NBA like now, so the guys in the neighborhood were the stars."

Stanley also enjoyed spending two weeks at Mott Camp. It was a big treat because his family could not otherwise afford summer camp.

"At camp, you had kids from the other side of town. It gave us a chance to interact," Stanley said, adding that he would like to offer today's urban children similar opportunities to spend time out in the country.

The community schools concept was thriving during Sondra Rawls' youth in the 1950s and 1960s.

"School was open all the time," she said. "They had a lot of family activities. It was like a ritual once or twice a week."

Like their north-side counterparts, south-side youth spent a lot of time on school playgrounds, at neighborhood parks and in organized activities at community centers.

The Clark School playground and the Clifford Street Center were favorite gathering spots.

They also swam in the pool at Lakeside Park or secretly took a dip in Thread Lake.

Like at Berston, blacks at one time were allowed to use the Lakeside pool on designated days during the week, said Fred Waller, who grew up in the 1920s and '30s. The injustice of that was that they were welcome any time to spend their money at Lakeside Amusement Park.

Waller also frequented Kearsley Park and other neighborhood gathering spots.

Tennis matches were played on courts at Liberty Street and later on Sixth Street.

For winter fun, prior to the 1960s, south-side youngsters enjoyed sledding on Harrison Hill at Seventh Street, behind Flint City Hall where the expressway is now.

Brennan Park Community Center, dedicated in 1971 on Pingree Avenue near Stewart School, offered various activities including softball games. The adjacent playground had been dedicated a park since 1957.

By the early 1970s, many of the favorite neighborhood and area parks were in decline.

Angela Sawyer remembers hanging out at Forest Park during her high school years at Northern, but the shady park was already past its glory days.

"There would be a steady stream of bumper-to-bumper cars and you'd drive through," Sawyer said. "It was just a thing of hanging out. That's why they closed Forest Park because they felt they couldn't control (the crowd). It was perceived as too many blacks in one spot instead of actual danger."

Sawyer's family spent a lot of leisure time in the Genesee Recreation Area off Carpenter Road, she said. They would picnic and fish.

Family gatherings also took place at Richfield Park or Bluebell or Goldenrod Beach.

Some outings took families to recreation areas outside Flint. Some of those mentioned were Metamora Park, Lobdell Lake, Shea Lake, Kensington Metropark, Belle Isle and the Idlewild resort near Baldwin.

IN THE BALLPARK:
'It was rough but it was fun."

All-around athlete James Luckado was a Northern track star in the 1940s and once pitted his speed in a friendly race against famed Olympics-medalist Jesse Owens.

One professional career was born on a hot July day in 1938, before a crowd of about 3,000 at Flint's Athletic Park.

The old ballpark, built in 1907, was located near Harrison Street and Fifth Avenue where the AutoWorld parking lot is now. It was home base for Flint's beloved Yellow Dogs.

Flint's famed Yellow Dogs were state baseball champions in 1940 and unofficially served as a farm club for several professional players in the late 1930s and '40s.

The semiprofessional Yellow Dogs were playing against a Detroit team organized by Joe Louis. Yes, the same Joe Louis who was the reigning world heavyweight boxing champion. In fact, Louis was playing first base that day.

The Dogs' home-run king, Eli Copeland, stepped up to bat, whetting the crowd's anticipation.

"I hit a ground ball and slid into first, crashing into Louis," Copeland said. "Joe fell and I ended up on top of him. He got up, pulled me up and shook my hand. Nobody was injured."

Louis' team won, 4-3, but the collision served as an introduction of sorts. Louis later hired Copeland to play with the Joe Louis Punchers from 1947 to 1950. It was a crowning achievement for an exceptional player.

Copeland, who is now listed in two sports halls of fame, started sharpening his skills at a young age by playing with neighborhood boys four or five years older.

"I was really competitive with them," he said. "Anything they had, they picked me to play with them. When I really realized I had talent was when I started traveling."

Copeland started with the Berston Midgets, playing sandlot ball. In 1934, he joined a Berston team called the Flint Pioneers and from 1935-36 was with North Michigan, the predecessors of the Yellow Dogs, for which Copeland played from 1937 to '41.

"We had a group of guys who were the best softball team in the state," he boasted. He led the team in batting statistics from 1937 to 1940.

The Yellow Dogs won the state championship in 1940.

One of the players, James Todd, claims credit for starting the team.

"A guy in the (illegal) numbers racket gave me $50 and told me to buy some balls and bats and shirts," Todd recalled. "A lady named Mrs. Harding was a seamstress and she sewed the name on them for us."

The uniforms were yellow with black letters. The name was the same as the sponsor's racket.

"The team went on to become famous, state champions and everything," Todd said. "They paid us at different times. Not much but $2-$3 was a lot of money in those days."

For a time, the Dogs traveled with a boys team called the Yellow Dogs Midgets. Sam Williams was one of them.

"They called us Midgets because we were kids, but we played teams a lot older than us," said Williams, a retired postal worker and radio personality.

"We traveled all around to play. Wherever they had a team that would play the Yellow Dogs, we'd go there. We'd play with their young kids before the big game. People paid to come to the game; it was that kind of professionalism.

"They got paid a small amount, but even they were playing for the sake of playing," Williams said.

"Every one of them had a (regular) job somewhere. They weren't playing for a living, they were playing for entertainment ... recreation, to have something to do.

"Some of the guys on the Yellow Dogs were recruited by Joe Louis to play on his team. Joe Louis had professionals. He got the best guys from everywhere. Our guys here, the Yellow Dogs, were good enough to play (Louis' team) but they always beat our guys. But it would be a tough battle."

The Yellow Dogs played from about 1936 to 1941. Members included Copeland, Todd, William "Bill" Hamilton, Robert Pea, Percy McClellan, Harold Johnson, Benny McCombs, Oliver Roland, Willie Moore, Floyd Bates Sr., Sonny Wells and Herschel Pritchard.

Copeland and Hamilton graduated to professional careers with the Joe Louis Punchers. Copeland also played part time for a year with the Ethiopian Clowns of Cincinnati in the Negro National League.

Copeland traveled and played with the all-black Punchers from 1947 until the

Major-league pioneer Dave Hoskins, who signed with the Cleveland Indians in 1953, is Flint's version of Jackie Robinson. He helped re-integrate baseball at great personal cost.

---

team disbanded in 1950. They played mostly big cities and did not experience the discrimination that some ballplayers of that era did.

"We didn't have problems getting waited on," Copeland said. "We avoided those places; wouldn't play in those places."

Bill Hamilton, who traveled with the Punchers in late 1940s, was named to the All-World Softball team in 1945 as leading hitter for the Flint-based M&S Orange team. His outstanding multiple-sport career began in high school.

He set a city football scoring records at Northern High in 1942 and won state track and field titles in long jump and high hurdles in 1941 and 1942, respectively.

A legend in his time, William Hamilton excelled in multiple sports at Northern, played professional softball and was director of Berston Field House for nearly 20 years.

He was named Michigan Athlete of the Year in 1942 and 1943, Rookie of the Year in the National Fast-pitch League in 1948 and Mr. Softball in 1949.

Also, Hamilton is listed in the Michigan Amateur Softball Hall of Fame, the Michigan Amateur Sports Hall of Fame and the Greater Flint Sports and Afro-American halls of fame. He was director of Berston Field House from 1967 to 1984 and directed Flint's Golden Gloves boxing tournament from 1974 to 1986.

James Todd, a Yellow Dogs' founder, claims credit for another piece of Flint's baseball history.

"One of my relatives told me he had a relative down South who was always in trouble, but he was a good ball player," Todd said. "So I sent for him. To make a long story short, he came here and was such an exceptional player, whites supported him."

That relative was David "Wahoo" Hoskins who became the first black from Flint to play major-league baseball. He signed with the Cleveland Indians in 1953.

One of Flint's first black professional baseball players was Houston McKell.

Triple-threat Floyd Bates Sr. played professional softball and basketball and set a hurdles record in track at Southwestern.

In the early 1930s, he was with the Cuban Stars of Tarrytown, N.Y., of the Negro National League.

Hoskins also paid his dues playing in the Negro League and with segregated minor-league clubs.

From 1942 to '47, he played in the Negro League for the Ethiopian Clowns and the Homestead Grays, sometimes called the black "Yankees."

From 1948 to '51, Hoskins played in the Central League and Michigan State League. In 1952, he joined the Dallas Eagles, becoming the first black player in the Texas League.

The Eagles were a Cleveland farm team. They were reportedly looking for a black player because managers had noticed that black players boosted ticket sales around the country.

Jackie Robinson planted the seed in 1947 when he became the first black player in modern major league play.

Hoskins arrived in Dallas in March 1952, and by May, more blacks than whites were attending the games for the first time in Texas League history.

Hoskins pitched shutouts and broke team records, but being the only black player had its drawbacks.

"He went through hell," said Cora Hoskins, his widow, who still lives in Flint.

"The team was segregated," she said. "He couldn't stay with the team (in hotels). He had to stay with a (local) black family."

Spectators shouted nasty remarks from the stands and sometimes players on the opposing team roughed him up, but Hoskins' teammates were supportive and he took it all in stride.

"I don't mind the segregation in the hotels and I just don't pay any attention to the name calling," Hoskins told The Flint Journal in a 1952 interview. At the time, he was sitting in the Negro YMCA while the rest of team stayed at a hotel.

"Now that I've more or less broken the ice, it'll make it easier for other colored players to come into the league," Hoskins said.

He got his big break in the majors on the recommendation of Satchel Paige, the renowned Cleveland Indians pitcher, who reportedly told the team's manager, "You better sign this boy; he can hit."

Hoskins played a year with the Indians and spent part of the second year on the injured list, but he received a full share of losers' pay from Cleveland's 1954 World Series loss.

From 1954 to 1960, he played for other minor league clubs, then retired to Flint and went to work in the shop. He died in 1970 at age 47.

Hoskins was born Aug. 3, 1922, in Greenwood, Miss., the youngest of nine children.

His brother William Hoskins remembered him playing ball behind the barn and "getting a whipping for not doing his chores."

Dave Hoskins came to Flint in 1936 at age 18. He played Class A ball in the Flint City League. A 1939 newspaper article said he was batting an even .500 for the Flint Aces. He later played for Buick CIO and the Flint Amateur Baseball Federation All-Stars.

He met and married his wife while playing with the Cleveland Indians. Cora Hoskins traveled with him until the births of their children – three daughters and one son.

The couple always called Flint home but spent part of the off-season in South America, where Hoskins played winter ball, Cora Hoskins said.

One of the main reasons The Greater Flint Afro-American Hall of Fame was established in 1984 was to recognize unsung hometown heroes like Grady Truss, shown here circa 1929.

Unlike baseball players earning millions today, Hoskins didn't get rich playing professional ball.

"Today you couldn't get an agent to talk to you for what he was paid," his widow said. "But it was what he wanted to do."

William Hoskins played baseball on an all-black team in Flint's City League. Opposing teams were all-white. The games were at Athletic Park, Atwood Stadium and Whaley Park, Hoskins said.

The team traveled all over the state.

"Everybody in Flint played softball," said Donn Kersey, who was born here in 1918. "We used to have lots of fun at Clark School, lots of ball games going on. I didn't play much but I participated."

At age 14 or 15, James "Red Horse" Wesley considered himself good enough to play softball with grown-ups. Baseball was his favorite sport, but he also excelled in football and boxing.

Wesley was a strike-out king when he pitched for the City League from 1936 to '40 and won an invitation to try out with the Homestead Grays of the Negro League. His overall record was good enough to get him listed in the Greater Flint Afro-American Sports Hall of Fame in 1989.

Wesley's team won a City League championship but couldn't participate in the state playoffs because amateur league rules barred black teams, he said.

"They used to bring the Tigers here and the Cubs," he said. "They never picked any of us half-breeds to play against them. We were good (but) we couldn't call our life our own then. No matter how hard we tried.

"Sometimes we weren't even allowed in the park when some of those (major league) teams came into town."

One game stands out in his memory. It was a Fourth of July. His team had traveled by car to a place near Cheboygan in northern Michigan to play the hometown favorites.

Wesley's all-black team was pitted against all whites. Both sides felt an undercurrent of having something to prove.

The score was tied at 9 when Isaac Truss came up to bat.

"He was a showman," Wesley said. "He waved them (to move) back. They called him all kinds of names.

"He said if they put the ball over the plate, he was going to hit it. Honest to goodness, he hit that ball (it was an enclosed park). I've never seen a baseball hit that far in my life."

It was a sweet victory for a minute. Then tempers flared.

"The people started coming out of the stands," Wesley said. Luckily, their opponents showed sportsmanlike conduct and calmed the angry crowd by telling them, "They beat us fair and square."

"They always say the further north you went the better you get treated," Wesley said. "Whoever put that lie out didn't know what they were talking about. We got treated like dogs up there."

Jimmy Jones sometimes experienced hostilities during his travels as a team manager for 13 years and a player for about 40.

"They wanted us to play ball out there at Owosso, but they wanted us out by sundown," Jones said.

And when an incident in Saginaw turned ugly, "it was the first time I had mud thrown on me," he said.

Some of the towns they played in were so small, their hosts would plow a field to make a ball diamond.

"I'll never forget that 60/40 deal," Jones said. "If we lost, they only paid us 40 percent of what they took up. (They) passed the hat. But they fed us good.

"Things have changed now. There are blacks living in Owosso, going to bars if they want to."

Despite the hardships, Jones was a devoted student of the game. He made a point of learning all he could from anybody with something to teach him.

When professional players came to Flint, instead of asking for their autographs, Jones would ask for pointers like how to hit a curve ball.

Jones said he learned a lot from Ug Davis who played with the Negro League. He picked up more tips locally from "Old Man Odom who knew baseball from A to Z."

Putting the knowledge to work, Jones was a leading hitter, base stealer and run scorer in Flint's amateur baseball leagues in the 1940s. He was inducted in the AAHF in 1989.

In his capacity as a black manager for 13 years, he had an insider's view of local talent.

"Some of the best (softball) players I've ever seen in my life couldn't make it as a baseball player," Jones said.

"They could play softball but couldn't handle baseball."

The difference is that a baseball can come across the plate at 90 miles an hour, he said.

In the early days, players didn't have protective equipment and could end up with broken ribs. Jones knew a few who died after getting hit in the head with a ball.

Luckily, Jones' mother sewed a pair of pants for him that had built-in pads, so he could slide, he said. They came in handy in base-stealing. Still, he'd come home so stiff sometimes, he could barely walk.

"It was rough but it was fun," he said. They didn't get paid; they played for hot dogs and soda pop.

Some of Jones' teams included the Buick 20, a foundry team; Buick CIO; and the Unique Baseball Club.

Semiprofessional leagues brought many black ball clubs to Flint including the Homestead Grays, Cuban Stars, Chicago Giants and the Joe Louis Punchers.

There were business-sponsored teams such as the St. Clair Oil Company team and M&S Orange.

In the 1940s, James Blakely played with the Flint Bluebirds, the Flint Giants (later Percy's Catering), and the Flint Indians, a tricounty team. He traveled some with the Kansas City Monarchs and rubbed elbows with many local players who became professional athletes.

Harold Johnson is remembered as the first black manager of a city league softball team. From 1931 to 1950, he managed many teams including the semiprofessional M&S Orange. He also played on the 1940 Yellow Dogs state champion team. In his career, he won 812 games and lost 120.

By the 1980s, local baseball interest had struck out.

In a Flint Journal article in 1977, former pro William Hamilton lamented the change.

As Berston's recreation director, Williams supervised young athletes on a daily basis. The youngsters idolized basketball stars like Julius "Dr. J" Erving but ignored baseball standouts like Reggie Jackson, Hamilton said.

"I question the kids after a baseball game the night before," he said. "I ask them if they know how many hits so-and-so got last night. They don't know. (But) let me ask them how many points Dr. J got and they all can tell me."

SHOOTING HOOPS:
"Everybody in the stands went crazy over it."

Abundant local talent could be found on company-sponsored teams like this one representing Caldwell's grocer in 1947.

Northern's Charles Teaberry was the first black player in Flint known to soar off the floor while shooting a basketball, introducing the jump shot.

"He made it famous around here," said Norm Bryant, co-founder of the Greater Flint Afro-American Hall of Fame. "That became the way to shoot."

Teaberry's trademark one-handed, overhead jump shot contributed to conference championships at Northern and Flint Junior College in the early 1950s.

Before Teaberry and for quite a while after him, white players regularly made jump shots, but blacks preferred the hard drive to the basket to score, said Kenneth Jackson, who played for Southwestern in the

Former Northern teammates and co-champions, Terry Furlow and Wayman Britt, faced off in college play with Furlow (left) in MSU Spartan uniform and Britt as a UM Wolverine.

---

late 1950s and early 1960s.

"It wasn't part of our game. Not that we couldn't do it but we didn't do it," he said.

The jump shot changed the game because it made black ballplayers more versatile, Bryant and Jackson said.

"After we saw the damage it could do, it loosened up the game," Jackson said.

All-around sharpshooting on Flint-area basketball courts has produced some of the most shining moments in local athletic history.

High school teams' five-year clamp on the state Class A title, from 1981 to 1985, speaks for itself. Central started the reign with three straight titles in 1981-1983 and Northwestern's dream team carried on the tradition in 1984 and 1985.

Northern's cagers first brought home state titles in 1933 and 1936 and, after a 35-year drought, won back-to-back championships in 1971 and 1972.

A parochial school shared the champion's spotlight in 1963, when St. Matthew Catholic High won the state Class D title, led by three-sport standout Craig Metcalfe.

Most championship teams had more than one exceptional player.

Northern's 1971-72 championship team had Terry Furlow and Wayman Britt. Central, in 1981, had Eric Turner, Marty Embry, Mark Harris and Keith Gray.

Northwestern's 1984-85 sweep included Glen Rice, Jeff Grayer and Andre Rison.

Credit is also due to coaches Bill Frieder of Northern, Grover Kirkland of Northwestern and Stan Gooch of Central.

The 1980s were prime time for Flint hoopsters. Flint prep teams made the final four in Class A eight years in a row. And Beecher High School won Class B state titles in 1985, 1987 and was a runner-up in 1986.

Even women's basketball heated up with state championship seasons for Northern, led by talent such as Leteia Hughley and Judy Tucker. Six-foot-three twins Pam and Paula McGee, who anchored Northern's 1978 and 1979 state title teams, were doing the same for the University of Southern California in 1983 and '84. Pam McGee made the U.S. Olympic team in 1984, winning the gold medal.

Northwestern's Tonya Edwards helped bring home the state trophy in 1983 and '84 followed by NCAA championships in 1987 and '89 at the University of Tennessee.

But Flint's exceptional basketball reputation goes way back. Among the first to make names for themselves were Floyd Bates Sr., who played professionally with the Harlem Globetrotters in 1942; the brothers, Dodson and Grady Truss, who led their respective Northern teams to the state title in 1933 and '36; and twins Oscar and Arthur Ingram who anchored Central's city and valley championship team in 1947.

Another court legend is Justus Thigpen, who is believed to be the first black from Flint to play in the National Basketball Association. A senior-year sensation at Northern High School, Thigpen starred on teams at Flint Junior College and Weber State in Utah before he was drafted in 1969 by the San Diego Rockets of the NBA. After being released, he had tryouts with the Carolina Cougars and the Philadelphia Pipers of the American Basketball Association.

In 1973, when playing semiprofessionally for the Flint Pros of the Continental Basketball Association, Thigpen joined the Detroit Pistons for a short time. Later that year, he played briefly for the Kansas City Kings.

Thigpen is well-known on the recreation circuit as a veteran player

Eric Turner's name comes up whenever local sports fans compare 'greatest ever' lists. He led Central High's 1981 state title team and was a promising starter at the University of Michigan before turning pro early and fading from the scene after an unsuccessful tryout with the Detroit Pistons.

---

and as director of Berston Field House since 1984.

Whenever talk turns to basketball lore, Terry Furlow's tragic story comes up. Furlow, 26, died in a car accident in 1981 after a stellar career at Northern (state champions 1971, 1972), Michigan State and five seasons in the NBA. He was a first-round draft pick by the Philadelphia 76ers in 1976. He later played for the Cleveland Cavaliers from 1978 to '79 and the Atlanta Hawks and was with the Utah Jazz at the time of his death.

Glen Rice (left), the state's 'Mr. Basketball' in 1985, was on Northwestern's state-title teams, and later turned up the heat for Miami.

He is remembered as a great shooter who could really light up the scoreboard. He was inducted posthumously into the Greater Flint Sports Hall of Fame in 1991.

Wayman Britt, Furlow's teammate on Northern's 1971-72 state championship squad, is cited for his leadership ability. In 1986, he was captain of the University of Michigan team that lost the national championship game to unbeaten Indiana.

Trent Tucker of Northwestern played for the University of Minnesota before becoming the New York Knicks' first-round draft choice in 1982. He was traded to the Phoenix Suns in 1991 but released. He briefly joined the San Antonio Spurs before linking up with the Chicago Bulls in time for their 1993 NBA championship.

In recent basketball history, Central's Terence Greene left his mark in 1985. He was a three-year starter at DePaul University in Chicago.

Eric Turner, a legendary Central guard, was known for his showmanship.

Jeff Grayer, two-time state champion, at Nortwestern, Iowa State standout and 1988 Olympic medalist, held his own in the pros.

"He made an outstanding play dribbling down court between his legs and behind his back to keep it away from opposing players," said Kenneth Jackson, who saw Turner in action in the regional finals against a Saginaw team. "Everybody in the stands went crazy over it."

Jackson blames more theatrical playing styles on televised sports. Local players would watch idols like Magic Johnson perform tactics such as passing off the ball without looking and they imitated them, Jackson said.

Turner and Northwestern's Andre Rison became masters of the blind pass-off, he said. After three outstanding seasons at the University of Michigan, Turner turned pro in his senior year. He was drafted by the Detroit Pistons but didn't make the final cut.

Grayer, Rice and Rison were the crown jewels of Northwestern's back-to-back state titles in 1984 and 1985.

Grayer played college ball at Iowa State and earned a bronze medal with the 1988 U.S. Olympic basketball team. He was a first-round draft pick by the Milwaukee Bucks in 1988. After becoming a free agent in 1992, he signed with the Golden State Warriors.

Rice's trophy case is crowded, too. Besides the twin state titles at Northwestern, he was voted "Mr. Basketball" in 1985 by the state coaches association. He was most valuable player in UM's 1989 National Collegiate Athletic Association championship victory over Seton Hall.

Rice became Flint's highest first-round draft choice in 1989 when the Miami Heat selected him fourth overall. He signed a multimillion-dollar contract.

Rison chose to pursue a career in football, signing first with the Indianapolis Colts and later with the Atlanta Falcons and Cleveland Browns.

FOOTBALL GREATS:
"If we won, we had bragging rights."

Before "Monday Night Football" or Astroturf or million-dollar contracts, there was a bunch of neighborhood boys with a pigskin and a love for the rough-and-tumble game.

Some of them earned nicknames like Freight Train and Steamboat because of their physical size or playing style. In one neighborhood game, two of those 6-foot, 200-pound Titans, wearing no protective pads or helmets, ran into each other with such force, they knocked each other out, recalled James Wesley, who was a noted football and baseball player in the 1930s.

"They got up (eventually), brushed themselves off and went back to playing," he said. "We had a lot of good, clean fun; nothing like it is today."

Young sportsmen played sandlot, pickup games all over the city. Many of their neighborhood scrimmages were played in the middle of unpaved residential streets.

When they played at "Thrift City," an area west of the Flint River near Davison Road, coaches from area high schools with an eye out for

Northern's Leroy Bolden is most often cited for a 79-yard, game-winning touchdown run in the final minutes of the 1950 Thanksgiving Day match-up against arch-rival Central. He went on to an outstanding career at Michigan State and as a pro with the Cleveland Browns.

new talent would sometimes go there to watch, Wesley said.

Berston's playground was popular. So were neighborhood parks and open fields near community centers. Atwood Stadium was the setting for organized sports and the annual Thanksgiving Day showdown between Northern and Central high schools was one highlight.

The Turkey Day contest was not only the season finale, it was the game of year, said Norm Bryant, a Northern alumnus and co-founder of the Greater Flint Afro-American Hall of Fame.

"You didn't have dinner until after the game," he said.

The games always started at noon. In its heyday, more than 20,000 fans crowded into Atwood, including many of Flint's most prominent citizens such as industrialist Charles Stewart Mott. Extra bleachers were erected on the field and there would be standing room only.

Some of those die-hard fans brought blankets and heating pads to stave off the bitter cold. But neither snow, rain nor complaints could stop the game from being played.

"Sometimes they had to have the guy with the snowplow (go) around the edge of the field so you could see the markers," Bryant said.

Other times the natural-grass field would get so muddy it was nicknamed the Mud Bowl. That was in the 1950s and '60s before artificial grass was installed, he said.

"It was a bitter rivalry," Bryant said of the Turkey Day game. "If you were married into a family from the south side (as he is), if they won, they had bragging rights. If we won, we had bragging rights."

Such deep pride was at stake that the contest could transform a mediocre team into a menace. Northern could have lost every game during the season and Central could have won every game, but that all went out the window when the teams faced off on Thanksgiving, Bryant said.

Those holiday classics delivered memorable moments like a 79-yard touchdown run in 1950 by Northern's Leroy Bolden to clinch a 20-13 victory over Central.

The Flint Journal described the tie-breaking run as the longest run from scrimmage in the 23 years of the annual contest. With the score tied and a record crowd of 20,600 watching, Bolden scored with less than three minutes to play. It was Bolden's 13th touchdown of the season. The Vikings won the state championship that year.

Bryant played on Northern's 1953 team that beat Central 15-13 on a safety. Central won the next two out of four Thanksgiving games, but the big payback came in 1958 when a halfback named Ron Watkins "ran wild," Bryant chuckled. "Central beat Northern that year 51 to nothing. That was the worst whipping."

The Turkey Day series ended in 1976, its 49th year. That game went into overtime but Central won, 7-6, capping a three-year winning streak. Overall, Northern won the series 28-20 with one tie in 1948. Northern also had the longest winning streak, a five-year shutout from 1949 to 1953.

Central's longest records of bragging rights in the ongoing rivalry came after the Thanksgiving Day games ended. They had four-year streaks from 1981 to 1984 and 1990 to 1993. But as of 1994, Northern still held the winning edge at 35 to Central's 31 total victories.

A dazzling list of African-American gridiron talent spans the decades

Central's Don E. Coleman was the first MSU player to have his jersey number retired and is listed in the National Football Foundation Hall of Fame.

---

like a long touchdown pass. There are record holders, state champions, all-staters, All-Americans and immortalized greats such as Michigan State's Don Coleman, who was inducted into the National Football Foundation Hall of Fame in 1975.

One of the earliest records in organized play belongs to Percy McClellan, a fullback for Central, who once punted the length of the field. He is believed to have been Central's first black athlete in 1917. Described as "a demon on running plays," McClellan played semiprofessionally with the Flint Bears in 1920 and professionally with the Flint Cardinals in 1921, according to his Afro-American Hall of Fame biography. He was also Flint's second black police officer.

Playing for Central in 1928, halfback Houston "Mickey" McKell set a school record of four touchdown passes in a single game. He was Central's first black all-state football player.

Al Washington, at right end, was Northern's first black football player. He played from 1928 to 1930, including on the undefeated 1930 state championship team.

James McCrary, a fullback, was Washington's teammate and Northern's first all-stater. He earned more praise as an outstanding player for Michigan State University and was an assistant coach there for two years. He was also coached at Arkansas A&M and Wilberforce University in Ohio.

James R. "Jimmy" Johnson loved football so much that as a boy of about 10 in the mid-1920s, he used to sneak through the cornfields on the Charles Stewart Mott estate to get to his "free seat" on a hilltop overlooking Central's football field.

Years later, when his turn came to play, Johnson earned a record 11 letters in four sports at Central, four of them in football. He was captain of the football team, played offensive and defensive lineman and was a member of Central's 1932 state championship team.

After graduating from Central in 1934, Johnson attended South Carolina State where he was named all-conference two years and a little All-American in 1938. He is also remembered as the director of the St. John Street Community Center (1951-1971) and the Brennan Park center (1971-1976). He is a hall-of-fame member in both the Greater Flint Area Sports and Afro-American groups.

His younger brother, Al Johnson, owns an impressive athletic record and is a local hall-of-fame inductee, too. Besides lettering in basketball and track at Central, he earned All-State football honors in 1945 and was a two-time All-Saginaw Valley Conference choice. An injury ended his promising career while he was playing for the Flint Falcons, a semi-professional team, in 1947.

He worked 30 years for the Flint Parks and Recreation Department, retiring in 1990. He became its first black basketball director in 1960 and later supervised flag football and softball as well. In 1985, the Michigan Amateur Softball Association named him softball commissioner of the year for the state and district.

At Michigan State, Leroy Bolden was the first black co-captain of the MSU team. He lettered all four years, once scoring three touchdowns in a victory over Ohio State and drawing praise from opposing coach Woody Hayes, who marveled: "He has to be the greatest football player I've ever seen. We set everything to stop him and we knew exactly what he was going to do. He still beat us."

He was named most valuable player in 1953 for his contributions to the Spartans' co-Big Ten and Rose Bowl championship teams. He played two years with the Cleveland Browns, after signing in 1958.

He was inducted into the Greater Flint Area Sports Hall of Fame in 1985 and the Afro-American Hall of Fame in 1989.

Bolden's 1950 state title teammates at Northern High included Ellis Duckett and Freddie Williams.

Williams, a multisport athlete, cinched his place in the legends book by scoring on a 52-yard pass in the final seconds of a 1950 game against Saginaw's Arthur Hill. With the score tied at 19, Williams caught the pass on the 10-yard line and ran with it through the end zone and into the stands. He was inducted into the Afro-American Hall of Fame in 1991 and the Greater Flint Area Sports Hall of Fame in 1993.

Bolden and Duckett teamed up for more championship play at Michigan State.

Duckett was All-Valley and All-State in high school. At Michigan State, he blocked a punt in the 1954 Rose Bowl against UCLA, then picked up the loose ball for a touchdown that won the game for the Spartans. The final score was 28-20. A blowup photo of Duckett blocking the kick was hung in the dining room in the Spartan Stadium press box.

Duckett was inducted in the Greater Flint Area Sports Hall of Fame in 1986 and the Afro-American Hall of Fame in 1989.

Central's Jesse Thomas also distinguished himself at Michigan State in the early 1950s and played professionally with the Baltimore Colts from 1955 to 1957. He's a dual Flint halls of fame inductee.

During Thomas' Central days, there used to be joke about him, said sports fan Kenneth Jackson. After a Central game, someone would ask who won the game. And the answer would be "Jesse won the game."

"They say he was that good," Jackson said.

Sheer talent helped Northern's Jay Watkins score in an upset victory over Saginaw's Arthur Hill in 1944, but it was by sheer cunning that he was wearing a Viking uniform at all. At 130 pounds, Watkins sat out his sophomore and junior year, before getting a beefier cousin to pose as him to get issued a uniform. Halfway through the season, the star halfback decided to let Coach Guy Houston in on his deception.

Houston, who was white, is mentioned often, both as a staunch crusader against racial discrimination and as one of the winningest coaches in Flint high school football history. During 24 years as Northern's coach, starting in 1928, Houston guided the Vikings through 10 unbeaten seasons and 12 Saginaw Valley Conference titles. He ended his coaching career in 1951 to become Northern's principal.

Don Coleman of Central's 1947 state championship team was a two-time All-American at Michigan State on his way to a berth in the National Football Foundation Hall of Fame for outstanding college players. He's also enshrined in MSU's hall of fame and several others. He was the first MSU gridder to have his jersey number, 78, retired.

MSU lost only four games during Coleman's playing days from 1949

Gene McFadden was a key contributor to Northern's 1956 state title and later earned All-State, All-Conference and MVP laurels at Hillsdale College.

---

to 1951. He earned a pro ball tryout but at 170-180 pounds was too light to make the team.

Injuries from a car accident got Northern track and football star Leon Burton dropped from the Michigan State squad in the mid-1950s. But he recovered and went on to help establish a winning football program at Arizona State. After a record-setting college career, he was drafted by the San Francisco 49ers but didn't make the final cut. He played professionally two seasons with the New York Titans.

Clarence Peaks, an ex-Central star quarterback, played pro ball 10 years with the Philadelphia Eagles and the Pittsburgh Steelers. The Eagles were the NFL champions in 1960 and Peaks was named All-Pro. At Michigan State, he was All-Big Ten and All-American. It was widely believed that he had the Heisman Trophy as good as won in 1956 had he not sustained a fluke knee injury. Michigan State's teams had been undefeated in 28 games and ranked No. 1 in the nation but with its star halfback injured, lost the game and its bid for the national title.

Gene McFadden added his name to a local Hall of Fame with an impressive career at Northern and Hillsdale College. At Northern, he played on the 1956 state championship team and, in 1987, earned All-City, All-Valley and All-State honors. At Hillsdale, his All-State and All-Conference performance earned him the Outstanding Freshman Award and, as a senior, team captain and Most Valuable Player honors. He later earned a doctorate in educational administration at Michigan State and served as chairman of the board of the Flint Blue Devils, an amateur football team.

Other gridiron greats of the 1950s included the multitalented Joe Quarles of Central, who also starred in basketball; Charles Thrash of Central, who also excelled in track; and Dalton Kimble of Northern, also a track standout.

Melvin Summers, co-captain of Central's 1963 team, was one of few in the Indians' history to win nine varsity letters. He was All-State and All-Conference in football and basketball and also ran track.

Jerome Oliver III, a 1973 Southwestern graduate, lettered three years for Purdue as a wide receiver. Since, he has worked on the coaching staffs at Davison High, Purdue, Eastern Michigan, Northeastern, Navy, Grand Valley State and Western Illinois.

By the 1970s, Flint had so many former high school players playing professionally that one wit quipped that NFL meant National Flint League instead of National Football League.

Ricky Patton, a Southwestern standout in 1973, played for the Atlanta Falcons, the Green Bay Packers and the San Francisco 49ers.

Reggie Williams, Patton's teammate at Southwestern, was an All-American at Dartmouth, played 14 years as a pro with the Cincinnati Bengals and started in two Super Bowls. In 1991, he became general manager of a World Football League team in New York. He was a 1990 inductee in the Greater Flint Sports Hall of Fame.

Booker Moore, a 1977 Southwestern graduate and standout at Penn

Southwestern's Reggie Williams played in two Super Bowls during a 14-year pro career with the Cincinnati Bengals.

State, was the top draft choice of the Buffalo Bills in 1981. He played with the team five seasons then tried out with the Detroit Lions in 1986.

An All-State high school running back, Moore set six records, earning frequent mention in the Colt best-ever hall of fame. One record was for 1,240 yards rushing in a single season, the most in Flint's prep history at that time. He also owned the Colt record for career touchdowns – 36. He was inducted in the Greater Flint Sports Hall of Fame in 1993.

Mark Ingram, a Northwestern and MSU star, was drafted by the New York Giants in 1987. The former high school quarterback played wide receiver in college and the pros. As a free agent in 1993, he signed with the Miami Dolphins.

Ex-Beecher High School and MSU standout Carl Banks was a first-

Beecher and MSU standout Carl Banks earned two Super Bowl championship rings during nine seasons with the New York Giants.

round draft pick in 1984 by the New York Giants and played for them nine seasons, including Super Bowl championships in 1987 and 1991. The star linebacker was named to the Pro Bowl team in 1987. He signed with the Washington Redskins in 1993 and went to the Cleveland Browns the following year.

Off the football field, Banks has garnered praise for his community work. He donated thousands of dollars to the athletic programs at his former high school and college and conducted local football camps for youth.

Lonnie Young, also a Beecher and MSU grad, has worked with former teammate Banks at football camps in Flint. He signed with the St. Louis Cardinals in 1985 and was traded to the New York Jets in 1991. He has played defensive back and free safety.

Known as a tough competitor on and off the playing field, Northwestern standout Andre Rison set records at Michigan State and made his mark in the pros.

Beecher and Michigan State also launched the professional career of Courtney Hawkins, now with the Tampa Bay Buccaneers.

The Indianapolis Colts claimed Andre Rison, formerly of Northwestern and MSU, as a late first-round draft pick in 1989 but traded him the following year to the Atlanta Falcons. He played in four Pro Bowls. After being released by the Falcons after the 1994 season, as a free agent, he signed a lucrative contract with the Cleveland Browns.

At Michigan State, Rison played wide receiver and walked away with records in pass receptions (137) and receiving yardage (2,740). As a Spartan, he played in the Rose Bowl in 1988 and the Gator Bowl and Hula Bowl in 1989.

An all-around athlete, Rison was also part of Northwestern's state champion basketball team in 1984 and 1985.

ON TRACK:
"We might see another state record fall."

When Southwestern's Floyd Bates Jr. clocked 14.9 seconds in the 120-yard high hurdles at a city track meet in 1961, he broke a 23-year-old record set by his father, Floyd Bates Sr.

"It was a quirk of fate," said Kenneth Jackson, a track competitor with Bates Jr. in the early 1960s. "Floyd had no idea he would do it. When (he) broke the record, (announcers) mentioned that his father was in the stands. I don't think you'll find that father and son situation today."

That's why it is necessary to ask which one when tracking the athletic career of Floyd Bates.

Bates Sr. and Bates Jr. were both outstanding hurdlers and high jumpers. Both set track and field records and were equally gifted on the basketball court. Both are in the Greater Flint Afro-American Hall of Fame.

In 1937 and '38, Bates Sr. elevated the word athlete to a new level at Central High. At the city meet in '38, he set the low hurdles record (15.0 seconds) that his son would finally break. He set regional and state records in the high jump and was being touted as a strong Olympics prospect in 1938.

In basketball he was a leading scorer on the 1940 city champs team.

Bates got a pep talk about going to college from Jesse Owens, the legendary runner who won four gold medals in the the 1936 Olympics, during an exhibition at Atwood Stadium in 1938, The Flint Journal reported. Owens said: "If you're a good enough athlete to have colleges hunting for you, trade your skills for an education. Father Time catches up with you athletically but they never can take that education away from you."

Bates didn't go to college but he played professional basketball and softball and earned spots in the Michigan Amateur Softball Association Hall of Fame in 1982, the Flint Sports Hall in 1982 and the Afro-American Hall in 1986.

Bates Jr. broke his father's low hurdles record on a soggy track in 53-

Like father, like son. Floyd Bates Sr. (above) handed off his 23-year-old hurdles record at Southwestern to his son Floyd Jr. (right).

degree weather. At that same meet, he posted a 20.0 time in the 180-yard low hurdles to topple a 20.3 record set four years earlier. He was the state low hurdles champion in 1961. In basketball, he was the top rebounder and scorer for the 1961 Southwestern team.

Central and Northern track teams dominated meets in the late 1950s and early 1960s, often finishing in first and second place. In 1959, Central won the state Class A title and Northern finished second. Northern's second-place finish at the state meet in 1960 was its seventh in a row.

Ron Watkins of Central and Maurice Pea of Northern would take turns in the winner's circle.

"People would come out just to see those two run against each other," Jackson said. "We might see another state record fall."

Watkins, running the 100-yard dash, the 220 and medley relay, helped Central bring home the state championship trophy in 1959. He attended Michigan State where he competed in football and track.

At the 1960 state meet, Pea tied a record of 9.8 seconds set in 1925. His record pace of 21.3 in the 220 was disqualified because of the wind.

Floyd Bates Jr. hurdles at Southwestern.

Herb Washington of Central High and Michigan State left a mark on sports history by becoming the first designated base stealer in professional baseball for the Oakland Athletics in 1974, and he played in the World Series that year. He had already tucked many speed records in his belt.

Jesse Thomas, a track and football star at Central High School and at Michigan State, qualified for an Olympic tryout in 1952 and briefly played professional football for the Baltimore Colts and Miami Dolphins.

At MSU in 1972, he set a world record in the 60-yard dash with a time of 5.8 seconds. That year he also won the Big Ten Medal of Honor for his outstanding record in sports and academics and began training for the Olympic trials. He had beaten Olympic medalists in 50- and 60-yard dashes in 1970 competitions.

Some earlier track and field stars were Joseph Lawson of Northern, who owned six city records in track in 1938 and ranked among the top three in the state; Arthur Ingram, who burned up the track for Central in 1946 and was a state champion at Michigan State from 1950-54 in the 60-yard dash; Sylvester Collins, a standout at Northern from 1948-50 and Michigan State Normal from 1951-53, who later became the first black high school track coach at Northwestern in 1971; and Jesse Thomas of Central and Michigan State, who qualified for the 1952 Olympic trials in the long jump and is considered by many to be the best track and field star Flint has produced.

Ulus T. Silk also burned up the track for Central High and Mott Community College in the early 1950s. At Central, he won city, conference and state championships in the 440-yard run in 1952 and '53.

In 1954, Northern's Art Johnson ran the 220-yard dash in 22.8, 1.6 seconds off a 1933 record set by Jesse Owens. He was voted most valuable honors for top points in sprinting, broad jump and relays.

James Luckado, a Northern track star in the 1940s, also has a Jesse Owens story. Luckado beat the Olympic medalist in an exhibition race at Atwood Stadium in 1945. Luckado finished the 100-yard dash about a half-step ahead of Owens. There was one small catch though: Luckado was running straightaway while Owens was running hurdles.

Norm Bryant, Northern's track team captain in 1954, was a star broad jumper and relay runner.

Northern's Anthony Hamm kept up the winning pace in the the 1980s. He was a repeat city and conference cross-country champion in 1984-86, making him the first three-time consecutive winner in local history. He was also state Class A champion in 1985 and finished second in 1986. He helped Michigan State to a fourth-place Big Ten finish in 1988.

In modern Class B competition, Beecher's boys and girls track team both won the state title in 1992.

Northern's girls team won the Class A state title from 1979-81 and in 1983 and dominated the Saginaw Valley Conference team title for 12 years, ending in 1990. Marjona Howard won 100-meter and 300-meter hurdles at the state meet in 1990.

By 1993, Southwestern Academy's Stacey Thomas was showing up regularly in the champion's circle at city, regional and state meets. As a freshman, in 1993, she was the state Class A high jump champion. She also won four events at the city championships in 1993 and 1994 to boost Southwestern's girls team to its third consecutive title. Thomas won the high jump and the 800-, 1,600- and 3,200-meter runs.

HER STORY:
"The McGee twins revolutionized women's sports here in Flint."

Paula (left) and Pam McGee nailed twin state titles for Northern's Lady Vikings in 1978 and 1979 and twin national titles for the University of Southern California women's team. Pam became Flint's first Olympic gold medal winner in 1984.

So far, Stella Williams Robinson is only individual female listed in the Greater Flint Afro-American Hall of Fame.

Inducted in 1990, Robinson is noted for her softball and basketball feats in the 1930s and '40s. She played for city and state softball championship teams. In 1944, she pitched against the Women's World Champions and in 1945 was named a Flint All-Star.

"From what I understand, she was a good all-around player," said Norm Bryant, co-founder of the hall of fame.

Robinson also played with the St. John Street Women's Softball team, which was inducted into the AAHF in 1994. The 16-member team won the 1940 city championship and was a semifinalist in the state tournament.

Between that women's softball team and the outstanding women's basketball teams in the late 1970s through 1980s, little information is available about female athletes.

Records are poor because women's sports have never had the recognition or attention given to men's sports.

High schools didn't have competitive women's sports in the early 1950s, Bryant said. Back then, women played half-court basketball with three players on each team.

"The three on one side did all the shooting and the others just played defense," Bryant said.

Most of games were played as part of gym class, he said.

Ruby Turner-Noble won three out of four letters in basketball at Central in the late 1930s, she said. Many of her contemporaries remember her as a gifted player, but there is no public record.

Frankie Wynn played on intramural women's basketball and softball teams in the mid-1940s. They were good enough to draw a crowd to the city lots and community centers where they played.

"When I was in high school, they didn't have any girls sports," Wynn said, adding that even all the cheerleaders were male.

Donna Rollins Sparrow was another multiple-sport standout of yesteryear whose reputation endures but whose record is lost to posterity.

Players such as Robinson, Turner-Noble, Wynn and in recent years Pam and Paula McGee and Tonya Edwards have demonstrated that athletic talent is not exclusively men's domain.

The 6-foot-3 McGee twins led the Lady Vikings at Northern to back-to-back state Class A championships in 1978 and 1979. They did it again in 1983 and 1984 to make the University of Southern California a repeat national women's champion.

"The McGee twins revolutionized women's sports here in Flint," said Kenneth Jackson, an avid sports fan who once watched them play in the state finals.

"Pam and Paula dominated the game. They were bigger than anyone on the opposing team."

In 1984, Pam McGee, an All-American, became the first Flint resident to win an Olympic gold medal. She played with the U.S. women's basketball team. Many may remember it as an emotional high point when Pam removed her gold-medal necklace and placed it around the neck of her tearful twin Paula immediately after the medal presentation ceremony in Los Angeles. Paula had been cut from the Olympic team, one of few times the talented duo was separated on the court.

The twins were profiled in Sports Illustrated magazine in 1982. In 1985, they tried out with the Harlem Globetrotters, in hopes of becoming the first women players in the 60-year history of basketball's clown squad. They competed against 21 hopefuls but ultimately lost out to Lynette Woodard of Kansas, who was captain of the winning 1984 Olympic team.

The twins played briefly in 1985 for the Dallas Diamonds of the short-lived Women's Basketball Association and later for European teams.

European women's teams grabbed other former Flint hoop stars such as Northern's Leteia Hughley, Sweden; Northwestern's Tonya Edwards, Turkey; and Hamady's Laurie Byrd, Switzerland, Sweden, Italy and Spain.

Edwards has been called Flint's greatest woman player ever.

Kenneth Jackson recalled the time she scored a career-high 39 points in a 59-54 victory over Northern during 1985 season play.

"That was unheard of for anybody at that time," he said.

Edwards played on Northwestern's 1983 and '84 state Class A championship teams. Northwestern was runner-up in 1985, her senior season, when she became the first four-time All-Stater in state prep history. She also finished second in polling for the 1985 Miss Basketball Award, voted by the State Basketball Coaches Association.

After a stellar college career at the University of Tennessee, including national championships in 1987 and 1989, Edwards was invited to the U.S. Olympic team trials in 1988 and also tried out for the women's basketball league before joining a professional team in Istanbul, Turkey.

In 1991, at age 22, she was named head women's basketball coach at her old high school, Northwestern. That set her up to become the first person to play for and coach a state championship team.

The unbeaten Lady Wildcats, coached by Edwards, won the state Class A title in 1993. Edwards' old NW jersey number – 33 – was retired in 1994 and she was voted state Coach of Year by the state coaches group.

Following Edwards' lead, in 1994, Northern's Leteia Hughley became the second person to play for and coach a state championship team. Hughley

Head and shoulders above the competition, Northwestern's Tonya Edwards is widely regarded as Flint's greatest woman player. She also coached the Lady Wildcats' state title victory in 1993.

Northern's Leteia Hughley played with the McGee Twins on Northern's back-to-back state Class A title teams in 1978-79. In 1994, she coached the Lady Vikings' state Class A title team.

played with the McGee twins on Northern's 1978 and 1979 state Class A title team. The Lady Vikings were riding a 69-game winning streak when they nailed a third straight state title in 1980, making Hughley the only player in the state to start on three consecutive title teams.

While she was at Northern, The Lady Vikings never lost a game. Also as a track champion, she never lost a meet, winning three straight state titles in 1979, '80 and '81.

"Leteia Hughley used to play down in UM-Flint recreation building with the guys and could hold her own," said her former Northern classmate, Angela Sawyer.

After a record-setting college campaign at the University of Washington, Hughley joined a Swedish women's pro team in 1987. She was named assistant coach at Northern in 1991, then head coach in 1993.

Hughley's Northern teammate Judy Tucker shares the distinction of being a member of three consecutive state title teams in basketball and track. The two women were also teammates at the University of Washington, where Tucker transferred in 1982 after an unhappy freshman year at Syracuse University.

Tucker is a cousin of professional basketball player Trent Tucker.

Laurie Byrd, a 1978 Hamady High graduate, once scored 41 points in a game. She was most valuable player in her freshman year and a leading scorer at Eastern Michigan University, averaging 20.4 points per game. Byrd, a member of boxing's outstanding Byrd family, tried out for the 1980 U.S. Olympic team.

In the early 1980s, she coached at Ann Arbor's Gabriel Richard High and played amateur league ball for the nationally ranked Detroit Cobras before turning pro and joining the Chicago Spirits of the Women's American Basketball Association in 1985. Later that year, she joined a pro team in Switzerland. In 1991, she signed with the Detroit Dazzlers of the short-lived WABA.

She was inducted into the EMU Sports Hall of Fame in 1993 and still holds the school scoring record.

More for the fun of it, athletically inclined women in Flint have swum, danced, golfed, bowled and racketed their way to laurels and trophies.

Ailene Butler swam in the Flint River near the five-mile bridge when city swimming pools were off-limits.

"I was a tomboy always, being that I had a bunch of brothers," she said. "I was always the leader of something."

Butler played softball and tennis, golfed and played tennis on Berston's courts.

As a member of the Vehicle City Golf Club until the late 1970s, Ruth VanZandt played on courses in an around Flint. It was an all-black club started by men but several women joined, she said.

At Flint Junior College in the 1930s, VanZandt was a runner-up in bowling and table tennis championships.

Sheila Miller-Graham has made her name for herself in competitive dance. She has been director of Creative Expressions Dance Studio, part of the city recreation program at Berston Field House, since 1985.

"I started at McCree theater when I was 14," Miller-Graham said, adding that she would have started earlier if her parents could have afforded it. McCree's program was free.

By her senior year in high school, Miller-Graham had become director of the McCree program. She majored in dance at UM in Ann Arbor, graduating in 1980.

Two of her former students, Shonte Walker and Cherisse Bradley, landed a coveted $9,000 one-year scholarship to the Joe Tremaine dance studio in Hollywood. Walker went on to dance professionally in Japan.

In 1994, Creative Expressions students beat out competitors from 230 schools to win best of show and 10 top awards including three first places at the National Joe Tremaine Competition in Las Vegas. It was their best-ever showing at the annual competition.

Miller-Graham and co-director Alfred Bruce Bradley are now drawing more male students.

"Parents are starting to realize that boys need it to," Miller-Graham said. "We get them in the young stages but by the time they get to junior high, they get teased and drop out. (Some) come back when they've matured enough to handle the teasing."

The studio offers an all-male class on Saturdays to preserve that macho male-bonding feeling of athletics. A few older men take ballet, tap and jazz.

IN THE RING:

"He taught us that you couldn't just go out into the streets and fight."

In 1942, Benny McCombs became the first Flint fighter to win a national Golden Gloves title.

Herb Odom, a successful Chicago dentist, holds the distinction of being able to knock out your teeth and then repair the damage. A champion boxer in high school and college, Odom's comeback bid at age 47 was featured in Sports Illustrated and People magazines.

In boxing, several Flint athletes have stood out in the crowd, nationally and internationally.

In 1942, Benny McCombs brought home Flint's first national Golden Gloves title.

In 1992, Chris Byrd punched his way to an Olympic silver medal in Barcelona, Spain, as part of a U.S. boxing team coached by his dad, Joe Byrd Sr. He was Flint's first Olympic medalist in an individual sport.

In 1962, Flint's Auburn 'The Flash' Copeland lost in a lightweight title bout in a split decision. Considered one of Flint's greatest boxers, his 17-year career record was 60 wins, 11 losses and two draws.

The national spotlight landed on Flint again in 1993, when Flint's Timothy Littles, the U.S. super middleweight champion, successfully defended his title and earned a shot at the world championship (which he lost).

Flint even has a Hollywood connection. Former city and state Golden Gloves champion Tony Burton, now an actor, appeared in five "Rocky" movies as the boxing trainer of the title character.

World Heavyweight Champion Joe Louis boxed three exhibitions in Flint in 1939.

And a slew of boxers helped put Flint on the map through competition in the annual Golden Gloves amateur boxing tournament, over its 60-year history. City champions went on to compete at the state tournament in Grand Rapids and the nationals in Chicago.

The Flint Police Athletic League (PAL) and the Berston Boxing Club groomed many individual Gloves' champions who went on to professional careers.

For many years, PAL coach Joe Byrd trained his Olympic-caliber stable, including four sons, in the basement of his home.

In 1989, Flint had won seven state Golden Gloves team titles in a row.

Until the mid-1980s, Golden Gloves competitions at the IMA Auditorium and later IMA Sports Arena drew as many as 15,000 fans. Then attendance plummeted to about 2,000.

Boxing has long been a constructive outlet for local youth.

Thanks to dedicated trainers and promoters such as Clair W. James, Dee Cavette, Floyd Fielder, Bill Hamilton and Byrd, African-American participation in boxing dates almost back to the first professional match in 1929 at the IMA.

James organized one of the first boxing clubs in about 1932. He trained many Golden Gloves champions who made names for themselves such as Cavette, Fielder and McCombs, Flint's first national Golden Gloves winner.

James co-founded a Big Brothers-sponsored boxing club on the north side and organized exhibitions to raise money to build a north-side community center for black youth.

The club entered 30 fighters into the 1939 Gloves tournament. It started out as such a shoestring operation that at one time only had three gloves, forcing one person to spar with one hand. Their borrowed training facilities were unheated and poorly lit.

Cavette once said about James in a Flint Journal interview: "He was a great character builder. He taught us that you couldn't just go out into the streets and fight. We should use that energy in the ring."

James trained state champions including Auburn Copeland and Jock Leslie, who fought in Flint's first title match (against Willie Pep) at Atwood Stadium in 1947.

Copeland, nicknamed "The Flash," is considered one of Flint's greatest boxers. His 17-year career included a world junior lightweight title fight in Manila in 1962. He lost by a split decision. His record was 60 wins, 11 losses and two draws.

Paul Wright won the Golden Gloves national middleweight title in 1954 and was the National Amateur Athletic Union (AAU) champion in 1955 and 1956. He turned pro in 1957, training under Cus D'Amato, and was a sparring partner for heavyweight champion Floyd Patterson.

Jay Watkins, a 1940s city and state Golden Gloves champion in the lightweight division, turned pro in 1950 and was once rankèd eighth in the world. Several of his brothers also ranked in state and national Gloves contention.

Benny McCombs' 1942 national Golden Gloves title launched a professional career that took him through many spectacular matches but never landed a title bout. He moved up his weight class to light heavyweight because his middleweight reputation scared away competition. He retired from the ring in the early 1950s.

Other noted state Golden Gloves champions include Dee Cavette, 1936; Leon Watkins, 1951-52, and Larry Watkins, 1951, both brothers of standout pro Jay Watkins; Tony Burton, 1957; and Richard Dicks, 1959.

Herb Odom, a city and state Golden Gloves champion in 1948 and 1949, owns one of the most unusual Cinderella stories in boxing.

Odom grew up poor on Flint's north side and was a high school dropout. Even his poor reading skills fit the dumb jock stereotype. But unlike the typical story of the has-been athlete, Odom's has a fairy-tale ending.

He returned to high school and graduated, all while working full time in the auto factory. Though he was a gifted athlete, a reading disability nearly prevented him from being admitted to Michigan State University, where he won NCAA boxing championships in 1954 and 1955.

Despite his reading disability, Odom went on to earn a degree in dentistry from Meharry Medical College. He became a successful dentist and millionaire entrepreneur in Chicago.

But Odom added a postscript to his boxing laurels when he returned to the ring in 1980 at age 47 to fulfill his dream of becoming a professional boxer. He fought about a half-dozen fights and even scored a few knockouts in a brief comeback bid that was unusual enough to rate feature stories about him in Sports Illustrated and People magazines.

More recent boxing champs include Tim Littles, a PAL and Golden Gloves standout, who lost a bid in 1994 for the world super middleweight title to champ James Toney of Ann Arbor. His brother Jonathan Littles also has earned recognition as a boxer.

Byrd is another well-known family name in boxing. Patrick Byrd, brother to Chris and son of trainer Joe Sr., is a professionally recognized fighter. Joe Byrd Jr., Tim and Ron Byrd have all been State Gloves champs.

The Byrd brothers learned from a pro. Joe Byrd Sr. boxed professionally for 10 years beginning in 1964. He won the 1963 state Golden Gloves heavyweight title on a fluke. Byrd arrived at the state meet in Grand Rapids as a trainer but agreed to fill in when one of the Flint fighters dropped out.

And in this corner Tim Littles, a product of Flint's Police Athletic League training club, became a U.S. super middleweight champion and vied unsuccessfully for the world title in 1994.

Byrd once boxed Sugar Ray Robinson in an exhibition in the IMA Auditorium.

In 1989, he was named chairman of the national coaches committee of the U. S. Amateur Boxing Federation. Then he was tagged to coach the 1992 U.S. Olympic boxing team. In 1993, he opened Joe Byrd's Boxing Academy and through the Team Byrd stable with his sons is working to promote Flint as a contender on the national professional boxing circuit.

The Byrds are carrying forward a proud tradition. In the 63 years since Clair James trained the first African-American Glovers, there has always been a boxing patriarch.

In the 1930s, Clair James trained Dee Cavette, who in turn groomed Floyd Fielder. Cavette and Fielder later worked with together for many

Contenders in boxing's Byrd family include patriarch Joe (left) who coached the 1992 U.S. Olympic team on which son Chris (right), won a silver medal. Patrick (center), also an accomplished fighter, tried out for the team.

---

years to train countless others at Berston. Joe Byrd Sr. worked with former state Gloves champion and police team trainer Richard Dicks in the late 1950s and early 1960s before becoming head PAL trainer in the mid-1970s.

Byrd helped organize a tribute to veteran trainer Dee Cavette after he died in 1978. Cavette had been involved in Berston's program for about 44 years, first as a boxer then as head trainer for 28 years.

Cavette introduced Fielder to the ring at age 13. Fielder fought professionally for a while then became a Berston trainer in about 1953. Their capable gloves successfully defended Flint's informal title as the home of sports champions.

Race Relations

Marchers and demonstrators wore a path from the Flint River to Flint City Hall during the height of civil rights activism in the 1960s.

Blacks and whites in Flint largely lived in harmony before World War II, said Katie Ellis Harper, born here in 1928.

"During the 1930s we all lived in the same neighborhoods," Harper said. "When I was younger, they used to have talent shows and minstrel shows at Haskell (community center). It was black and white together on those shows."

Donn Kersey, born in Flint in 1918, described pre-1940s race relations the same way. His best friends, "the Talarico boys," were Italian. Another Italian friend taught him to swim.

Ruby Turner-Noble said she lived harmoniously among whites from the time she came to Flint as a baby in 1923.

"We didn't know what prejudice or segregation was," she said. "We could go to the white people's house and stay or they'd come to my house and stay."

Her best friend was white. That was Irene Bokor, whose father owned a north-side grocery.

"I'll never forget her as long as I live," Turner-Noble said. "She'd bring me candy bars because I didn't know what a nickel was. We sat on the bus side by side. I didn't know anything about the back of the bus."

"After all this (discrimination) stuff started happening, we couldn't understand it. Things changed when all these Southerners came up to work for Buick."

Like Turner-Noble, Sam Williams grew up in the St. John Street neighborhood's ethnic melting pot, arriving as a baby in 1927. His family rented an apartment in a white family's home.

"There were a lot of situations like that," Williams said. "It wasn't black against white. They were having a hard time, too."

His white neighbors were mostly Eastern Europeans who settled in St. John to be near their jobs at Buick. Blacks living in the St. John area also worked at Buick and across town at Chevrolet or AC Spark Plug. They walked, rode the bus or, in rare cases, drove to work.

So friendly was the neighborhood that Williams played on an interracial softball team, which traveled the state.

"Those were the good days," Williams said. "You won't see that again – the mixing of the races."

Those good old days of racial harmony in Flint had faded by the 1950s. In the turbulent years ahead, Flint would come close to having race riots on several occasions. There would be pickets, protests and legal battles over discrimination in housing, employment, education and human relations.

But some older black residents said racial friction did not suddenly descend on Flint after World War II. Instead, discrimination was passively tolerated or ignored before then.

"There was discrimination, but we didn't think anything of it," said Bessie Owens Brooks, born in Flint in 1906. "I don't even think we heard that word."

Besides, social conditions were better in Flint than in the South where blacks would be lynched for a minor offense such as not stepping off the sidewalk to let a white person pass, said Williams Hoskins, a longtime Flint NAACP member, originally from Mississippi.

Northern blacks traveling to the South packed lunches because they knew they couldn't stop to buy food along the way, except at a few places. Those using public transportation sat at the back of the bus or in the "colored car" at the rear of the train.

Southern Jim Crow laws segregated all public facilities including restrooms, drinking fountains, schools and voting sites.

The Emmett Till story illustrated the dramatic difference between conditions in the North and South, Hoskins said. Till was a 14-year-old black boy from Chicago who was killed by a white mob while visiting relatives in Mississippi in 1955.

"He'd been free to play with white kids (in the North)," Hoskins said. He went down South and (allegedly) whistled at a white woman. They took him out of his home at night and killed him."

In the North blacks had more freedom of movement and better opportunities to make a decent living, Hoskins said. They faced a more subtle kind of racism.

James Wesley, who moved to Flint in 1929, recalled: "Back in the 1930s, people who came up here to get away from the South didn't know what they were getting into. Only thing they didn't have up here was lynching. (But) the police used to beat blacks for the fun of it."

At one time, blacks did not venture north of Pierson Road or east of Boulevard Drive, he said. They would get chased back home, or worse, if they ventured outside of those boundaries.

"Fortunately, the kids could go to public school, but downtown was so segregated, it made you sick to think you lived in a place like this," Wesley said. "You couldn't eat any place. The Durant Hotel – you could go in there and sweep floors or tend bar, but as far as going in there to sleep, forget it."

Blacks had problems getting service in downtown stores for many years, some said. They complained that blacks were not allowed to try on shoes or hats before buying them and were waited on only after whites had been served.

But Anna L.V. Howard, who's lived in Flint since the 1920s, said she never had any of those problems.

"When my mama took us shopping, we tried on shoes," Howard said. "We were always clean when we went anywhere. We had on clean socks when we were going to try on shoes."

Howard said they shopped in all the stores and were waited on when it was their turn. Nor would they have stepped aside to allow whites to be served first, she said.

The main problem downtown was job discrimination, Howard said. At one time, a general perception among blacks was that when Michigan National Bank would hire blacks at all, it would hire only light-skinned women. Even so, the only jobs they could get were elevator operators or cleaning women, Howard said.

Blacks could shop at Smith-Bridgman's, the leading department store, but could not get a job there, she said.

"If you got hired at anything downtown ... they didn't hire clerks, it was just washing dishes, cleaning the women's restrooms or running the elevators," she said.

Certain neighborhoods practiced unwritten rules as well.

During his 1930s boyhood, Eugene Simpson said, blacks couldn't walk down Welch Boulevard unless they were going to work for whites.

"They see you walking down the street; they'd ask what you were doing there," he said.

Milton Port, born in Flint in 1912, recalled: "Some neighborhoods you could go to jail for just walking through." He said he knew a man, an upstanding citizen active in the church, who spent a night in jail for walking one night in a white neighborhood.

James Todd adopted a passive attitude to keep himself out of trouble. He was 15 when he moved to Flint in 1929.

"My father once told me: 'A man is like steel. If he loses his temper, he wasn't no good.'" Todd said. "I lived by that (rule). A lot of times when I should have been insulted, I just smiled, and that got me along, kept me out of trouble.

"The discrimination bothered us, but we knew we had to go along with the flow. You get used to it after a while."

Disparate treatment carried over into areas such as campgrounds, school dormitories and entertainment facilities.

Black children were not allowed to go camping until about 1925, said Ruth Owens Buckner. She remembers being about 14 the first time she went to camp.

"They decided to let the black girls go to an all-black camp," she said. But years passed, she said, before black girls were allowed to go to camp with white girls at Tyrone Hills.

While on a class field trip to Lansing in the early 1920s, Bessie Brooks said she and a friend had to spend the night with relatives after being turned away from the dorm where their white classmates and teacher stayed. The teacher apologized because she had not known of the policy barring blacks.

Many businesses in Flint were segregated.

For years, blacks had to sit in the balcony at the Michigan Theater on S. Saginaw Street, right in their own neighborhood, Dorothy Parks said. One day a man named Simms refused to sit up there and was forcibly removed, she said. Not long after that, blacks sat anywhere they wanted, she said.

Before World War II, downtown restaurants would only serve take-out meals to blacks, it is widely recalled. A few who insisted on service said they ended up with food that had been oversalted or tampered with in some other way.

After the war, James Todd said he noticed a gradual improvement in the reception blacks got downtown.

" 'Course you could always go anywhere and spend your money," he said. "We had clothing stores, and hardware stores and garages ... black businesses ... grocery stores."

It took awhile for blacks to wake up and understand that they could change things by banding together, James Wesley said.

Civil rights work ignited in Flint at about the same time as it did on the national front. The Rev. Martin Luther King Jr. lit the fuse in 1955 with a boycott that ended discrimination on city buses in Montgomery, Ala. Rosa Parks gained recognition as the "mother" of the civil rights movement when she sparked the protest by refusing to relinquish her seat to a white passenger on a crowded city bus.

In what is remembered as one of Flint's first civil rights demonstrations, in 1958, pickets marched at Flint City Hall to protest police brutality. During the following 10 to 15 years, local activists often used nonviolent tools – pickets, marches and sleep-ins – to effect social change.

"I'm old enough, and yet young enough, to remember the trials that many of us had," said Lennetta Bradley Coney, born in Flint in 1955.

"I was talking to some of my co-workers ... a lot of them don't remember when Martin Luther King was alive and the struggle that went on.

"I can remember when it (racism) was real flagrant, real overt, no coverup like it might be today."

When she was about 10, Coney said, a teacher at Scott Elementary singled out black students to criticize their speech patterns, telling them they were dropping endings and not using verbs correctly.

"As an adult, I felt maybe she meant well, but I don't agree with her strategy. It made me so angry."

When Coney told her parents about it, her mother went to talk to the teacher.

Black protesters in the 1960s and early 1970s generally made progress toward achieving social and economic equality with whites. But Coney wasn't the only one to describe the new racism as more subtle.

Said Angela Sawyer: "It's not something that you can prove; it's something that you feel." Born in 1963, Sawyer essentially cut her teeth on the enlightened civil rights era.

"You have to keep in mind that Flint is the new Old South," she said. "The people are primarily from the South – black and white – but they brought all those negative attitudes with them."

Recalling a conversation with a friend, she said the question arose whether institutional racism is perpetuated by whites who dominate decision-making positions or ingrained by long practice into every aspect of society from employment to housing, politics and education.

"We both agreed," Sawyer said, "that it's something you can feel, not something tangible you can put your hand on – lots of little things that form the bigger picture of being discriminatory."

PREJUDICE:
"I didn't know my dad was that way."

In his famous speech, Dr. Martin Luther King Jr. dreamed a day would come when his four children would "live in a nation where they will not be judged by the color of their skin but by the content of their character."

King's leadership helped to raise consciousness and improve race relations in the 1960s, but warped attitudes continued to hamper full equality in America.

Virginia Lewis Heller learned that cruel truth as a teen-ager in the early 1960s. She realized the subtle difference in the way she had been treated on her job at a bank one day.

"I can remember being on the bus and coming home and thinking, this is what prejudice is about," she said.

Heller was hurt because prejudice had been so foreign to her upbringing. Her parents, Henry and Bessie May Lewis, were respected Flint business owners.

"My mom and dad would bring anybody into the house," Heller said. "You never knew who was going to be there and who was going to be at the table eating. I can't ever remember my parents using a negative word to identify a person of another race. I do not ever remember either of them saying, 'John is white.' There was never any mention of color, and everybody was a person."

But sometimes it is parents who poison their children's minds, as Karen Aldridge learned in the mid-1960s from a friend's father who prejudged her because she was black. The two junior high school girls liked the same books and shared other common interests.

"We decided to visit each other's homes after school, but her dad vetoed it," Aldridge said. "I felt worse for her than for me. She apologized and said, 'I didn't know my dad was that way.'"

Sondra Rawls' father enlightened her about prejudice during that era.

"I recall telling him that I really didn't know anything about racism until junior high school," Rawls said. "He said, 'It was only because you were too young to know.'"

Then he reminded her of her playmates next door when they lived in the St. John neighborhood.

"He said: 'You remember how they always had to eat dinner just before their father came home. It wasn't by accident. The father didn't allow them to play with black children.'"

Rawls doesn't count that as a bad memory. Rather, she dismissed it as "a part of life."

By other accounts, some white parents still were pointedly separating their children from black playmates well into the 1970s. And living with such irrational color bias has been said to harm self-esteem in some black children.

"I can remember wanting to be white, but I think all black kids go through that," said Lena Pridgeon, who grew up in the 1960s. "I can remember not being able to get a black doll because there wasn't any."

Some fair-skinned blacks saw a different side of color prejudice.

Ruth Owens Buckner recalled a childhood incident when a door-to-door salesman came to their house. Her mother's family was of Irish ancestry, making it difficult to tell they were black just by looking at them. The salesman made the mistake, Buckner said, of asking her mother: "What's a lady like you doing living next door to niggers?"

Buckner's mother responded by going to the kitchen to get the tea kettle boiling on the stove. Returning to the door with it, she told the salesman he had one minute to get off her porch. In his hasty departure, his papers went flying all over, Buckner recalled with a chuckle.

Still not realizing what he had said was wrong, the salesman yelled back at Buckner's mother: "Are you crazy?"

On the other hand, Buckner said her uncle used his fair skin to advantage. Accepted as a member of the Ku Klux Klan, he once secretly warned the black community of the Klan's plans to burn a cross on the grounds of Clark School, she said.

Fair-skinned James Wesley's beef is with people who try to classify him by race. Once while renewing his drivers license, he had a run-in with a clerk who insisted that he identify himself as black or white.

"When she asked me what to put down I said b & w, for black and white. She said, 'Are you trying to be funny?' I said, 'No, you're trying to be funny (by) asking silly questions.'"

Some black high school classmates called Sondra Rawls disparaging names like "high yellow," she said.

"They'd say it like they were spitting it out." But in elementary school, the insensitive remarks had come from white classmates. Some asked Rawls questions like, "Why does your mother press your hair?" she said.

Musician Sherm Mitchell maintains a color-blind philosophy about race in his life and in his music and believes too many blacks are preoccupied by it.

He said: "I could have said, 'I'm not going to play anything but black music. I'm not going to play anything but music that represents my ancestry.' I probably wouldn't be as far as I am right now. ... I play all types. I play American music.

"I'd like to live my life thinking of myself as an American. ... Why do we recognize ourselves as anything different? ... If we really want to be African-American, how come we're not learning African languages? So why take part of it if you're not going to take the whole thing?

"If you go to Canada, you see black Canadians; they're just Canadians. You go to South America, you go to Brazil, ... they're not black Brazilians. You go to Mexico. They've got a lot of black Mexicans, but you don't hear about black Mexicans. They're just Mexicans.

"You can't run from being of African origin, but you don't have to keep putting that up in people's faces either. ... Yes, the slaves were from Africa, but I tell you what, you go to Africa. They'll tell you that 'you're not one of us.' When they come here, they are treated differently than we are."

Karen Aldridge reached a similar conclusion in the 1970s while working in Liberia for the National Baptist Convention.

"When I got to Africa I was an American, but when I got back here, I was black," she said. "So we're like people without a home. Here, white people don't accept us. You go over there and expect to be accepted and they say you're not African, you're American. It's a strange feeling."

Aldridge noted that prejudice sometimes works in reverse in Africa. She saw black store clerks take their time about approaching white customers or they would serve Aldridge ahead of whites. But they would wait on a black African before a black American, she said.

Most shocking, Aldridge said, was seeing black Africans mistreat other black Africans, based on economic status.

"If you were poor and uneducated, you were treated like dirt," she said.

The same is often true in the United States where prejudice is sometimes based on social class or religion.

Jimmy Jones, a black factory worker, married a young Jewish woman in the 1930s.

"They had her (symbolic) funeral the next day," he said. "She was dead to the family.

"Every time I went downtown, I never got away without a fight. Wherever we went, we had to carry our marriage license to prove it."

Fred Waller, a retired pharmacist, learned the hands-off-white-women lesson at Central High School in the late 1930s.

"As part of gym class, we were supposed to learn to dance," he said. "But in the gym class opposite mine, there were no Negro girls."

The student body was probably about 5 percent black then, he said. Rather than allow Waller to be the partner of a white girl, the teacher pulled a black girl out of English class to dance with him, he said.

Some blacks are equally disdainful of interracial couples. Critics said they interpret it as a traitorous disregard for the injustices blacks have suffered at the hands of whites.

Because of the prejudice shown to her, Annalea Bannister, a 1943 Flint Central graduate, said she has few fond memories of her high school classmates.

"If I never saw some of those people, it wouldn't bother me," she said. "We (blacks) were just there. We were students. If you were friends with whites in elementary school, by the time you got to junior high they didn't even want to acknowledge that they knew you in the halls."

When Norm Bryant played football for Arizona State in the 1950s, black players were housed in the black community while white players and the coach stayed in a hotel, he said.

James Wesley recalled when blacks could swim in the pool at Berston Field House only on Fridays.

"Then on Saturday, they'd drain the pool and put fresh water in," he said. Only after black leaders made a fuss was the swimming time expanded to two days, he said.

During the 1940s, Freddie and Shirley Williams said they experienced racial prejudice at school and in public accommodations and employment.

Racial tensions smoldered between white children who lived east of the Flint River and black children who lived west of it, Shirley Williams said. But black children had to cross the river to attend Lowell Junior High School on the east side.

Many of the whites were transplanted Southerners, she said. There would be racial name-calling and fights would break out.

Racially insensitive situations occurred regularly in schools when black students and black teachers were few.

Eugene Simpson told of the times a teacher at Fairview Elementary School would have him stand and sing for his predominantly white classmates: "I'm My Mammy's Pickaninny, Blacker Than a Crow."

"I didn't know they were making fun of me," he said of the epithet. "I was glad to sing it for them because I thought I had a pretty good voice."

There were no black teachers then. By not having any, Fred Waller feels that something was lacking from his education.

"I thought that black instructors, hopefully, would look after their own," Waller said. He graduated from Central High School in 1940, a year after Marian Coates, who would become Flint's first black classroom teacher in 1943, graduated from Northern.

When Freddie Williams attended Northern High in the late 1940s to early 1950s, there were more black students but still no black teachers.

There, the "man-made" distinctions between races created a bad memory for him. Prejudice turns so many positives into negatives, said Williams, who was a former star athlete at Northern. One of them was "finding out that no matter how much better you were in school, when you got out, you started back at day one."

His wife-to-be, Shirley, attended Central during the same time.

"It was quite prejudiced, even for the poor whites," Shirley Williams said. Blacks were steered to general courses and some were told they'd never be able to get a job in fields such as music, she said.

Most school perks, outside of basic instruction and athletics, were off-limits to blacks.

To this day, Fred Waller does not know the location of Central's swimming pool because he and other blacks were not allowed to use it in the late 1930s. Waller didn't mind except on principle.

"Primarily, the reason it bothers me is that people came North for the freedom and weren't free," he said.

His wife, Dorothy, added that her sister is still feeling the insult 70 years later.

"She still talks about that all the time so it must have really bothered her," Waller said. "She and two other girls bought swimming suits but were not allowed to swim."

Blacks could not participate in many school activities, said Ruth Owens Buckner, who attended Central in the late 1920s. For a long time, there was only one black girl in the school choir and she was very fair-skinned, Buckner said. One or two black guys were on the football team.

College experiences were not much better for some.

In the mid-1930s, Ruth VanZandt said she got a D in European History at Michigan State Normal College in Ypsilanti, because she wouldn't laugh at a professor's "darkie joke."

"It made me so mad," she said. "I got up, slammed my books down and walked out." A girl who laughed at the joke got an A, VanZandt said.

"There was nothing you could do, you just had to take it," she said.

In the early 1970s, at the University of Michigan in Ann Arbor, Karen Aldridge had a professor whom she felt bent over backward to emphasize stereotypes. His mind-set appeared to be that all blacks were poor and their parents illiterate, Aldridge said.

"A lot of the whites (on campus) had had no contact with blacks," Aldridge said. "For some of them, it was a learning experience and some didn't want to deal with that at all."

That was made all too clear by the parents of her first dormitory roommate who insisted on a room change as soon as they saw Aldridge. She overheard them saying to someone at the front desk, "She's not staying in that room with her." To have their way, they agreed to pay for the room without using it.

Aldridge's next roommate would carry her purse with her every time she went to the bathroom, she said. And, at first, the house mother seemed uncomfortable dealing with young black women but softened up when she got to know their families, Aldridge said.

In life, in general, racial prejudice has shown itself in stereotyping, distrust and hostile, hurtful actions.

Lois Shaw, a registered nurse at St. Joseph Hospital in the late 1940s, lost a patient who refused her care because she was black.

"There were really racist folks here in Flint," Shaw said. "Lots of them came from Arkansas, Mississippi, Texas. We had a situation where the blacks were afraid of the whites and the whites hated the blacks."

Shirley Williams resented the disregard shown to black patrons at the neighborhood Columbia Theater on St. John Street.

"I can see now the bathroom in the basement," she said. "There was never any toilet paper. He (the owner) would hose it down, so the floors were always wet. It was uncomfortable to go down there because you'd get your clothes wet.

"We were used to it; we hadn't been introduced to anything else."

Her husband Freddie added: "Our parents taught us that. They'd grown up under prejudice. So to keep you from getting in trouble, they drilled into you how to respect the white folks. That's how we were taught."

Woodrow Stanley, who would become Flint's mayor in the 1990s, experienced a form of stereotyping while in high school. He had taken a summer job at Gilbert Shoe Stores at N. Saginaw and Wood streets.

When school resumed in September, Stanley continued working part time, at the manager's request. Normally, the store did not employ part-timers.

So when it became necessary for the store to lay off some employees, the foreman offered the hard-working Stanley a deal: Quit school and come to work full time as a foreman. Stanley told him he couldn't work full time because he had to go to school. The foreman argued that he could get a diploma any time.

"He wanted me to quit school," Stanley said, incredulously. "I don't know if that was something related to stereotyping. I was upset that he would even think I would quit school. It may not have had anything to do with the fact that I was black. On one hand, it was a compliment; I'd done a good job there, but I wasn't planning on making it a career."

Prejudiced attitudes created tension in some Flint neighborhoods, even those where people generally got along.

Sondra Rawls recalled a hostile neighbor in the St. John area. Neighborhood children had to walk past her house on the way to school, Rawls said. For no reason, the woman would come out of her house and yell racial slurs at them.

She'd taunt them, saying, "Go back to Africa where you came from." And the children would yell back: "Sorry, I came from South Carolina," Rawls said.

As a child, Karen Aldridge had a white neighbor on Marengo Street who would throw rocks at black children and threaten to shoot them, she said.

Angela Sawyer's family experienced an example of well-meant stereotyping when they integrated a Beecher neighborhood in the 1970s. The Sawyers did not fit the image of blacks held by the mostly Southern whites already living there, she said.

"One of our neighbors told my dad ... about his brother who'd moved into a neighborhood that had some niggers next door," Sawyer said. "My father reared back. The man said, 'Oh no, I don't mean you.' I guess he thought he was paying my father a compliment."

The man explained: "There's a difference between living next door to niggers and living next door to colored folks."

Charlotte Williams recalled that Lapeer Street once was jokingly called the Mason-Dixon line. The reference was to the geographical line between Pennsylvania and Maryland, dividing Northern states from Southern states.

William and Bertha Simms were the first blacks to move across Flint's "Mason-Dixon" line in the early 1950s, Williams said, adding that they were helped by whites. William Simms was a dentist and his wife was in real estate.

The second couple to cross the line were the Rev. Robert Turpin and his wife, Annie. Whites interceded for them, too.

But in 1953, Alexander Jones moved in unassisted, though intolerance had not abated.

"When I first moved in, everything around here was white," Jones said. "Now look at it. I don't know of one white family in the neighborhood. They don't want to live around blacks."

Despite such attitudes, Jones believes neighborhood race relations were better in the old days, and particularly during the Great Depression of the 1930s when money, food and other necessities were scarce.

"Back then, you could count the blacks who owned a home," Jones said. "Black and white (neighbors) helped each other. You almost had to lean against each other to stand up."

In the early 1960s, Charlotte Williams and her husband met mild resistance when they decided to build their present home in the "Sugar Hill" neighborhood off Lapeer Road, immediately west of S. Dort Highway. At the time, there were about 11 houses in the area.

The Williamses chose a model they liked and made the required $5 deposit. But the real estate agent held the deposit for a year while showing the couple houses all over the north side of Flint.

Williams said her husband correctly predicted that the agent would soon be begging them to move to Sugar Hill.

In 1968, Sam Williams encountered no overt prejudice when he built a home in the Evergreen Estates subdivision, near the east city limits at S. Center Road. The Williamses were the second or third black family to move in and were treated OK by white neighbors.

"The only thing, they always moved away," Williams said. "(Now) this is a black neighborhood."

Lois and Edgar Holt, with Lois' sister Ruth VanZandt, crashed a barrier in the late 1970s when they built a house on Crapo Street between E. Court and E. Second streets.

"The powers that be weren't too happy with a black family being this close to the cultural area," VanZandt said. Their occupancy of the three-unit frame house contradicted one white woman's conviction that they'd "never get over there," VanZandt said.

"We didn't have the laws against housing discrimination at that time," she said. "People have always thought that once you're in the North, you can do anything. But that was not true."

Reality was "colored housing" ads in the newspaper, Freddie Williams said. Also, in a practice called racial steering, real estate agents would show houses to blacks only in certain neighborhoods. And while blacks were being steered in, whites often were being steered out.

"Some announced plans to move even before they got to know their new black neighbors," Shirley Williams noted.

Norm Bryant said there used to be a map showing which neighborhoods that blacks could live in. For a long time, most of them were "by the (railroad) tracks and by the river," said Bryant, who moved to Flint at age 6 in 1942.

"Any time you'd go to any big city, that's where you'd find black people, near the tracks and the river.

"We were very limited as to what we could buy. They listed in the paper, 'This is for colored.' You could maybe get a white person to intercede for you in some cases."

That's what Fred Waller's father did in the 1930s when he wanted to buy a house on Ninth Street at Broad where the I-475 and I-69 interchange is now. The owners wouldn't sell it to him. So, Waller said, a white friend named Mrs. Knight bought the house then resold it to his father.

And Dorothy Waller recalled a white neighbor in the E. Court Street area who went out of her way to show sensitivity, shortly after the Wallers moved there in the mid-1960s. The neighbor, who lived a few doors away, stopped by their home to explain that her family was moving because of a job change, not because the Wallers had moved in.

"She didn't have to do that," Waller said. "She could have moved and said nothing."

"Coloreds welcome" signs, posted on rental houses in the 1950s, marked other receptive whites.

So did the '60s-era gesture of Karen Aldridge's neighbors, an older white couple, who generously shared fruit from their orchard with black neighbors.

In the Mt. Morris area during the 1940s, sisters Marion Wright Quinn and Rachel Wright James enjoyed cordial relationships with their white neighbors.

"Most of them seemed to be middle-class people," Quinn said. "They'd come and have dinner with us and we'd visit with them. We'd visit their churches and they'd visit ours."

One secret to getting along with whites, some successful blacks have said, is to refuse to accept racism as an obstacle.

That's how Dolores Watkins Ennis handled a professor in the early 1950s who tried to dampen her career goals. Ennis was a Latin major in her senior year at the University of Michigan.

"He said to me, 'Miss Watkins, where are you going to get a job teaching Latin?' " Ennis recalled. "I told him that was my problem, not his." About two years later, she became Flint's first black secondary-level teacher.

"No one should be shocked at some of those things going on," Ennis said, adding that "you don't have to cave in to it."

Said Charlotte Williams: "Even growing up, we knew there was racism, but we didn't call it that. My church (Quinn Chapel AME) was very instrumental in helping us adapt."

She "put up with it" when she encountered racism, but never let it become a personal problem.

"We had lots of white friends, (but) we never spent the night at each other's houses because you just didn't do that," she said.

In reviewing her life, Williams said she couldn't identify many negative experiences that she would say happened because she was black. That has also been true for her daughter whose husband is white, she said.

On the other hand, Woody Etherly Jr. believes he has cause to be bitter, but said he isn't, about the militant label placed on him because of his outspokenness on racial issues. Etherly, who served as a Flint city councilman from 1970 to 1983, describes himself as a "softie" until it comes to policies detrimental to blacks.

"Basically, I am a very peace-loving person ... but I have the ability to change and meet fire with fire," he said.

Many of his battles stemmed from the inability, or refusal, of power brokers, who usually were white, to understand and address the needs of the black community.

"White folks still think they know what's best for us (blacks)," he said. "I have a problem with that. I have a problem when I sit down and tell you that we as black folks don't condone all these people standing on the corner pushing drugs. We don't condone all the break-ins and the murders in the black community. We don't like that."

His concern is that those problems appear to get resolved faster when they occur in white neighborhoods, Etherly said, noting that blacks pay taxes, which should entitle them to the same prompt police and city services that whites get.

"If you get in the car with me and come to the black community, I can show you what I'm talking about, OK?" he said. "But they (policymakers) don't want to do that. Now, they'll get on a bus with all the dignitaries and police escorts ... and they'll ride through the community and ... talk about how bad it is. It didn't have to be that way. So I get upset with people that play these intellectual games with me."

He berated "pseudo-liberal" politicians who respond to problems in the black community only when it suits their political agenda. Flint needs "true" politicians committed to an interracial coalition for change, he said.

For example: "I went to the councilmen's ball, at least, I thought it was the councilmen's ball," Etherly said. "Come to find out, it was four black councilmen. No white councilmen (nor) white staff from the councilmen's office. And it was called a Unity Ball. Now where's the unity?"

Etherly said his role models were Adam Clayton Powell Jr., a former U.S. representative from New York City, and Coleman Young, Detroit's former mayor. He admired them as uncompromising politicians who were faithful to black interests. White society prefers to uplift black leaders whom they can control, he said.

"White folks ... try to put you in a little mold, and they don't want you to break out. I never could fit, so I always broke out; so people say I'm militant. But let me tell you, I've got two things in life I love – politics and religion. And the reason I like both of them is because both of them deal with helping folks.

"I've been a fighter all my life on behalf of black folks."

DISCRIMINATION:
"You knew where you could go and couldn't go."

Melvin McCree, son of Flint's first black mayor, believes in confronting racial discrimination head-on.

"I've always taken the attitude that if I want to go into a a bar or a restaurant, I'm going," he said. "If you don't like me ... tough; and if you treat me bad, I'll probably come back again."

McCree was born in 1953 and came of age during the era when anti-discrimination battles were being fought and won. But his forebears had lived in a different Flint when discrimination was common and generally tolerated.

"You didn't dare go into certain establishments," said Lois Shaw, who came to Flint, at age 27, in 1946. "They didn't have signs up saying you weren't wanted, but you knew better than to go in there because they wouldn't serve you."

And Sam Williams, a Flint resident since 1927, commented: "You guys (younger generations) have a lot to be thankful for compared to the people who went ahead of you, who tried to open up the way.

"At (one) time, you couldn't stay at the hotels, you couldn't eat at a lot of restaurants, either."

The Durant Hotel downtown was no exception. The landmark opened in 1921 and closed in 1973. In its heyday, it was the hub of civic and social events in Flint. And being at one time the only major hotel in town, the exclusionary policy against blacks added insult to injury.

"When (black) entertainers came to town, they couldn't stay there," Ruth Scott said. "They stayed at somebody's house. That's just the way things were."

Possibly the first black guest to stay at the Durant was Jimmy Carter, the world lightweight boxing champion, said Norm Bryant. He couldn't pinpoint the date of that historic visit, but newspaper accounts indicate that Carter was on tour from 1954 to 1955, during the height of his acclaim.

Blacks at the Durant held menial jobs such as elevator operators, shoeshine boys, busboys, maids and janitors, but, by the late 1940s, were allowed to attend conventions and other social events at the hotel.

Before and during World War II, however, The Purple Cow coffee shop at the Durant did not want to serve blacks.

Annalea Bannister said she and a group of friends, including two Army lieu-

The Durant Hotel, a premier establishment, did not accept black guests until the 1940s.

---

tenants on leave, were ill-treated at the Purple Cow. After spending the early part of the evening at a downtown bowling alley, the group wanted a bite to eat, Bannister recalled. They went to the Purple Cow across the street.

As soon as they walked in, they noticed the waitresses huddling in a corner, giving them strange looks.

"We knew they were talking about us," she said. But the waitresses would not come over to take their order. Soon, word had spread all over the hotel that some blacks in the coffee shop were causing trouble, Bannister said.

Her uncle, who was a waiter at the hotel, came to see what the fuss was about and was shocked to find his niece and daughters at the center of it. They sat there for an hour and a half without getting service, Bannister said.

It drove home the injustice of racism, seeing that Bannister's escorts were fighting in a war on behalf of all Americans. But in that regard, segregation in Flint was not much better than the "Jim Crow" practices of the South.

"You know how you say, (if) you lived up north, you were free," Bannister said. "You weren't free. You knew where you could go and couldn't go."

Katie Ellis Harper was shielded from that knowledge for years after being born in Flint in 1928.

"When we were younger, we didn't know what our parents were going through and the places that were closed to blacks," she said.

But Ellis Harper found out when she was older, at a popular downtown confectionery.

"They would take the black people's money for candy and peanuts up front, but they wouldn't serve the blacks in the restaurant part in the back," she said. Challenging that policy turned out to be a mistake.

"They put so much salt in our hamburgers we couldn't eat them," she said.

Ellis Harper had another brush with discrimination at a downtown hat store. The proprietor did not want blacks to try on hats without a hair covering because she said they had greasy hair. But her complaints stopped after customers protested, Ellis Harper said.

Elnor Pea said she'd heard similar stories but never had a problem shopping at Schiller's Millinery Store on S. Saginaw Street from 1926 to about 1953. Some of the clerks were receptive and some weren't, Pea said, adding that she didn't care one way or the other.

"If they had a problem, that was their problem," she said.

Charlotte Williams tasted discrimination at a diner on the corner of First and S. Saginaw streets. She and a friend who went there for lunch were so engrossed in conversation that it took a while for them to notice that people who had come in after them had been served and were leaving.

Williams complained to the proprietor, who made it clear that blacks were not welcome. They left and told their story to Dr. Jesse L. Leach, a civic and NAACP leader, who had been the first in Flint to file a complaint under a new civil rights law in 1937.

Williams isn't sure what Leach did, but the next time she went to that particular diner, she had no trouble getting served. Still, it was a hollow victory. Williams said she no longer wanted to eat there because she could not be sure that the food served to her would not be tampered with.

"It wasn't arrogance," she said. "But you had a good feeling about yourself, that you didn't go where you weren't wanted."

Alexander Jones, who was 78 in 1994, still won't patronize businesses where he doesn't feel welcome. He followed a personal "buy black" campaign long before it was touted as an economic improvement strategy in the 1970s.

"You can say what you want about the (anti-discrimination) law, but I'd just as soon stay as I always was," Jones said. "I still say they (some businesses) want my dollar but they don't want me on account of the color of my skin. So I keep my green dollar with my black skin. Just like they passed this integration law that blacks have to be served (in restaurants). Uh-uh. I'm still segregated, because I feel more comfortable going where I've always gone."

Layton Galloway recalled that blacks were unwelcome at a movie theater on Hamilton Avenue near Lewis Street, on the city's east side. But they had several other options at theaters on the north side, south side and in downtown Flint, though they had to sit in the balcony for many years, he said.

The Capitol, the State and the Strand theaters in downtown Flint became more popular with blacks in the 1950s, Galloway said.

"I never went to the Capitol until I was grown," he said. "But when I was a young boy, 13 years old (in the late 1930s), we'd go down to the Capitol lobby and shine white folks' shoes."

During the first decades of the 20th century, some said that blacks were assigned certain days to visit amusement parks, community centers, roller rinks and recreational parks. Also, concerts and other events held at the IMA Auditorium were segregated for many years. Blacks attended IMA events at midnight, after whites had used the facility during the early evening hours.

Shirley Williams complained about city bus service. She remembered waiting downtown a long time for the St. John Street bus, which served the north-side neighborhood where many blacks lived. Many buses would pass by, some of them empty, but when the St. John bus arrived, it would be filled to capacity, she said.

Buses were the main mode of transportation for many blacks in the 1940s and 1950s. Few could afford cars. So it seemed illogical and unfair to Williams that fewer buses were assigned to the route that had the most riders.

Widespread housing discrimination lasted well into the 1960s. Blacks knew and generally accepted the invisible lines cordoning off neighborhoods where they could not live.

Eighth Street was "kind of a boundary line, going toward town," said Anna L.V. Howard, who grew up in the 1920s and '30s. In those days, only whites lived east of Lapeer Street. Blacks lived west of Lapeer back to South Saginaw, she said.

Ruth Owens Buckner was a newlywed in about 1930 when she and her husband were turned away from a rental house in Elm Park, an all-white neighborhood west of Howard Avenue on the south side.

"A poor white woman told me she couldn't rent to us because it was a restricted area," Buckner said. "There was hardly anything out there, so there was no reason for it to be restricted."

Elm Park reluctantly accepted Carl and Lois Shaw in the 1950s. Lois Shaw, a registered nurse, arrived in Flint in 1946 and soon learned that she couldn't rent a house anywhere she wanted. The Shaws were able to buy the Elm Park house because her husband knew the real estate salesman, she said.

Regardless of restrictions, Dolores Watkins Ennis "went where I wanted to go."

But she conceded that, in the 1950s, many neighborhoods resisted blacks, including the neighborhood adjacent to Elm Park where hers was the first or second black family on their block. Ennis still lives in the house she and her husband built in 1958.

"This was like farm land," she said. "There were no houses here. A bunch of us got together and bought it."

Meanwhile, by 1960, blacks on Flint's north side had begun to spread west of N. Saginaw Street. But no Welcome Wagon greeted the first wave of black newcomers that included the Rev. Eugene Simpson.

"I was trying to buy a house by (old) Northern High School, and those white Realtors kept trying to sell me a house over in Beecher," Simpson said.

"I finally bought the house on Genesee and Bonbright. When I moved, there were only two black families living there. I was treated all right by my neighbors, but they all (eventually) moved." In 1972 Simpson moved to Grand Blanc.

Lennetta Coney called up a vague childhood memory of an aunt and uncle who were the first blacks to move to Grand Blanc's Ottawa Hills subdivision in the mid-1960s. The couple were forced to move to make way for freeway construction in their south Flint neighborhood. To penetrate Grand Blanc, they had to resurrect a time-tested strategy.

"They managed that by asking a white friend to be their front," Coney said. Reportedly, some folks were upset about a black family moving in, but what was done was done.

ON THE JOB:
"The last hired and the first fired"

Early in her working life, Dorothy Waller, now a retired math teacher, was "shocked" to be turned down for an ironing job at a Chinese laundry. She is convinced it was because of her race. Waller was accustomed to being accepted in interracial circles.

Unfair hiring practices disillusioned the Rev. Albert C. Lee before he had even finished college. In the mid-1950s Lee was a business administration and accounting major at Flint Junior College.

"I was about the No. 2 student in my accounting class," Lee said. "A job opened for a student accountant. I applied for a job, and the instructor informed me that he did not believe that this company would be (receptive) to a black student in accounting."

In 1986, the Flint advertising industry refused to open to Lennetta Bradley Coney, an articulate, personable and well-groomed black woman in her early 30s.

"I couldn't understand and still can't put my finger on it, not getting hired in the advertising business here," she said. "I did feel there was some discrimination in not hiring me because I clearly had the credentials and the experience."

Coney, who is executive director of multicultural affairs at Mott Community College, does not appear to be the type to frivolously cry job discrimination or even to expect it to happen to her.

She was born and raised on Flint's south side, in a respectable, middle-class family. A well-rounded childhood included enrichment programs in sewing, modeling, dance and foreign travel.

After graduating from Howard University with a bachelor's degree in journalism, she lived and worked in New York City for seven years, where she was a senior account executive for an advertising agency. But after marriage drew Coney home to Flint in 1986, she learned that her national and international work credentials were not enough to open doors at local advertising agencies.

"I remember going for a job interview," Coney said. "I won't say which agency, but the person who interviewed me said: 'Wow, your salary was higher than mine.' Now naturally, with the cost of living being higher in New York, it had to be more."

That fruitless interview left Coney with the impression that it wasn't because her resume wasn't good enough, but that it was too good. She had been perceived as a threat.

Coney's story is one of many told by African-Americans who have tried to find good jobs or to keep them. Her best friend since kindergarten, Debra Taylor, also has stories.

Taylor, who holds a bachelor's degree in telecommunications and a master's in public administration, left Flint for several years after a few discouraging job experiences.

Taylor was fired from two jobs – one right out of college and the other while working in the shop. She remains convinced that being fired from a factory job in the early 1970s was "definitely illegal and racially motivated."

In Taylor's view, blacks sometimes experience job discrimination in the form of being qualified but never given a chance.

Typical job discrimination patterns are showcased in expressions such as "the last hired and first fired," "the dirty jobs nobody else wants," and the "token- or super-Negro" who gets hired because of lighter skin, docility, overqualification or as a political favor. Also, some said a double standard for measuring ability is unfairly applied to blacks.

"Even now, you still got to be better than the whites," said Dolores McGowain, who can trace her family back to Flint's first black residents.

Her grandfather, George W. Artis, moved his family to Flint from Dresden, Ontario, in 1889. He was a highly respected contractor said to have built several Flint-area barns.

His three sons – William R., Arnold E. (McGowain's dad) and Leroy H. – later formed the Artis Construction Co., which built the old Regent Theater Building in downtown Flint. The family construction trade was passed down to William's son, George Robert Artis.

"Dad was one of the few black business people in downtown Flint, back in the mid-1950s," said Ronald Artis, an industrial electrician. He speculated that his dad being fair-skinned worked to his advantage.

Annalea Bannister also theorized that her sister got hired at Peck's drug store downtown "because they couldn't tell she was black. If they had, she would never have gotten it."

Pre-World War II, blacks could shop downtown, but few were hired, except for menial jobs.

The first black person to work behind a counter downtown – Mildred Todd's fair-skinned daughter – was hired by Smith-Bridgman's department store, Dorothy Parks recalled. The date is uncertain.

"A lot of people didn't like the idea that she was fair (complexioned)," Parks said. "They thought they should have hired a darker person." For darker-skinned blacks, "all you could get was a broom, sweeping jobs," Parks said.

Parks said she would be told there were no openings when she applied for jobs at downtown stores, which she dismissed as "a polite excuse."

"They wouldn't say you couldn't have it because you were black," she said.

Her husband, Leonard Parks, added that color consciousness in hiring was not limited to downtown stores.

"They had quite a bit of that going around even in the shops," said Parks, a Buick retiree. But in the shops, the fair-skinned blacks were sweepers, too.

"Even back in the 1940s, they gave me the broom and slop jar," Parks said. "I told them I was more qualified than that." He had to produce trade certification papers to get reassigned to a better job.

By the time his wife, Dorothy, got hired in the 1950s, blacks were being hired to work on the assembly line, but she started out cleaning bathrooms, too.

Some blacks who were the first of their race to hold various jobs in Flint were well-received by co-workers and employers; some were not.

Flint's first black classroom teacher (1943), Marion Coates-Williams, had co-workers who went out of their way to make her feel welcome.

"When the teachers were planning parties, they'd always make sure it was someplace I would be accepted to eat," she said. "It was a good staff. I really enjoyed working with them."

Coates-Williams was only 21. So the older teachers took her under their wings. One, who owned a car, even gave her rides to work every day.

But Hurley Hospital did not exactly roll out the red carpet for Lois Shaw, who said she was its first black registered nurse in 1947. But Shaw got hired, thanks to Zolton Papp, chairman of Hurley's board of directors.

When she applied for the job, Shaw had been told she was "overqualified." She interpreted that to mean "because she was black."

But Papp, a white civic leader and pharmacist, went to bat for her. A day or two later he called Shaw to offer her the job, she said.

Being the "first and only" and unwelcome on top of that, Shaw had to prove herself. At first, her co-workers questioned everything she did, she said.

"I had to be twice as good as anyone else," she said. But it only took about a year to establish herself with the doctors, she said. Many would ask for her.

For others, job discrimination led to legal challenges.

Layton Galloway, one of the first black postal workers, confronted prejudice when he was assigned to the branch office at Franklin and Leith in the 1950s.

"The first day of work I went across the street to the Chuck Wagon for lunch and I wasn't served," he said. "They said I could take the sandwich, but I couldn't eat it in there."

Galloway filed a civil rights complaint.

"We ran him (the owner) out of there," he said. "He moved up on Dort Highway." Before moving, he offered Galloway a voucher for six months worth of free meals. Galloway declined.

"I didn't want to have anything to do with it," he said.

Others perceived discrimination in deceptions.

Several years ago, Mayor Woodrow Stanley said he heard a rumor about college athletic scholarship offers not being disclosed to designated recipients.

"They discovered a lot of letters sent to black athletes, and the coach never gave the kids the letters," Stanley said. "What he didn't want (was for) these black kids to get these scholarships."

Flint's dominant industry, the auto plants, generated the most job discrimination stories. It dates back to the early decades when blacks were assigned to work in Buick's hot, dirty and dangerous foundry where steel was melted and poured into molds.

Milton Port worked in the foundry about eight years, hiring in in 1934.

"When I went in Buick, a black couldn't work in the core room," he said. "They had white women working in there, but they didn't have blacks unless they were sweeping. You didn't get a job as a core setter or inspector.

A mixture of races, nationalities and faiths worked at Buick circa 1916.

(Blacks) only got the back-breaking jobs until the union came in.

"When they put you on a job, you (stayed until you) died on it. You weren't supposed to ask for more."

But Port did get a better job during the World War II labor shortage. After the war, however, management tried to send him back to the foundry, so he quit.

"I figured, if I can work this job during wartime I ought to be able to work it during peace time," Port said. "I told the man what he could do with his job.

"Even when I left Buick and went to Chevrolet, and asked for better jobs there, (the) foreman told me, 'As long as I'm foreman you'll never work that job.'"

Port had worked his way up to metal finisher by the time he retired from Chevrolet Metal Fabricating. Before that he was a die setter.

For a long time, though, they wouldn't let him handle tools. One white co-worker went so far as to tell Port to never to touch his tools. So Port had to learn by observing. By the time he was promoted to die setter, he also knew how to do press jobs and the guy with the hands-off tool policy didn't.

Port said he would be called down to the white man's work area whenever a press had to be set up. And he made sure to not let his old nemesis watch him do it, he said.

Unionization improved working conditions for blacks, Port said. Union rules helped them land jobs as electricians, millwrights, tinsmiths, pipe-fitters, foremen and general foremen. White workers generally had an easier time getting the jobs they wanted, he said.

"Years ago, they'd put (a white male) on the job, if he could do it or not, and showed him how to do it," Port said. "Some couldn't read and write."

He recalled one illiterate foreman at Buick who got the job because he was white and knew how to push people, Port said.

Twenty years of working at Buick did not exempt Jimmy Jones from discrimination.

"I learned how to do every job in GM," Jones said. "I'd break guys in on the machine, and six months later, they were foremen. That was an accepted way of life. I never got used to it."

The Rev. Eugene Simpson's run-in with discrimination at Buick happened about 1978, just two years before he retired.

"I worked on the repair floor as a repair man," he said. "It was a high-paying job." A white male co-worker was assigned the job of installing car tapes. Simpson asked for the job because he had more seniority. The foreman told him he couldn't have it because it was a job for a driver. A few months later, the foreman told another worker it was a job for a repair man.

A union committeeman was called in to resolve the dispute. He said the job didn't have a classification, meaning it had been open all along according to seniority.

Robert Pea was among those who discovered that, when it came to getting a factory job, it wasn't what you knew, but who you knew. When he sought a position at AC in the 1930s, Pea asked his former high school coach, Guy Houston, to put in a good word for him. He got called to work the same day. When his wife got hired in the 1940s, somebody vouched for her, too.

"You could make good money if you could get in the shop," Freddie Williams agreed. "The trouble was getting in. You had to know somebody already in."

Whites could more easily get jobs in the factory after graduation because their fathers or other family members were already working there, he said. In some cases, there were white shop foremen who did not have a high school diploma, he said.

But after the war started, even underage blacks were being hired. Williams said he knew a few 16-year-olds working in the shop.

Getting hired was one hurdle, and moving up another.

Williams worked in the shop 36 years, 18 of them on production before being offered a supervisory position. Suddenly, he had become qualified with no additional education, he said.

His wife Shirley, a 30-year shop veteran, explained it this way: "When the government came in and said they had to have black supervisors, they had no problem choosing them, because they had been qualified all along, just never given the opportunity."

James A. Sharp, a former Flint mayor, still is wondering why he had to do three tours of duty in Vietnam while others did only one.

In the early 1970s, Sharp, a sergeant in the Marine Corps, had been to Vietnam twice. When his number came up a third time, he balked. With help from a friend in the data processing division, Sharp investigated records and found that 225 first sergeants had done only one tour of duty plus had been back in the United States longer than he had.

Complaining didn't do Sharp any good. He was sent back again. Luckily, he came home for good after only nine months because a political friend pulled some strings.

Becoming Flint's first popularly elected black mayor in 1983 thrust Sharp under a "vicious" spotlight, due to political enemies and the media.

"It's just an incredible job, in any of these cities, to be the first black executive of the city," Sharp said. "It's incredible because you have all these people not wanting you there, working against you, ... second-guessing and undermining, because they don't want you to have a second term."

Some underminers were entrenched civil servants at Flint City Hall, inherited employees who could not be fired or replaced, he said. Sharp had authority to appoint new department heads but, to a large degree, the rank and file were the cogs that kept the wheels of municipal government turning.

"It (also) didn't help that I tried to hire black people," Sharp said, of his affirmative action efforts. Almost everything he did was publicized as being "racially motivated," he said.

"Word got out fast that there was nothing but black people at City Hall, that I had hired all black folks. And that rumor sort of ran through town. And it stuck."

Most unjustly, that conflicted with his personal history and beliefs. Sharp grew up in an integrated New York neighborhood. He began his political career in 1971 as a district representative for U.S. Rep. Donald W. Riegle Jr., a Flint native.

As mayor, Sharp received death threats and was targeted for hate campaigns, but his outlook on racial discrimination is remarkably tolerant.

"I know that when you get most of the hard-core people, who make judgments based on race, in a one-on-one situation, they soften up," Sharp said. "They'll convert."

On the other hand, Sharp accuses the media of staging photographs, misquoting him and one-sided reporting. He said the media never associated him with good news or showcased the accomplishments of his administration.

Into the 1980s, perceived job discrimination was less blatant and thus harder to prove.

Robert Matthews, a UM-Flint graduate student, said he sensed something fishy when he responded to a newspaper ad for an apartment rental agent. Though he had prior experience, he didn't rate so much as an interview. Instead, he was told the job had been filled.

"I noticed the ad ran in the paper another couple of weeks so that sort of piqued my curiosity as to why they'd continue running the ad if the job was filled," Matthews said.

Matthews had left his resume with the company in case a position opened up later but never heard from them again, he said. So that left him forever wondering if he had not been considered for the job because he is black.

LEADERSHIP:
"A common man trying to do common good."

Woodrow Stanley is officially Flint's third black mayor but at least four or five others have worn a version of that title before him.

Decades before Flint's official African-American mayors – Stanley, James A. Sharp and Floyd J. McCree – local blacks elected their "Mayor of Brownsville."

"That was a title, more or less, given to Negro leaders," said Fred Waller, a retired pharmacist, recalling that the 1930s-era honorary title was decided in newspaper balloting.

"At the time, there were no official black leaders," Waller said.

Magnus Clark, a restaurant owner, was voted the first Mayor of Brownsville, according to old newspaper articles. The last was Samuel T. McClarin, head porter at the Durant Hotel and at that time the only black supervisor there.

The Mayor of Brownsville was popularly elected by the 20,000 subscribers to the Brownsville News, a black newspaper. Editor Henry G. Reynolds created the "election" to stimulate reader interest and to fill a void.

In those days, blacks had little or no voice in local government. The

Mayor of Brownsville's duties were mainly social. He wore a badge inscribed in bronze and bestowed in an inauguration ceremony.

"It sort of faded out when blacks began to be elected to things, probably in the '40s," Waller said.

In the 1930s and '40s, the who's who list of black leaders in Flint included prominent business owners, doctors, lawyers, social workers and ministers.

Officials of the Flint NAACP, founded in 1922, and the Flint Urban League, founded in 1943, also played important leadership roles.

Jesse L. Leach, a surgeon, appears to have been Flint's first black government official. He served on the Genesee County Board of Supervisors (now Commissioners) from 1927 to 1948.

Leach was once described as the most important black person in Flint history. A 1914 graduate of Meharry Medical College, he came to Flint in 1920 and remained here until his death in 1981 at age 85.

He served five terms as president of the NAACP Flint chapter, several years as state president and 18 years on the national board. He is on record as the first person to file a civil rights complaint under a law enacted in 1937. That was after a restaurant on Dort Highway refused to serve him.

Leach worked to improve the quality of life for blacks in housing, employment and business. He held local and national leadership positions in health, civic and church organizations.

Blacks needing a job or legal assistance sought his help. And whites reportedly consulted him as a liaison to the black community.

He promoted and built the Flint Community Building on Dewey Street where he and other black professionals had offices and community events were held. Also, he was president of the South Side Improvement Corporation, working to improve available housing for blacks.

Many who knew him described him as a doer and a motivator.

The first black woman to hold public office was Georgia M. Hyche, who was appointed to the County Board of Supervisors in 1957 and served three two-year terms.

Hyche was an active Republican from 1934 to 1946, but is best remembered as a tireless Democrat. From 1948 to 1960, she was a state delegate and president of the New Era Democratic Club. She also was active in the women's division of the Genesee County Democratic Club, the NAACP, PTA and service groups.

Hyche's political activity left an impression on Flint mayor-to-be Woodrow Stanley who lived on her street when he was a boy.

"She was probably one of the most prominent black leaders," Stanley said. "On election day she would be speeding through the streets picking up people to take them to the polls. That left an indelible imprint on my desire to run for public office."

And Melvin P. McCree said: "Georgia ... would serve as a liaison for whites looking for black voters' support. My father (Mayor Floyd McCree) liked her a great deal and worked with her for many years."

Like Hyche and Leach, many of the first black politicians got their start on the county Board of Supervisors. George Friley, Flint's second black police officer, was elected in 1951. Floyd J. McCree joined in 1956.

Until about 1930, most Flint blacks were Republicans in allegiance to Abraham Lincoln, who abolished slavery. But voting records in the mid-1930s indicate that most Flint blacks had switched to the Democratic Party.

Bessie Brooks said she shocked her mother by voting Democrat in 1927.

"She said my grandmother would turn over in her grave if she knew I voted for a Democrat," Brooks said. "See, then they all voted Republican. My mother was a Republican. They followed the leader. I had a mind of my own when I got grown."

Flint's first black state representative, John F. Young, served from 1949 to 1952. Roger Townsend was second, from 1952-64, and Floyd Clack, third, was re-elected to his fourth four-year term in November 1994.

Floyd J. McCree, the first black to serve on the Flint City Commission, was elected in 1958, after serving a two-year term on the county Board of Supervisors. In 1966 McCree was chosen by his fellow commission members as Flint's first black mayor – the first black nationwide to head a major city.

Black government leaders in the 1960s often coalesced with civil rights leaders. Prime movers and shakers were Harold R. Hayden, Flint NAACP president; C. Frederick Robinson, an attorney and chairman of the Community Civic League; John Mack, executive director of the Flint Urban League; and John Hightower, a factory worker and president of the Flint Trade Union Leadership Council in the auto plants.

The Community Civic League was a civil rights umbrella group founded by Robinson, Hightower, the Rev. Alfred L.C. Robbs of Canaan Baptist Church and Earl Crompton, a UAW leader.

"At that time there was total segregation between professional blacks and nonprofessional blacks and the union blacks," Robinson said. "So what we did was made an effort to get everyone involved – the professional people sitting in the same room with the union people and making joint decisions about what collective efforts we should make."

The NAACP became more aggressive and the Trade Union Leadership Council fought discrimination in the plants, he said. The Community Civic League spearheaded voter education drives and tackled legal issues.

Hightower added: "We combined our resources and made a big difference in Flint. Fred fought it from a political point of view, Harold fought it

The outspoken Rev. Alfred L.C. Robbs, pastor of Canaan Baptist Church and later Christ Fellowship, was one of the founders of the Community Civic League.

---

from a civil rights point of view, and I fought it from a jobs point of view."

The Rev. Robbs tackled the religious and moral perspective, spurred by the shockingly backward social conditions he found when he came to Flint in 1957.

"I've been in cities in the deep South that were not as prejudiced," said the outspoken Robbs. "I said, Lord if you'll help me, I'll try to face it."

Besides Robinson and Hightower, his partners in civil rights leadership included Edgar Holt, a Flint and state NAACP president; and James Crichton, a business owner.

"These were guys that the Lord used me to bring out of the cupboard,"

Several civil rights leaders worked together under the umbrella of the Community Civic League. John Hightower (right) headed the Trade Union Leadership Council in the factories and Harold Hayden was president of the NAACP.

Robbs said.

Robbs, Crichton and Robinson organized what is remembered as the first civil rights protest in Flint.

In the fall of 1958 they picketed Flint City Hall for a month to protest the arrest of a young black woman accused of loitering. The young woman claimed she had been merely walking home from church.

"The police tried to say the girl was prostituting," Robbs said. "They could pick up black women anywhere and make it the same charge as prostitution."

The case against the young woman was thrown out of court. Police apologized and said it was a case of mistaken identity, according to The Flint Journal's files.

Robbs said the matter was settled because U.S. Vice President Richard M. Nixon was coming to town for a political rally and city officials did not want to be embarrassed by the picket.

"The things you all have now, that you take for granted, we fought every inch of the way for it," Robbs said. "We suffered for it."

Blacks had many causes to fight for in the late 1950s. According to Robbs, there were no black salespeople; domestic work and operating elevators were the main jobs open to women, and teachers at one predominantly black school did not have college degrees.

Attorney C. Frederick Robinson was a pillar of Flint's civil rights' activism in the late 1950s and '60s. He organized the first protests and won legal remedies in court.

"We fought 'til we got college-degreed teachers in every school in Flint," Robbs said. "We kept fighting until we got a black principal."

In the mid-1960s, Robbs' group "took to the streets and demanded that we have equal rights to live where we wanted to live," he said.

Mayor Floyd McCree was recognized as a key spokesperson for fair housing, but C. Frederick Robinson initiated it, Robbs said. Being vocal about civil rights caused problems for some of the leaders.

Hightower was branded a communist. He said federal authorities threatened to arrest him for no reason because he helped lead a weeklong picket at Michigan National Bank to get black tellers hired.

"Once you acted in an outspoken way in those days, you were (called) a Communist," Hightower said.

Two white civic leaders – Flint Mayor Robert J. Egan and Genesee County Prosecutor Robert Leonard – came to his defense.

According to Hightower, Leonard, who was a strong civil rights supporter, said: "I see no reason why this man should be arrested. All they wanted to do is to be able to have the same service as anyone can have."

Flint industrialist and philanthropist Charles Stewart Mott interceded and saw to it that the bank hired Pauline Pryor, the first black teller, Hightower said.

Robbs added: "Mr. C.S. Mott was one of the great benefactors of Flint. So much so until I told him one day there was no way Flint could come into its own without his support. Not only blacks but whites also looked on him as a great white father."

Robbs said Mott praised him for his candor.

"He said, 'You tell me what I need to hear, not what I want to hear, and I thank you for that.'"

The group picketed for black hiring at other large companies including Consumers Power Co. and the local Sears, Roebuck & Co. department store.

Hightower said he stood outside of Sears one day to count black shoppers. He wanted the count to use in arguing that Sears should hire blacks in proportion to the number that shopped there.

The committee took on restaurants, skating rinks, bowling alleys and other public places known to exclude blacks.

"We broke down all of Industrial Avenue," Hightower said, explaining that the street had been lined with bars and diners where blacks could not eat or drink.

They met some resistance, such as from the owner of the Colonel's Drive-In restaurant on N. Saginaw Street. According to Hightower, the owner said, "Before I serve niggers, I'll close down." And he did.

But first, Hightower's group staged a demonstration in the parking lot of the business. Each time a patron drove out, a protester moved into the vacated parking spot. They sat all day and ordered only a cup of coffee, Hightower said. That went on for a week before police were called. But the group's attorney successfully argued that no laws were being broken.

In another demonstration, an interracial coalition desegregated a bowling alley, Hightower said. The whites would go in first and set up leagues. Then the blacks showed up as their guests. That challenge was successfully settled in a lawsuit, aided by attorney Otis Smith, who later became Michigan's first black Supreme Court justice, Hightower said.

About 75 activists, blacks and whites, traveled to Alabama in 1965 to support the historic Selma-to-Montgomery march led by Dr. Martin Luther King Jr.

One of the leaders, Edgar Holt, took out a second mortgage on his house to raise the money to charter a plane, his widow, Lois, said.

Holt, a Buick foundry worker, came to Flint in 1950 and was an avid civil rights worker until his death in 1984.

He was president of the Flint branch of the NAACP in 1958-59 and again from 1967 to 1970. He served as state NAACP president from 1964 to 1966 and was active at the national level where he received several awards.

Among his many good works, Holt organized youth programs, fought for school integration and fair housing and started drug rehabilitation and ex-offender programs. He was also a founder of the interracial Urban Coalition in 1969.

Like Hightower, he was investigated for Communist involvement. Lois Holt recalled when FBI agents visited their home for a private chat with her husband.

In 1948 the NAACP Youth Council had also been investigated, but charges were never proven, according to old newspaper clippings.

Back then anyone who was outspoken about civil rights was considered a subversive, Lois Holt said. Years later, Holt declined an offer to review copies of the files the FBI had kept on him.

"Edgar said they'd just make him angry," Lois Holt said.

Holt sometimes received threatening calls about his civil rights activities. The death threats never bothered him; he was fearless, Lois Holt said. She admitted to being afraid at times but supported her husband's efforts "100 percent, if he was right."

Holt developed his civil rights conscientiousness while a young man. He suffered a severe racially motivated beating at age 25 that was written about in the book, "We Charge Genocide: The Crime of Government Against the Negro People," edited by William L. Patterson.

An excerpt states:

"Edgar B. Holt, a vice president of the Southern Negro Youth Congress, was beaten on July 25, 1946, at Newport News, Va., by a foreman and several other whites while he was on a construction job. Holt had asked a foreman for a drink of water, but was told that whites drank first. When he objected, the foreman struck him in the face and several whites joined in to beat him. The men then dragged Holt to a road and left him lying there."

Holt never talked much about that incident, but it was said to have affected him profoundly.

"He was deeply hurt over it," said Ruth VanZandt, his sister-in-law. "It was an emotional thing for him to think about how he had been treated and then knowing that other people had been treated that way and worse."

His empathy with other victims led him to organize a fund-raiser in Flint for the mother of Emmett Till, the Chicago boy who was murdered in Mississippi in 1955 for allegedly whistling at a white woman.

A vicious beating at the hands of a white mob shaped the conscience of Edgar Holt, who was a local and state NAACP president and a fearless defender of equal rights.

As far as Lois Holt knows, her husband was jailed only once in his life, after a black minister in Flint accused him of "desecrating" the church property. Holt had posted an election campaign sign on the church lawn in protest of the pastor's decision to allow a white political candidate to post signs while refusing the same privilege to a black candidate, who happened to be Floyd McCree.

Holt was outraged. McCree was not well-known then and Holt was trying to publicize him, Lois Holt said.

"Edgar could see the potential of blacks being in politics in Flint, and he pushed him (McCree)," she said.

"Edgar didn't like to be in the limelight. If he could help black people, he would do that. He didn't care about getting the credit himself."

She described her late husband as calm and comical, personable and lovable "unless you misused someone. Then he was fierce."

A wall in Holt's home is covered with plaques and awards he received during his lifetime. The two he most treasured are from the national NAACP and the Flint Human Relations Commission, Lois Holt said.

Forty boxes of his personal papers have been turned over to a local historian who is writing a book about him.

Kindred spirit Woody Etherly praised Holt as "a war horse."

"He was very knowledgeable, and you couldn't play games with him," Etherly said. "He would fight with General Motors. He would fight with the Board of Education. He would fight with anybody and everybody on behalf of black folks."

Because of his activism, Holt was kept in one of the dirtiest jobs in the auto plant, Etherly said.

"He understood they were making him pay for his fighting, but he kept the fight going. To me, he was another great man in the city because it made no difference what they did to him. He was right back on the scene."

Past presidents of the Flint NAACP have included labor leaders, educators, attorneys and business owners.

When Holt was elected Flint chapter president in 1958, the NAACP leadership roster read like a civil rights who's who. Attorney C. Frederick Robinson was first vice president, and the executive board included the Rev. Alfred Robbs, Floyd McCree, James Crichton, Ailene Butler (who became Flint's first black city councilwoman in 1973), Sam Duncan (a labor leader and future local NAACP president), Chester Simmons (a future city councilman and administrator) and Max Dean, a white attorney.

The NAACP Flint branch was organized in 1922, according to Jesse L. Leach, who was its president in 1951. Other records indicate that the chapter started in 1918.

Among numerous NAACP causes have been a successful drive to hire black drivers for the Flint Trolley Coach company in 1943, support of the Fair Employment Practices Law in 1956 and the nationally prominent campaign for a fair-housing law in 1967-68.

Police brutality became a concern in the late 1950s, triggered by a wrongful arrest case. That's when discussions began about starting a Flint human relations commission.

NAACP president Eugene Miller, elected in 1960, co-chaired a steering committee to establish the Urban Coalition. In 1968 he pushed for more black history being taught in Flint schools.

NAACP youth members participated in many of the marches and

Fifth Ward City Councilman Fred Tucker was known as shrewd politician and businessman. The murders of Tucker and his bride, Louise, in 1980 remain unsolved.

pickets of the 1960s. State Rep. Roger Townsend was one of the Youth Council advisers.

"We picketed banks. We picketed everywhere that black people did business that did not hire us," said Woody Etherly, a council member.

"And another thing, we would compare prices. We'd go in the white community and see what (merchants) were charging white folks. Then we'd come into the black community and see what (they) were charging black folks. We found that white folks was paying less for their food than we were."

Etherly was among the demonstrators at the Colonel's Drive-In. When police arrived wearing riot helmets and toting automatic weapons, he decided it was time to go home.

"We didn't have not one gun," he said. "We didn't have anything. It did-

Ailene Butler, funeral home owner, was the first black woman elected to the Flint City Council, representing the First Ward.

n't make any logical sense to me. ... I made up my mind then that I would get into the political arena and try to effectuate change from the inside instead of taking to the streets and doing the violent thing."

Etherly organized a youth sleep-in on the front lawn of Flint City Hall in 1967 to protest housing discrimination. He was elected Third Ward council representative in 1970 and held the post 13 years.

After Floyd McCree became mayor in 1966, the role of blacks in city government expanded a great deal.

In 1968, Fred Tucker became the second black elected to the City Council. He served until 1979. Eddie Little served on the council from 1970 to '73 and Ailene Butler became the first woman to serve, 1973-75.

Since, five blacks have served as council president and as many as four have served simultaneously on the nine-member panel.

Etherly shared his recollections of a few of them.

Butler was a victim of character assassination, he said.

"There was a belief that no woman should sit there, or no black woman, I should say." Butler had some unusual ideas, but some of them made a lot of sense, he said.

He described Fred Tucker as the "smartest politician" he's ever known.

"Fred knew how to put things together," Etherly said. "He was a natural negotiator. ... That came from his UAW background as a shop committeeman.

"We got a lot of things done on behalf of black folks. People were basically afraid of me because of the sleep-in. In their view, I was such a bad guy. I used that fear they had of me to get them to a place they wanted to talk to Fred."

Etherly described Mayor McCree as "a giant in more ways than one."

"Floyd was the kind of council person and mayor that this city needed because Floyd was the kind of person that could build bridges on all sides," Etherly said.

"People think of Floyd as a gentleman and gentle person, but Floyd did what Floyd had to do behind closed doors. He was very articulate behind closed doors, and he would sit down, and if he had to, you know he had to fire up sometimes; he did it in such a way that it was not magnified, like the kinds of things I did."

A cross-burning at Clark School in the early 1920s influenced Ailene Butler's decision to become politically active.

"I never will forget it," she said about witnessing the cross-burning. Her father and other black men went to put out the fire while Butler, then about 4 or 5, watched with her mother from their yard.

Her grandmother had told her about the mistreatment of black slaves. Then in high school, Butler said she wondered why only whites belonged to Northern's Glee Club and only white girls could go to camp.

So, "everything that could be headed up in Flint, I was in it," she said. She owned one of Flint's first black funeral homes.

Fred Tucker came to Flint in 1949 from Albion, Mich. He died violently at age 49 in a double homicide that was never solved. His body, and that of his wife of four days, Louise, were found dumped in a field in Toledo, Ohio. Police speculated that the couple had been abducted from their Flint home.

At one time Tucker owned more than 200 houses in Flint. One political opponent accused him of being a slumlord.

Floyd McCree began his political career at his wife's urging, his son Melvin said. He had been involved in labor union politics in the factory.

After a term on the county Board of Supervisors, McCree ran for the Flint City Commission in 1958, causing one local doctor to declare that no shop worker should be an elected official, Melvin McCree said. Floyd McCree served on the commission 12 years, including as Flint's mayor in 1966.

Back then, the mayor was the equivalent of the council president, Melvin McCree explained. Mayor McCree, a shop worker who had dropped out of college because he couldn't afford it, received national publicity after becoming the first black to head a midsized U.S. city.

McCree made many sacrifices as mayor, his son said. He was required to live in the deteriorating ward he represented, though he could afford to move. His council salary was $600 a year. So he lost money every time he took off work to perform a community service.

He lost his privacy and uninterrupted sleep nights. There were times when murderers and rape victims ran to Mayor McCree's home for help, Melvin McCree said.

Mayor McCree also received hate mail. Melvin McCree recalled one strange letter stating that "black music was destroying minds and leading kids to crime."

In 1971 Floyd McCree became County Register of Deeds and served until 1988 when he died while sitting at his desk.

He instilled in Melvin, who now holds that office, a firm belief in the power of the political process.

And mirroring his father, Melvin McCree served on the Flint City Council from 1983 to 1987 and was its president. He became Register of Deeds in 1990.

"My father used to say bad officials are elected by good people who fail to vote," McCree said. "Black folks ought to be really sensitive about that. There is a requirement to get off your butt and do something for yourself.

"The bottom line is he (Floyd McCree) was raised up with the principle of work. He thought you should give back more than you take. He was a shop worker who felt strongly enough to give up some of his pay to attend council meetings to talk about dealing with community issues. That's the sense of commitment that his family instilled in him. We're not talking about a super-hero or super-intelligence, though he was bright. We're talking about a common man trying to do common good."

Flint City Council alumnus Floyd Clack served from 1979 until 1982 when he was elected to the Michigan House of Representatives.

Clack grew up in Texas, intending to become a lawyer. Instead he became a teacher and taught for 16 years in Flint schools.

Involvement in the United Teachers of Flint and in the NAACP, as president and vice president in the early 1970s, marked the beginning of his political career.

Clack was the first black to represent Flint's second ward. He lost his first bid in 1977 but won two years later.

Police and community relations were a hot issue during Clack's council term.

State Rep. Floyd Clack is at home in the classroom where he taught for many years before entering politics.

"Shoot first and ask questions later" seemed to be standard police procedure in those days, he said.

As a state representative, Clack focuses more on helping people than on shaping laws, he said. Getting local banks to improve a dismal record of loans to eligible minorities was one major accomplishment.

He hopes to someday organize a coalition of African-American professionals. Flint has a cross-section of professional people who are not networking to effect change, he said.

"There should be an umbrella group for the NAACP, Urban League, the Greek organizations and everything else," he said.

He would also like to establish more youth leadership training programs to replace older black leaders as they retire.

Black women have held key leadership positions in government, education, business, churches and more.

Pioneers include Olive Beasley, executive director of the Michigan Civil Rights Commission Flint district office from 1964 until 1980; Odell Broadway, a school social worker; Ophelia Bonner, a civic worker for whom Bonner Park is named; and Charlotte Williams, a member of the county Board of Supervisors from 1966 to 1980 and president of the National Association of Counties in 1979.

Williams was one of three African-Americans and the only black female

Charlotte Williams served on the Genesee County Board of Supervisors and became the first black woman elected president of the National Association of Counties in 1979.

on the former 68-member county supervisors board. Being the sole female posed more obstacles for her than being black, she said.

"I have been a token female and a token black," Williams said. "But I never minded it because they use tokens to open up gates."

In 1979 she became the second black and second female president of the 42-year-old National Association of Counties, comprising 1,300 counties nationwide.

A highlight of her one-year term in office was to introduce U.S. President Jimmy Carter on national television. Carter appointed her to a presidential policy-making board and invited her to a conference at Camp David, the presidential retreat, she said.

Beasley came to Flint in 1964 from Detroit where she had been director of a statewide coalition that pushed through passage of the Fair Employment Practice Council – a 13-year effort.

Beasley was then named the first black female head of the Flint civil rights office.

"When I came here, (Flint) was a very ugly factory town," Beasley said. The Flint Cultural Center was newly built and T. Wendell Williams newly elected as the first black member of the Flint Board of Education. But,

Ollie Bivins Jr. is sworn in as Flint's first black municipal judge in 1968. He was first elected to Flint District Court and four years later moved to Circuit Court.

overall, blacks held very few leadership positions.

By the early 1990s Beasley had seen tremendous growth in the number of elected black officials and black professionals.

Before her retirement in 1980, Beasley had chaired the Flint Urban League, worked for passage of Flint's fair housing ordinance and processed numerous discrimination complaints. Her personal papers are archived at Wayne State University and in the Olive Beasley Collection at UM-Flint.

As civil rights activism picked up steam in the 1960s, so did black political clout.

In one political first in 1968, Ollie Bivins was elected a Flint District Court judge. In 1972, he was elected to circuit court and served until 1982.

In 1992 Larry Foster was elected the first black supervisor of Mt. Morris Township.

Blacks have served at various times on school boards in the Beecher, Clio, Carman-Ainsworth, Flint and Westwood Heights school districts.

Marion Coates-Williams takes pleasure in remembering when her husband, T. Wendell Williams, became the first black elected to the Flint school board in 1963.

"You talk about black people getting out voting," she said. "The lines were so long they couldn't close the polls (on time). You've never seen so many people active. I heard one man talk about the Williams machine. That was people coming together. It was a landslide. It was really something."

Williams served on the school board until 1966. He was also a medical doctor and active in the NAACP, the Urban League and church.

As Flint's black population approached 50 percent, black mayors – James A. Sharp and Woodrow Stanley – won election in 1983 and 1991, respectively.

Sharp was the first popularly elected black mayor, seated nearly 20 years after Floyd McCree. He reflected on his four-year term with mixed feelings.

On the one hand, he said he was proud of accomplishments such as hiring the first female firefighters in the state, but on the other, he felt unfairly criticized for innovations such as hiring "gang leaders" to head a grassroots effort to reduce nighttime crime.

His administration oversaw the opening of the Water Street Pavilion festival marketplace in downtown Flint and laid the groundwork for the formation of GEAR – Genesee Economic Area Revitalization Inc. – an umbrella group to promote economic development countywide.

Also during Sharp's term, planning began to build a new Bishop Airport terminal and a bid failed to have a new Saturn auto factory built in Flint.

Sharp had an open-door policy to encourage blacks to take an active role in local government. He also secured funds to restore a portion of the historic Berston Field House, which serves Flint's predominantly black north side.

Sharp said the only thing he would change about his mayoral term would be to pay closer attention to politicking. Winning a second term would have allowed him to finish the programs he started, he said.

During Stanley's first term, one of his concerns was to find a new use for the closed AutoWorld theme park. The ultimate decision was made to raze it and turn the property over to the University of Michigan-Flint.

Stanley also dealt with proposals to turn AutoWorld into a casino or to generally allow casino gambling in the city. Both questions were defeated in a referendum.

Stanley placed stronger emphasis on mandatory city residency for police officers and other city employees. He strengthened ties with state and national leaders, and in the 1994 governor's race was considered as a running mate to Democratic candidate Howard Wolpe.

Stanley also spearheaded the drive to renovate Atwood Stadium.

Among other 20th century black leaders in Flint were Wesley T. Cobb, John W. Mack and Melvyn S. Brannon, executive directors of the Flint Urban League; Archie Parks and George Friley, Flint's first and third black police officers, respectively; Leo A. Greene, a prominent business owner; Henry Horton, a social services administrator; and Sylvester Broome and

The Jobs Central training center (fomerly Dewey School) is named for the late Sylvester Broome Jr., a county commissioner and community leader in the 1980s.

Chester J. Simmons, a county and city elected official and civic leader.

Cobb directed the Urban League from 1962 to 1965. Mack succeeded Cobb and served until 1969 when Brannon was installed. Cobb and Mack guided the organization through one of the most racially tense eras ever seen in Flint.

Cobb once compared race relations in Flint to a man who has cancer but refuses to see a doctor.

"Too many people still look at race relations as a Negro problem when in reality it is a struggle for survival of all citizens," he said.

He sponsored hearings about improving community race relations. In the spring of 1964 he warned city officials of ripe conditions in Flint for a racial revolt.

After leaving Flint Cobb became an executive at the United Nations. Mack, his successor, left Flint to become president of the Los Angeles Urban League where he has attained national prominence.

During his Flint tenure, Mack dealt with issues such as fair housing, affirmative-action hiring of black police officers and improving human relations. He was among black leaders on the streets to keep the peace when

Urban League of Flint leadership over the past 33 years has been manned by Wesley T. Cobb (above), John Mack (opposite page top) and Melvyn S. Brannon (opposite page bottom).

---

a race riot threatened in the summer of 1967.

Though racial conflict is an ongoing concern, the League's focus in the 1970s and thereafter shifted to improving education and employment opportunities. Under Brannon's leadership, the League initiated an annual Salute to Black Scholars to showcase graduating high school seniors who had earned good grades. Also the League purchased and converted the old Selby Elementary School into a job-training and education center.

John Mack

Melvyn S. Brannon

Brannon has sat on several health and civic bodies, and beginning in the mid-1980s, he framed the League's response to retrenchment of civil rights laws.

Greene wore two hats – business owner and political leader.

In 1949, he opened Greene Home for Funerals at 2505 St. John St. It has relocated to 2210 King Ave.

Republican Gov. George W. Romney, elected in 1963, appointed Greene as his assistant on minority group relations. But Greene resigned in 1967 citing his dissatisfaction with the administration's responsiveness to minority concerns.

In 1964 Greene helped to establish and served on the Flint Human Relations Commission. He sat on the county Board of Supervisors from 1961 to 1965 and was named to the Genesee County Social Welfare Board in 1965.

He supported the open-housing fight and criticized the lack of diversity in the membership of the Flint Rotary, Kiwanis and Optimists service clubs.

Simmons served on the County Board of Supervisors from 1961 to '68 and was an administrator for the Model Cities program and the Genesee County Community Action Agency. Simmons served three terms as a Flint city councilman, representing the First Ward, and was twice elected council president. He also served on numerous civic boards, ran unsuccessfully for Flint mayor in 1983 and at the time of his death in 1989 he was the city's affirmative action officer during the administration of former Flint Mayor Matthew Collier.

Among black labor leaders in Flint, four often singled out for recognition were Earl Crompton, Sam Duncan, Eugene Miller and Ruben Burks.

In 1989, Burks was elected the first black director of UAW Region 1-C. He had served as assistant director since 1983. As a member of Local 598 since 1955, Burks served in various elected capacities including executive board member. He also has been very active in community service.

Crompton was an international UAW representative for almost 20 years and a member of several community groups including the NAACP, Urban League and Community Civic League

Duncan, president of UAW Local 598 at the Flint Truck Assembly Plant from 1963 until his death in 1979, was the first black elected to head a local union and had the longest tenure. He first ascended to leadership in 1962 as vice president of the local, which was considered quite a feat seeing that black membership was less than 10 percent, and Duncan had just completed a term as president of the Flint NAACP.

Despite being in a wheelchair during most of his presidency, as a result of a war injury that left him with a limp, Duncan represented hourly workers so wonderfully he was all but idolized.

He was eulogized as a man who helped everybody, even those who did not work in the shop. His funeral was held at the union hall because the crowd of mourners was too large for any funeral home. In a tribute to him published in

The Flint Journal a week after his death, one admirer said: "I'd have to say he was a very smart political person because to be elected a black president (of) our local union at that time, there were very few blacks in power."

In 1982 a memorial scholarship for disabled students was established in Duncan's name.

Miller, a factory worker and later supervisor, was elected NAACP president in 1960, chairman of its publicity committee in 1961 and education committee chairman in 1964. As president he protested the exclusion of NAACP members from a committee planning the Flint Human Relations Commission and led a Flint contingent to Lansing to push for stronger civil rights laws.

Testifying in 1965 before a U.S. House of Representatives subcommittee on education, Miller blasted inferior conditions in Flint schools serving mainly black students and criticized Mott Foundation-sponsored programs that he said detracted from basic education. As a candidate for the Flint Board of Education in 1967, he criticized racial imbalances in school facilities and programs.

In 1969 he was named temporary cochair of a steering committee to form the Urban Coalition. He also worked on programs to benefit youth, health, community service and education.

Perhaps best summing up his outlook, he once gave a speech titled: "Know Your Geography: Is Flint North or South of the Mason and Dixon Line?"

PROTEST:
"No one had ever dared to challenge the establishment."

The "funeral" took place on the patio between Flint City Hall and the police department. About 200 "mourners" listened to a passionate eulogy, then followed a slow-moving hearse up S. Saginaw Street from city hall to the Flint River, the final resting place.

In a symbolic gesture, pallbearers heaved the casket over a bridge railing into the river. They were burying the "faith and hope of the city," said the Rev. Alfred L.C. Robbs.

Butler Funeral Home had provided a hearse and donated a cheap casket for the staged media event.

"Man, the cameras were just clicking while we buried the city, while we threw it over the bridge," Robbs chuckled, reminiscing. He noted that the protesters took the precaution of tying a rope around the casket to retrieve it afterward. Otherwise police would have arrested them for littering.

"People in town were so upset ... said, 'You better settle this thing or this town will go up in smoke,' " Robbs recalled.

It was a volatile era. Job and housing discrimination, police brutality and unequal opportunity in education were among the burning civil rights issues. In the mid-1960s rioting erupted in several major cities across America. Though the 1960s and into the early 1970s, agitation by the Black Panther Party and other militants inflamed simmering black frustration with social conditions.

The outspoken and controversial black leader Malcolm X spoke at Flint's IMA during a Black Muslim rally in 1963.

Rallying cries of "black power" and "we shall overcome" signaled a change in passive attitudes.

Most protesters, however, followed the nonviolent example set by Martin Luther King Jr. Their weapons were symbolic – sit-ins, rallies, marches and dramatic gestures like Flint's mock funeral.

If a store didn't serve blacks, it was boycotted. If a business didn't hire blacks, it was picketed. Sympathetic media coverage focused national attention on the issues.

"Most of the progress and efforts to secure the rights of black people started right here in this (law) office," said attorney C. Frederick Robinson, noting that blacks in Flint seemed complacent about social inequality when he arrived here in 1956.

"No one had ever dared to challenge the establishment. That was the mentality of that time," Robinson said.

He and others formed the Community Civic League to forge civil rights activists into a unified body.

One of the first battles, against the Flint Board of Education, abolished separate screening committees for hiring black and white teachers, Robinson said.

Next came the 1958 protest at Flint City Hall after a young woman was arrested and falsely charged with prostitution.

Blacks, led by Robinson and others, picketed at Flint City Hall for about six weeks, sometimes in the rain.

"There were efforts to get rid of us by both blacks and whites," Robinson recalled. "Blacks would come down and say, 'Ya'll don't know what you doing. Get on away from here. You're just causing trouble.' "

Robinson and crew succeeded in getting the city's loitering ordinance declared unconstitutional.

Malcolm X (center, above), then a controversial minister of the Nation of Islam's black nationalist movement, came to Flint's IMA Auditorium (bottom) in October 1963 for a gathering sponsored by the Black Muslims.

Olive Beasley, executive director of the Michigan Civil Rights Commission Flint district office from 1964 until 1980, was the first black female to hold the position and was respected and admired for intelligent, effective leadership.

"Loitering was when you were doing nothing, and doing nothing constituted a crime," he said. "You and I could be standing on the corner talking, and they would say we were doing nothing, and that was a criminal act. It was just a tool used to arrest people when they wanted to. (The law was) designed to be used against vagrants and prostitutes, but the end result was that none of us had any rights."

In those days, blacks and whites were buried in separate cemeteries. The Civic League put a stop to that by filing a lawsuit with J. Merrill Spencer, a funeral director, acting as plaintiff.

The Civic League mounted the campaign to elect the first black to the Flint Board of Education.

"That was through the cooperative efforts of people working together, passing out fliers, knocking on doors, deciding first of all who ought to be the candidate," Robinson said.

They chose T. Wendell Williams, a physician, because he seemed to have the most electable qualifications and commitment to black concerns, Robinson said.

Leaders from many aspects of community life worked with the Civic League. Flint Mayor Floyd McCree was one of them. Others included local ministers and labor leaders Earl Crompton and John Hightower. NAACP and Urban League officials also were involved.

"I think everybody felt the need that black people ought to get together and make their own decisions and not be dictated to by white folks, whether it be the Chamber of Commerce or the union," Robinson said.

"We were pretty aggressive statewide and were instrumental in founding a Black Caucus as well as the Democratic Party black caucus."

As the group's momentum and successes grew, some local white leaders tried the "divide and conquer" strategy to break its solidarity, Robinson said. One such challenge came from labor leaders. White union leaders demanded that black union members side with the union's view on issues instead of the Civic League's.

"I said, 'No, that's not true,' " Robinson said. "Black people must be black first and union second. They're born black and they will die black, (but) they will go in and out of the union during the course of their lifetime."

But, he added, it was a tough decision for black union members.

Police brutality was another long-standing concern the Civic League took on, said A. Glenn Epps, who was an assistant prosecutor in the 1960s.

"Part of our big fight was to stop police from arresting (black) people on Friday night and not arraigning them until Tuesday," Epps said. The group influenced a decision for district court to hold weekend arraignments, he said.

Local civil rights supporters also participated in national civil rights efforts such as the March on Washington in 1963 and the Selma to Montgomery (Ala.) March in 1965.

In 1967 a campaign for Flint's open-housing ordinance forged an interracial coalition that won a national first. But Robinson rated it a hollow victory.

"It espoused a principle," he said. "But there was no penalty, no enforcement." Blacks continued to have difficulty moving into some neighborhoods.

Olive Beasley viewed passage of the ordinance more positively. As director of the Michigan Civil Rights Flint office during the fair-housing campaign, she took pride in Flint becoming the first city in the nation to successfully defend a fair housing law.

NAACP leaders teamed up with civil rights activists in the factories to demand better jobs and working conditions.

"There was a long, hard struggle, maybe a year or more, to get the (city) council to pass the ordinance," Beasley said. Mayor Floyd McCree had to threaten to resign before the commission would seriously consider it.

But after the commission approved the ordinance, a group called the White Citizens Council circulated petitions demanding that it be put to a vote.

All three major networks, national magazines and The New York Times and New York Post sent reporters to cover the story, Beasley recalled.

Dorothy Waller campaigned door-to-door to persuade voters to support the ordinance. Having been born in Flint, she had lived under housing restrictions all her life.

"My brother would drive me over in this area, but I never thought it would be possible to live here," she said of the upper middle-class south Flint neighborhood where she's lived for more than 25 years.

Future politician Woody Etherly was a member of the NAACP youth group during the fair-housing battle. When the City Commission at first refused to consider the proposal, Etherly, then 23, organized a sleep-in on the lawn at Flint City Hall that drew national media attention.

Etherly said he conceived the idea during a visit with hospitalized Mayor Floyd McCree. The two men discussed the need to do something dramatic to attract attention to the fair-housing fight.

"After I left the hospital, I went and got some young people – six of us – and we sat down and talked," Etherly recalled. "Then we went over to

Job discrimination at factories and other large employers was frequent target of NAACP protests like this one in April 1964.

Canaan Baptist Church in the basement. Rev. Robbs was there. And Ailene Butler who owned the funeral home was there. And I believe Fred Tucker (councilman) was there, and some others. We told them that we were going to organize a sleep-in."

The adults opposed the idea at first, Etherly said. Some of the NAACP leaders said they did not want that sort of demonstration associated with its youth group, so Etherly and some others turned in their membership cards, he said.

"So ... the six of us got together and called all the major (TV) networks – Detroit's Channel 2, NBC, everybody. And I told them if you want to see something interesting, be at City Hall, and I gave them a time to come to City Hall and then the six of us showed up.

"Amazingly all the networks came. And we came in with our little sleeping bags and stuff. We went down to City Hall and began to spread our sleeping bags and the city (officials) cut on the water (lawn sprinklers) and were up on the roof with their guns looking down on us. That went across national news, and when people saw the news, people began to come."

According to newspaper accounts about 200 young blacks and some whites took part in the sleep-in. It lasted about 10 days, ending when the City Commission agreed to reconsider the open-occupancy proposal.

Etherly's cousins, the children of Mayor Floyd McCree, also were youth activists.

"I think my sister Marsha and I chose to go and sleep on the lawn," Melvin McCree said. "Most of the people sleeping on the lawn was young people. It was kinda cool."

Being active in the NAACP youth group also meant getting up early in the morning to go picket, McCree said.

"We did that on a continuous basis, as if it were a job." He said he picketed at Buick to demand more blacks in supervision and at Michigan National Bank to get black tellers hired. Also he supported the farm workers' grapes and lettuce boycott.

"My feeling is that you don't just fight for one group of people. If you believe in a certain principle, you fight for everyone," McCree said.

About 20 young people made up the core group of NAACP youth activists, he said.

"What we'd do is meet at church beforehand to get warm. Sometimes we would picket in the dead of winter. It could be half a day or all day, whatever to show we were serious about wanting change in Flint."

The restless mood of the 1960s and 1970s had a notable effect on youth. Some marched and demonstrated alongside their parents or adult mentors; others protested in rebellious behavior.

"We followed the action of the Panthers, Stokely Carmicheal ... these people were our heroes," said Karen Aldridge, who studied Afro-American culture at the University of Michigan in Ann Arbor in the early 1970s.

"You listened to the Last Poets' 'When the Revolution Comes' and you believed that."

Martin Luther King Jr. was a respected leader, but a strong nationalistic focus marked a cultural awakening.

"We read black poetry, took classes, knew about the Harlem Renaissance writers," Aldridge said. She rose at 5 a.m. every day to lead a black culture program for children in the community.

"You really had a sense of who you were, but you were angry, too,"

Aldridge said. To this day, she said she won't watch a movie like "Mississippi Burning," because it is too painful a reminder of racial discrimination at its ugliest.

Angela Sawyer, another young witness of '70s unrest, recalled how newscasters daily recited the grim death toll of Vietnam casualties. Rebellion was a trendy thing to do, like getting a tattoo or wearing a nose earring.

"Kids in my neighborhood would be walking around barefoot in dirty jeans and high as a kite and would tell you what they were on," Sawyer said.

"They wouldn't go to school; thought it was cool."

Some also considered it "cool" to drop out of school, run away from home or be sent to a juvenile home. A counter-culture revolution was in full swing.

Flint's tense racial climate in 1967, while rioters looted and burned Detroit, created a bad memory for Gregory Pridgeon, who was 13.

"The police was stopping everybody," he said. His parents went out of town and had to show identification to be allowed back into the city.

Mayor James A. Sharp recalled that his son Owen, 18, was minding his own business, eating a hot dog at a downtown coney island restaurant, when he was arrested one night in a police sweep.

"There were a lot of arrests made and my kid was one of them," Sharp said. "They were just locking people up off the street for whatever reason."

Flint's most intense period of unrest occurred on a Monday night in July. It was the night after rioting started in Detroit. Black leaders were called to Stewart and Industrial avenues to quell a disturbance threatening to get out of control.

John Hightower, the Rev. Alfred Robbs, Harold Hayden and Mayor Floyd McCree were among the black leaders called.

The angry crowd refused to listen to Robbs or Hightower, but Hayden, who was head of the NAACP, was making headway when an agitator tossed a brick through a drugstore window, Hightower said. As he put it, "all hell broke loose."

Police began making arrests indiscriminately, including some of the peacemakers. Hightower said one officer put a gun to his head and called him a nigger. He said he tried to show the officer his deputy's credentials but was knocked to the ground. In the ensuing mayhem, some members of the unruly crowd fled and some turned violent.

They tossed gas bombs, smashed store windows and pelted cars with rocks, news reports said. A few stores were broken into, but nothing on the scale of looting in Detroit and other riot-torn cities.

More than 100 people were arrested in Flint during the two-day disturbance. All were set free the next day, as a show of faith by Genesee County Prosecutor Robert Leonard, who freed them with the understanding that they would work as peacemakers. Leonard's action drew harsh criticism from law enforcement officers and others.

That was not the first racial disturbance in Flint. Decades earlier, schoolyard brawls and other confrontations at public facilities would sometimes escalate into a full-blown racial conflict.

Eugene Simpson recalled two disturbances in the 1940s. Nobody was killed, but numerous injuries were reported, he said. The National Guard was called in for about a week until tensions cooled down.

In 1965 a rumor about a riot planned for Labor Day heightened fears to the point that turned the city into an armed camp, The Flint Journal reported. According to one rumor, Flint police were advising white residents to leave town and store owners to board up windows. In the week leading up to Labor Day, more than 150 uneasy residents telephoned the Flint Urban League seeking information and advice.

Gun sales reportedly escalated and several whites were arrested for carrying a concealed weapon. Gun owners said they were sleeping armed.

But Labor Day came and went peacefully. City officials and black leaders theorized that subversives had deliberately started the riot rumor to stir up dissension and stifle civil rights progress.

Urban League Executive Director John Mack said overreaction to the rumor showed a lack of respect for and distrust of the black community. He recommended a redoubled focus on ending housing discrimination, preserving the Human Relations Commission and hiring more black police officers.

By the 1970s, political awareness and activism spilled over into public schools.

Lennetta Bradley Coney and Debra Taylor recalled their involvement in the Black Cultural Movement at Southwestern High School.

"At that time, it was right after the '60s, that spirit was still there," Taylor said. "There was mood in the community and in the country of newfound black pride." A clenched fist raised in the air symbolized unity and empowerment.

Southwestern High School blacks founded the Black Cultural Movement to sponsor activities aimed at boosting black pride, Taylor said.

Southwestern's black enrollment was only about 30 percent then, though the school's assistant superintendent was black.

"We got together on our own and decided we wanted to be active in student government," Taylor said. "So we developed a slate for student council at every (grade) level. It was sort of a coup in that white students were not aware of our organization."

Blacks voted as a bloc while the white vote was split among several candidates, she said. As a result, the black students won several seats on the student council. That did not go over well with the predominantly white student body.

Coney was elected 10th-grade president, and the class vice president and secretary also were black. She recalled an editorial in the school paper that belittled their victory.

Blacks had not been attending Southwestern long enough to feel welcome there. Coney, who lived within walking distance of Central High School, had agreed to be bused to Southwestern to help integrate it, she said.

Taylor summed up poor student relations as a case of blacks and whites not being accustomed to interacting with each other socially.

At least one major racial altercation resulted. Black students and whites were injured when chairs were thrown.

At one point white students left the building, gathered on a hill outside and told the blacks to go home, Coney said.

In the following weeks parents and police patrolled the halls. The police were there to keep the peace. The parents, mostly black fathers, including Taylor's and Coney's, were there to keep an eye on the police.

Police brutality was reportedly a common complaint in those days, so the fathers wanted to make sure their children were safe.

The black community was much more unified then, Taylor noted.

"They (dads) took off work and monitored the hallways to make sure the black students wouldn't be mistreated."

Genesee County Prosecutor Robert Leonard organized conflict resolutions sessions that brought black and white students together to resolve their differences.

Flint high schools had been disrupted by racial tensions before.

In 1963 an anti-black poster and a racial altercation between two male students at Central High led to several students being injured or arrested. Afterward school and city officials organized programs aimed at improving race relations.

In April 1968, students reacted angrily to news of the assassination of Martin Luther King Jr. A student fight at Northwestern High led to an early dismissal, according to newspaper reports. Then some Northwestern students went to Northern High where a disturbance broke out. Police used tear gas to disperse the crowd.

Karen Aldridge, a Northern sophomore, recalled running to her uncle's nearby home when the trouble started. Though Northwestern students had congregated at Northern, she said, they were not causing any problems until the police arrived with tear gas.

"It was handled very poorly and caused a ton of confusion," Aldridge said. The high schools were closed two days to allow a cooling off period.

In December 1975 an incident that made national headlines stemmed from an argument between a black female Flint police officer and her white male partner, which led to both being wounded. The case involved officers Madeline C. Fletcher, 20, and Walter Kalberer, 34. During an argument over who would drive the cruiser, Fletcher shot Kalberer and was in turn shot and wounded by other officers.

Fletcher was charged with assault with intent to do bodily harm but was found not guilty in a trial that concluded in June 1976.

Racial unrest simmered through the 1970s and 1980s, but appeared to be on the rise nationally by the early 1990s, as demonstrated by rioting in Los Angeles in 1992. Flint, however, experienced no major incidents.

While the need for civil rights agitation still exists in Flint, the unity and commitment of the 1960s-era movement are missing, Robinson said. More blacks are going to college and getting professional jobs, but, collectively, blacks still are at the bottom, he said.

Young blacks living on the lowest rungs of society rarely get a chance to see or interact with those who are successful, he said. That separation didn't exist in the old days when social status didn't make much difference in how blacks lived.

"You were black irrespective to whether you were an attorney or a doctor," Robinson said. "You were just a black doctor or a black attorney.

"So you could see where we had something to fight for."

Now, "we're aimless. ... We have no national sense of direction. We're just floundering about."

Legacy

Flint's history shows it's a comeback city.
It came back after the demise of the lumbering era in the late 1880s with a bustling carriage-making industry that led to the birth of General Motors in 1908.

Now the Vehicle City seems to be bouncing back from a sharp downturn in the automotive industry during the 1980s that severely hurt the local economy.

But there is a less-noted angle to Flint's comeback tradition.

"One thing I noticed about people in Flint is they'll go away for a number of years but they often end up back in Flint," said Melvin McCree, Genesee County's Register of Deeds.

As he sees it, they come back because Flint offers affordable housing, convenient transportation and a tolerable crime rate. And it's conveniently close to large metropolitan cities such as Chicago, Toronto and Detroit yet small enough to drive across town in 10 minutes.

"I think you have to see the world to know what you have (at home)," McCree said.

"I remember walking in downtown Chicago, Phoenix and other places. They have just as many boarded-up buildings as we do. If you could confine visitors to (just) seeing Miller Road, they (would) go home raving about Flint."

Marion Coates-Williams, born and raised in Flint, said she has never wanted to live anywhere else. In her 60-plus years, she's seen Flint change from a small, friendly, close-knit town to a midsized city where neighbors are often strangers. Her brother moved away but she stayed and made a good life here, she said.

Lolita Hendrix, born in Flint in 1964, remembers growing up in "a safe, fun city to live in." She's traveled some and lived in other places but always considered Flint to be her home.

"Wherever I was, I always wanted to be back in Flint," Hendrix said.

"I can remember people from outside of the area having a negative view of Flint. And that's something we have now, (the view) that Flint is this godawful place. I can remember being in Mississippi or St. Louis. That was before the (movie) "Roger & Me" days. I can remember adamantly defending Flint."

Even now, Hendrix said she has friends who have moved away asking her, "How can you stand living there?"

"And I'm still defending the heck out of it," she said. "It's certainly not the place it used to be, but it's still a nice place to live."

Norma Fairhurst takes a similar stand and regrets the one time she agreed to deny her Flint heritage. That was while she was singing professionally with the Velvelettes. As one of the first non-Detroit groups to sign with Motown, they were instructed to say they were from Detroit instead of Flint supposedly because "no one knows where Flint is."

"I wouldn't do it (now) because I am very proud to be from Flint," Fairhurst said. She's since spent eight years promoting Flint while working for the Flint Area Chamber of Commerce and Convention Bureau.

Sheila Miller-Graham, a national-award-winning dance instructor, said she, too, knows former Flintites who disown it.

"They make it big and tell people they're from Detroit," Miller-Graham complained. "Why not give Flint the credit?"

Young people often tell her, "I don't want to be in Flint all my life," she said. Her response is that there is more than one way to leave town. One of her ways of leaving is through the experiences of former students studying or performing in such far-flung places as Hollywood, Calif., or Japan.

Nor does Miller-Graham understand why Flint people feel that they have to go to Detroit, Lansing or Saginaw for entertainment.

"A city is what you make it," she said. "If you decide to become involved in it, you'll get more from it. If you decide to sit back and not get involved, you won't.

"A lot of people say there is not enough to do. My problem is that I don't have enough time to do it all, especially if I've got some money."

But she noted that many things-to-do in Flint are free. For example, she filled up one summer by taking her daughter, nieces and nephews to a different park every day. They also visited Mott Hashbarger Farm and the Pennywhistle Place playground in the Genesee Recreation Area; the Flint Children's Museum on West Third Avenue; and Longway Planetarium in the Flint Cultural Central, some of which charge a small admission.

Part of Flint's image problem is because many people don't like to read so they don't know about special events unless they hear about them through the grapevine, Miller-Graham said.

Karen Aldridge is one of Flint's comeback kids. She lived in Africa for a few years after college in the 1970s and commuted from Flint while working in Lansing during the 1980s. When Aldridge took a job in Flint, she said some of her Lansing acquaintances teased that, "I don't know whether to give you a congratulations card or a condolence card."

But Aldridge saw them as the disadvantaged ones. Many Lansing residents, who work at Michigan State or in state government, tend to live in isolated cliques, she said.

"I like having a defined black community," she said of Flint. "In Lansing, it's not as integrated."

Also, living in her hometown gives Aldridge more opportunities to be a role model for youth. It's important for them to see successful black people who aren't dealing drugs, she said.

Similarly, positive youth development is a key interest for Debra Taylor, another Flint comeback kid.

A 1973 Southwestern graduate, Taylor lived in Lansing, Detroit and Washington, D.C., before returning to Flint in 1991.

As senior program officer for the Flint Community Foundation, Taylor is helping mastermind Flint's rebirth. She is co-chairperson of the committee working to restore Atwood Stadium and is active in other community development and civic groups.

"Flint is at a critical point, Taylor said. "It can come back or become a has-been like the coal mining towns in West Virginia."

Taylor is betting on the comeback. Several of her peers who left Flint found themselves drawn back despite other intentions, she said. Taylor calls that "the Lord's plan."

"These are people who benefited when Flint was bustling," she said, referring to an era of abundant enrichment programs such as Stepping Stones, Tot Lot, police cadets, camping and after-school activities sponsored by the Mott Foundation.

"If not for some of those programs, we wouldn't be where we are," Taylor said.

"I'm just looking now for a way I can give something back. We African-Americans here, we have our destiny in our own hands. But we need to look beyond GM to entrepreneurial effort and to cultivate younger leadership to take up the mantle."

Index

A
Atherton East, 27-31
Athletic Park, 200, 203, 210

B
Banks, Carl, 192, 227, 228
Banner, Melvin, 86
Bates, Floyd Sr., 192, 205, 208, 215, 230, 231
Bates, Floyd Jr., 230, 232
Beasley, Olive, 11, 290-292, 301-303
Berston Field House, 18, 150, 178, 187-188, 192, 197-198-202, 205, 207, 212, 216, 220, 240, 247, 258, 293
Bolden, Leroy, 192, 196, 220-224
Brannon, Mel, 293-295, 297
Broadway, Odell, 112, 123, 183, 290
Bronze Reporter newspaper, 86
Brownsville News, 85
Buick 20 softball team, 212
Birch, Joseph, 76
Butler, Ailene, 1, 84, 91-92, 132, 159-160, 199, 240, 285, 287-288, 304

C
Capitol Theater, 35, 166-167, 184-185
Cavette, Dee, 196, 244-247
Clack, Floyd, 46, 47, 83, 278, 289, 290
Clark, Magnus, 159, 276
Clark Elementary School, 18, 19, 70, 96, 97, 101, 117, 157-158, 188, 202, 210, 256, 288
Clifford Street Center, 9, 17, 18, 35, 36, 137, 178, 183, 202

Cobb, Wesley, 293-295
Coleman, Don, 192, 197, 222, 224
Columbia Theater, 13, 15, 70, 166, 167, 260
Concerned Pastors for Social Action, 86, 139, 140, 146, 179
Copeland, Auburn, 192, 244, 243
Copeland, Eli, 204, 205
Courts, Rev. Thomas, 139
Crompton, Earl, 278, 297, 302

D

Dewey Woods, 188, 200
Dukette, Father Norman A., 137-139, 146

E

Elks Club, 157
Elm Park, 17-19, 268, 269
Etherly, Woody, 11, 13, 22, 42, 63, 89, 112, 113, 143, 144, 263, 264, 285-288, 303-305
Evergreen Estates, 16, 18, 21, 262

F

Fairview Elementary School, 54, 82, 96, 99, 100, 105, 181, 258
Fielder, Floyd, 192, 244, 246, 247,
Flint Community Center, 13, 137, 178
Flint fair-housing sleep-in, 140, 143, 287, 288, 303
Flint Junior College, 65, 114, 115, 125, 126, 269
Flint Negro Business and Professional Women's Club Inc., 178
Flint Park & Amusement Co., 36, 150, 164, 165, 187
Flint Spokesman newspaper, 86
Flint Urban League, 65, 73, 74, 107, 118, 128, 139, 179, 278, 292-295, 307
Friley, George, 67, 72, 79, 278, 293
Floral Park, 17-19
Furlow, Terry, 214-217

G

Garden Theater, 35, 36, 166, 167
Golden Leaf Club, 19, 144, 157-159, 160, 161
Grayer, Jeff, 192, 215, 218, 219
Greater Flint Afro-American Hall of Fame, 194, 210, 213, 220, 230, 236
Greene, Leo, 145

H

Hamady House, 176, 177
Hamilton, Bill, 192, 205-207, 212, 244
Hamm, Anthony, 234
Hayden, Harold, 278, 306, 280
Hightower, John, 64, 85, 118, 119, 146, 278-283, 302, 306
Holt, Edgar, 23, 85, 123, 179, 262, 279, 282-285
Holt, Lois VanZandt, 21, 82, 85, 93, 103, 104, 112, 123, 179, 283-285
Horton, Henry, 21, 22, 27, 46, 83, 84, 91, 147, 293
Hoskins, Dave, 192-194, 206-210
Houston, Guy, 151, 274
Hughley, Leteia, 215, 237, 239
Hyche, Georgia, 277, 278

I

Idlewild, 152, 189
IMA Auditorium, 9, 41, 150-156, 160, 170, 173, 180, 187, 200, 244, 246, 268, 299

J

Joe Louis Punchers, 204-206, 212
Johnson, Al, 223

K

Kimbrough, Clarence, 20, 105

L

Leach, Jesse L., 51, 75, 169, 267, 277, 278, 285
Luckado, Jim, 192, 203, 234

M

Mack, John, 278, 293-295, 307
Mallory, Dudley, 50, 51, 76
Mayor of Brownsville, 80, 276, 277
McClellan, Percy, 79, 195, 205, 222
McCombs, Benny, 192, 205, 241, 242, 244, 245,
McCrary, James, 101, 195, 196, 222
McCree, Floyd, 22, 23, 78, 80, 123, 278, 281, 284, 285, 287-289, 293, 302, 303, 305, 306

McCree, Melvin, 22, 23, 94, 113, 125, 156, 265, 288, 289, 305
McGee, Pamela, 192, 215, 235, 236, 239
McGee, Paula, 192, 215, 235, 236, 239
McKell, Mickey, 195, 2074, 222
Metropolitan Chamber of Commerce, 51, 73, 74, 85
Michigan Theater, 165
Miller, Eugene, 114, 285, 297, 298
Mitchell, Sherm, 39, 42, 52, 86-88, 96, 115, 121, 122, 151, 156, 159, 169-171
Moore, Booker, 226
Moore, John W., 50, 51
Mt. Olive Baptist Church, 131, 136, 139, 140, 142

O
Old Timers Club, 181

P
PAL Club, 244, 245, 247
Palace Theater, 166, 167, 184
Papp's Drugstore, 11, 12, 92
Parkland School, 82, 90, 96, 101, 115, 200
Parks, Archie, 14, 78, 79, 293
Patton, Dorothy (Dottie), 87, 88, 151, 159, 161, 162, 168-170
Patton, Ricky, 226
Peaks, Clarence, 226
PMAC, 62
Potters Lake, 130

Q
Quinn Chapel AME Church, 131, 135-137, 142, 144, 146

R
Rice, Glen, 192, 215, 217-219
Richard Theater, 13, 166, 167
Rison, Andre, 192, 215, 218, 219, 229
River Park, 28-30
Robbs, Rev. Alfred L.C., 132, 133, 137, 140, 146
Robinson, C. Frederick, 20, 43, 44, 74-76, 116, 117, 122, 278-281, 285, 299, 302
Roosevelt Elementary School, 96, 99, 108

S

Schiappacasse's Candy Kitchen, 185
Sharp, James, 31, 32, 78, 84, 85, 275, 276, 293, 306
Shook's Confectionary, 68
Spencer, Edith, 20, 72, 92, 94
Spencer, J. Merrill, 72, 79, 94, 103, 301
Sportman's Club, 18, 156, 160, 179
St. John Street neighborhood, 2, 7, 10-18, 30, 32-35, 37, 41, 43, 45, 124, 152
St. John Street Community Center, 9, 12
Stanley, Woodrow, 15, 52, 67, 68, 86, 113, 124, 130, 187, 260, 272, 276, 277, 293
Stepping Stones Club, 176, 177
Sugar Hill, 8, 17-20, 261

T

Thigpen, Justus, 192, 215
Thomas, Jesse, 192, 196, 224, 233, 234
Tom Thumb Weddings, 141, 142
Townsend, Roger, 64, 82, 278, 286
Tucker, Fred, 84, 286-288, 304,
Tucker, Judy, 215, 239, 240
Tucker, Trent, 217
Turner, Eric, 192, 215-218
Turpin, Rev. Robert, 21, 139, 261

U

Union Picnic, 130, 131, 146

V

Van Dyne, Roy M., 51, 76
VanZandt, Ruth, 54, 82, 103, 113, 115, 123, 126, 144, 240, 259, 262, 283
Velvelettes, 88, 151, 155, 169, 171-174

W

Washington, Al, 73, 101, 151
Weaver, Wrex, 68, 72
Williams, Charlotte, 90, 112, 115, 116, 125, 144, 160, 183, 261, 263, 267, 290, 291
Williams, Marion Coates, 20, 82, 103, 105, 114, 144, 179, 182, 184, 271, 272, 292

Williams, Reggie, 196, 226, 227
Williams, T. Wendell, 20, 72, 105, 291-293, 302
Woodlawn Park, 17, 18, 20, 21
Work Projects Administration, 53
Wright, Marie, 125

Y

Yellow Dogs softball team, 203-205, 207, 212
Young, John F., 82, 278

Z

Zags (Zeta Alpha Gamma), 181